INTERNATIONAL POLITICAL ECONOMY SERIES

General Editor: Timothy M. Shaw, Professor of Political Science and International Development Studies, and Director of the Centre for Foreign Policy Studies, Dalhousie University, Halifax, Nova Scotia, Canada

Recent titles include:

Pradeep Agrawal, Subir V. Gokarn, Veena Mishra, Kirit S. Parikh and Kunal Sen
ECONOMIC RESTRUCTURING IN EAST ASIA AND INDIA: Perspectives on Policy Reform

Steve Chan (*editor*)
FOREIGN DIRECT INVESTMENT IN A CHANGING GLOBAL POLITICAL ECONOMY

Jennifer Clapp
ADJUSTMENT AND AGRICULTURE IN AFRICA: Farmers, the State and the World Bank in Guinea

Seamus Cleary
THE ROLE OF NGOs UNDER AUTHORITARIAN POLITICAL SYSTEMS

Edward A. Comor (*editor*)
THE GLOBAL POLITICAL ECONOMY OF COMMUNICATION

Robert W. Cox (*editor*)
THE NEW REALISM: Perspectives on Multilateralism and World Order

O. P. Dwivedi
DEVELOPMENT ADMINISTRATION: From Underdevelopment to Sustainable Development

Jacques Hersh and Johannes Dragsbaek Schmidt (*editors*)
THE AFTERMATH OF 'REAL EXISTING SOCIALISM' IN EASTERN EUROPE, VOLUME 1: Between Western Europe and East Asia

Noeleen Heyzer, James V. Riker and Antonio B. Quizon (*editors*)
GOVERNMENT-NGO RELATIONS IN ASIA: Prospects and Challenges for People-Centred Development

David Kowalewski
GLOBAL ESTABLISHMENT: The Political Economy of North/Asian Networks

Staffan Lindberg and Árni Sverrisson (*editors*)
SOCIAL MOVEMENTS IN DEVELOPMENT: The Challenge of Globalization and Democratization

Laura Macdonald
SUPPORTING CIVIL SOCIETY: The Political Role of Non-Governmental Organizations in Central America

Stephen D. McDowell
GLOBALIZATION, LIBERALIZATION AND POLICY CHANGE: A Political Economy of India's Communications Sector

George McMahon (*editor*)
LESSONS IN ECONOMIC POLICY FOR EASTERN EUROPE FROM LATIN AMERICA

Juan Antonio Morales and Gary McMahon (*editors*)
ECONOMIC POLICY AND THE TRANSITION TO DEMOCRACY: The Latin American Experience

Paul J. Nelson
THE WORLD BANK AND NON-GOVERNMENTAL ORGANIZATIONS: The Limits of Apolitical Development

Archibald R. M. Ritter and John M. Kirk (*editors*)
CUBA IN THE INTERNATIONAL SYSTEM: Normalization and Integration

John Sorenson (*editor*)
DISASTER AND DEVELOPMENT IN THE HORN OF AFRICA

Howard Stein (*editor*)
ASIAN INDUSTRIALIZATION AND AFRICA: Studies in Policy Alternatives to Structural Adjustment

Larry A. Swatuk and Timothy M. Shaw (*editors*)
THE SOUTH AT THE END OF THE TWENTIETH CENTURY: Rethinking the Political Economy of Foreign Policy in Africa, Asia, the Caribbean and Latin America

Kenneth P. Thomas
CAPITAL BEYOND BORDERS: States and Firms in the Auto Industry, 1960–94

Geoffrey R. D. Underhill (*editor*)
THE NEW WORLD ORDER IN INTERNATIONAL FINANCE

Sandra Whitworth
FEMINISM AND INTERNATIONAL RELATIONS

International Political Economy Series
Series Standing Order ISBN 0–333–71110–6
(*outside North America only*)

You can receive future titles in this series as they are published by placing a standing order. Please contact your bookseller or, in case of difficulty, write to us at the address below with your name and address, the title of the series and the ISBN quoted above.

Customer Services Department, Macmillan Distribution Ltd
Houndmills, Basingstoke, Hampshire RG21 6XS, England

Subsidy Regulation and State Transformation in North America, the GATT and the EU

Robert O'Brien
Lecturer in International Relations
University of Sussex
Brighton

First published in Great Britain 1997 by
MACMILLAN PRESS LTD
Houndmills, Basingstoke, Hampshire RG21 6XS and London
Companies and representatives throughout the world

A catalogue record for this book is available from the British Library.

ISBN 0–333–69246–2

First published in the United States of America 1997 by
ST. MARTIN'S PRESS, INC.,
Scholarly and Reference Division,
175 Fifth Avenue, New York, N.Y. 10010

ISBN 0–312–17513–2

Library of Congress Cataloging-in-Publication Data
O'Brien, Robert, 1963–
Subsidy regulation and state transformation in North America, the GATT and the EU / Robert O'Brien.
p. cm. — (International political economy series)
Includes bibliographical references and index.
ISBN 0–312–17513–2 (cloth)
1. Subsidies—United States. 2. Subsidies—Canada. 3. General Agreement on Tariffs and Trade (Organization) 4. Subsidies–
–European Union countries. I. Title. II. Series.
HC110.S9027 1997
338.9'22—dc21 97–7120
CIP

This book is printed on paper suitable for recycling and made from fully managed and sustained forest sources.

10 9 8 7 6 5 4 3 2 1
06 05 04 03 02 01 00 99 98 97

Printed and bound in Great Britain by
Antony Rowe Ltd, Chippenham, Wiltshire

To my parents and Angela

Contents

Acknowledgments

I first became interested in the issue of subsidy conflicts in 1987 while working as a parliamentary intern in the Canadian House of Commons. Over the past decade numerous people helped me pursue the subject matter, leading to the publication of this book. Members of my PhD committee from York University will recognize large sections of the work. Robert Cox, Daniel Drache and David Leyton-Brown all took an interest in the project and offered assistance. The Walter Gordon scholarship at York University facilitated my early field research in the United States. In Washington I was able to rely upon the assistance of Robert Meuser for practical guidance through the trade maze and physical provision during my research trips. Thanks are also due to people in the US, Canadian and EU bureaucracies, interest groups and political parties who took the time to speak to me. The intellectual atmosphere stimulated by my new colleagues Zdenek Kavan, John MacLean, Jan Aart Scholte and Marc Williams at the University of Sussex helped me look at the same issue in a different light. Angus Cameron kindly assisted in the preparation of the manuscript. Finally, my greatest debts are to my parents and to Angela who provided me with moral support, financial security and the example of a steadfast work ethic.

Abbreviations

AAA	Agricultural Adjustment Act
ACOA	Atlantic Canada Opportunities Agency
BCNI	Business Council on National Issues
CAP	Common Agricultural Policy
CBC	Canadian Broadcasting Corporation
CIT	Court of International Trade
CMA	Canadian Manufacturers Association
CRTC	Canadian Radio and Television Commission
CVD	Countervailing Duty
DOC	Department of Commerce
DREE	Department of Regional Economic Expansion
EC	European Community
ERDA	Economic and Regional Development Agreements
EU	European Union
FDI	Foreign Direct Investment
FTA	Canada–United States Free Trade Agreement
GATT	General Agreement on Tariffs and Trade
IMF	International Monetary Fund
IR&D	Independent Research and Development Program
ITA	International Trade Administration
ITC	International Trade Commission
ITO	International Trade Organization
MOU	Memorandum of Understanding
MPEAA	Motion Picture Export Association of America
NAFTA	North American Free Trade Agreement
NTBs	Non-Tariff Barriers
OECD	Organization for Economic Cooperation and Development
PEI	Prince Edward Island
R&D	Research and Development
SDI	Strategic Defense Initiative
SEA	Single European Act
TNCs	Transnational Corporations
UK	United Kingdom
US	United States
USTR	United States Trade Representative
VERs	Voluntary Export Restraints
WTO	World Trade Organization

Introduction

Many people traveling around England take time to visit the ancient monument of Stonehenge and marvel at its size and meaning. Venturing three kilometers northeast they would come across a less famous site which serves as a symbol for the present international system – Woodhenge. Woodhenge is comprised of three rings of wooden posts protruding a couple of feet from the ground. It is not a very impressive sight. There is speculation that the posts may have stood as individual markers linked by other posts or as the foundation of a roofed building which served as a temple or a meeting place. One sees the elements of a foundation for some structure, but it is not clear of what form, size or purpose. Similar to Woodhenge, discussions about the international system are also concerned with posts and foundations. Numerous writers from different perspectives have suggested that we are living in an era that has broken from the past, but are unable to identify its present or future form. The international system has been described as post-hegemonic, post-Westphalian and post-modern (Keohane, 1984; Zacher, 1992; Walker, 1993). The end of the Cold War has made it clear to even the most conservative analysts that this is a period of great change. Yet, it is difficult to say with clarity what the system is changing to or what will rise from these various posts and foundations.

This study contributes to the discussion by providing some empirical work on an issue which allows us to discern emerging trends in a reconstituted system. The attempt by state and business elites to resolve subsidy disputes by redefining the role of the state and transferring the location of decision–making power offers clues to the direction we are traveling. Numerous areas of investigation could highlight the contradiction between a global economy and national political structures, but the subsidy issue is a particularly useful example of the attempt by political and economic elites to construct international institutions that limit domestic autonomy on a sensitive issue.

The conflict between states over subsidization of domestic economic activity has been of interest to those concerned with trade issues over the past twenty years, but has recently taken on a greater public profile. With the gradual demise of tariff barriers since the Second World War, attention has shifted to non-tariff barriers to trade (NTBs). The practice of subsidizing industry has been an unfair trade practice of great concern to the US. These subsidies are often seen to be giving industries based in a particular country an advantage over similar industries in other countries. Subsidy disputes exacerbate political conflict on two planes. Nationally, they pit groups favoring US style liberalization against those protecting other values. Internationally, subsidy disputes may lead to conflict between representatives of rival states and rival development models influenced by domestic pressure. In times of slow growth, these issues take on increased importance.

This study has two prime investigatory tasks. The first is to explain what subsidy issues are about and why they are difficult to resolve. Subsidy issues arise from the continuous pressure for economic liberalization and are a source of conflict because they challenge local and national autonomy. The second is to consider the implications of subsidy disputes for our understanding of the global political economy. These disputes highlight the tension between globalization and demand for local control and diversity. This book does not provide many policy recommendations for resolving disputes. In many circumstances subsidy dispute resolution would require political integration. In other cases the disputes are not really about subsidies, but concern commercial advantage, adjustment policies, socio-economic organization, or state power. Their significance lies in that they serve as signals of a much deeper issue or contradiction. That contradiction is between the globalization of production and finance and the continued nationalization of legitimate political authority. The attempts at internationalization of authority in this issue area are timid, difficult and lacking in accountability.

The primary argument emerging from the subsidy case studies is that our understanding of what a state is and what a state does is changing in response to global economic pressures. The subsidy issue is only one aspect of this changing nature of the state, but it provides a particularly stark and important illustration. Our understanding of what a state is changes because bodies other than the state are taking vital decisions about how governments can spend tax revenue. Our understanding of what a state does changes because subsidy rules redefine legitimate state activity on a more liberal or laissez-faire trajectory. However, state mutation is not identical in every geographic area. The West European and the North American entities may face similar problems, but have devised different solutions.

This study begins by reviewing the process of globalization and liberalization in the fields of production and finance, as well as the more limited internationalization of the state and authority. It proposes that there are two contradictory forces at work in the global economy. The first is pressure for increased liberalization and the second is the backlash against the ravages that increased openness and competition has imposed on some members in each society. The implications of this dialectic process for the key concepts of autonomy and sovereignty are outlined, demonstrating how the globalization of the economy has altered our understanding of the state.

The second chapter examines US trade law and the operation of its antisubsidy policy. The countervailing duty process is explained and an illustration is provided of its controversial operation. Issues that make their way through the US courts became global trade issues. The fragmentation of the US political system and its sensitivity to distressed industry has global impact in that any country wishing to export to the world's wealthiest market must be wary of legal and political backlash. An understanding of international subsidy or other trade issues therefore requires an understanding of US trade politics.

Chapter 3 highlights the domestic roots of subsidy practices by focusing on key Canadian and US public policies. Policy differences in the areas of national security, regional development, subnational economic policies, culture, and healthcare are shown to be embedded in different historic experiences. They are a product of political struggle in each country, reflecting competing forms of liberal models.

Chapter 4 examines the role of subsidy disputes in the Canada–US Free Trade Agreement (FTA). A series of cases launched in US courts in the 1970s and 1980s raised fears in Canadian elite circles about US protectionism. Canada's aim was to restrict a policy tool that the US Congress considered vital in its dealings with unfair trade and domestic constituent pressure. The subsidy issue proved so contentious that the parties agreed to implement a temporary dispute settlement process and return to the subsidy negotiations within seven years.

Chapter 5 follows the subsidy issue into the negotiations on the North American Free Trade Agreement (NAFTA). Canadian and US negotiators put the subsidy issue on a back burner hoping that a solution would emerge at GATT. Bilaterally the obstacles were too great and a number of legal cases created more tension. The final NAFTA subsidy provisions largely mirrored those of the FTA with some minor administrative changes. The thorny issue of which government intervention policies are legitimate, and who makes that decision, was avoided by agreeing to enshrine subsidy provisions similar to the FTA's.

Chapter 6 moves the analysis to the multilateral level by examining attempts to deal with the subsidy issue at GATT. As attention moved to NTBs the subsidy issue was brought to the fore by the US. The Tokyo Round provisions are examined in an attempt to understand the origins of the issue. The Uruguay Round subsidy negotiations are outlined and the successful conclusion is linked to a change in US policy. The new agreements will bring in stricter disciplines to subsidy practice, but the question remains whether the US itself is ready to abide by such a system.

Chapter 7 examines the origins of GATT agricultural policies and the conflict in aviation high technology. It reveals the strong domestic opposition to free market principles in the agricultural field in various powerful states and the belief by some policy makers in strategic trade industries. The attempt to include agriculture in a strict subsidy regime revealed the fundamental contradiction in the GATT structure – the imperative of liberalization and the need for domestic autonomy. The EU–US aerospace dispute highlights the clashes resulting from varying forms of government intervention as US indirect subsidies are pitted against direct European intervention.

Chapter 8 considers the EU's policy towards internal subsidization. In comparison to the GATT and North American arrangements, the EU has had a great deal of success dealing with subsidy (state aids) issues. With the EU renaissance in the mid-1980s, officials only had to enforce rules that were already on the books. Yet even this accomplishment is threatened by the clash of economic models between southern and northern EU member states.

The concluding chapter argues that the dispute over subsidy practices raises vital questions about the evolution of the state, sovereignty, autonomy and democracy. The ability of subnational and national groups to pursue particular policies is threatened by the transfer of sovereignty to unrepresentative institutions at the regional and global level. The attempt to create regional and global institutions is undermined by their distance from the people and their lack of democracy. Sovereignty transfer to supranational levels is frustrated by some of those groups that have experienced a reduction in autonomy and control. The difficulty of legitimating these supranational entities or subjecting them to popular control suggests continued conflict and instability in the global political economy, as other issue areas such as competition policy, labor and environmental regulations spark similar controversies.

1 Globalization, the State and Subsidies

This chapter sets the context for the studies in the following pages. It makes three primary arguments. Firstly, economic, and to a lesser extent political, life in OECD countries since the late 1940s has experienced increased globalization. Secondly, this globalization has raised questions about our understanding of the state. Thirdly, subsidy disputes are a product of this globalization, as is the ensuing redefinition of the nature and role of the state through subsidy negotiations. The major part of the chapter outlines the phenomenon of globalization in production and finance and considers the social forces, ideas, and institutions crucial to that process. Resistance to globalization in the form of protectionism is also examined. This is followed by a section considering the changing nature of the state with regard to sovereignty, autonomy and democracy. The concluding section locates the issue of subsidies in this framework suggesting how the study of subsidy conflicts may throw light on crucial changes in the global political economy.

GLOBALIZATION

When using the term globalization, this study is referring to three related processes: the expansion and integration of the production process to many countries, the liberalization of finance and the internationalization of the state.[1] Finance and production have become globalized in that they transcend state boundaries that previously restricted them, while the state has become internationalized – its authority moving to a higher level. Production and finance have become integrated on a global scale, but the state has not. Together they constitute an attempted shift from an *international* to a *transnational* liberal economic order (Gill, 1990: 209). Movement is from economies that were primarily nationally based with external linkages, to highly integrated structures of production and finance alongside a limited internationalization of political authority and legitimacy. The causes for this shift can be found largely in the dominant social forces (transnational capital) and a particular form of the state (hyperliberal).

Developments in the areas of material capabilities (economic slowdown), ideas (liberalism) and institutions (OECD, G-7) on a global level also assist the transformation of the world order.[2] The transnational order is centered in the US, but spreads out to incorporate elite sections of other countries. Its configuration is closer to that of an empire than a nation state (Strange, 1988a: 10–11).

The origins of this transnational order lie in the postwar structure designed by the US. Originally planned to allow for stability and American expansion, the liberal international economic order also planted the seeds for a transnational order. Protected by American military power, and financed by American economic surplus this liberal order allowed for the globalization of production and finance (Cox, 1987: 244–64). Indeed, the particular form of the US state is crucial in the transition from an international to a transnational world order.

The US resembles the ideal type of a hyperliberal state. The hyperliberal strategy attempts a return to nineteenth century economic liberalism to encourage prosperity. State activity in the economy is seen as inherently inefficient and every effort is made to separate state activity from economic activity (with the exception of defense spending). Such a strategy favors less redistribution of income, privatization, deregulation, decreased spending on social services, and an appeal to traditional values. Labor is viewed as an input to production and must find a market-determined price. Thus, steps are taken to make the labor market less rigid with regard to falling wage levels. Indeed, high wage levels are seen as a strong factor in uncompetitiveness (this does not apply as rigidly to executives). Social consensus does not figure prominently in this strategy; opposition groups are to be rendered impotent or relegated to an insignificant role in society. The key elements of hyperliberalism are the increased role of the free market in decision-making, the decreased role of the state in the economy and a flexible labor market. The United Kingdom under Margaret Thatcher and the United States under Presidents Reagan and Bush in the 1980s are prime examples of this form of organization.

A contrasting approach is that of state capitalism.[3] In this model the principal economic actors (business, labor, state) hammer out and pursue an industrial strategy. Rather than letting the free market of international competition determine a nation's role, specific sectors are targeted for assistance and development. The welfare of principal workers (those in the targeted industries), whether it be financial, physical or educational is seen to be linked with the success of the internationally competitive sectors. A country following this strategy creates 'a dualism between, on the one hand, a competitively efficient world market oriented sector, and on the other, a protected welfare sector' (Cox, 1987: 291–2). Japan, Sweden, and France have followed this model in different forms.

The concepts of hyperliberal and state capitalist forms of state are used as ideal types. There is no perfectly hyperliberal state; it is an abstraction that allows one to discover tendencies within states and to differentiate between distinct forms of development. One can compare a particular state with the models to improve understanding of its structure relative to these ideal types. Thus, while the US may resemble the hyperliberal model, an argument can be made that it has an *ad hoc* industrial policy. Canada appears to contain elements of both models, but has more state capitalist features than the US. Both forms of state are coming under continuing pressure to adapt to the increasingly competitive global economy. Hyperliberalism and state capitalism are also ideas that inform groups of people about how society should be organized. Their ideal form is one that various groups or social forces strive to recreate. They are a response to the competitive pressures of a global economy and variants of liberalism as described later in this chapter.

Production

Many explanations for the internationalization of production focus on economic factors such as the product cycle theory, vertical integration, and economies of scale (Vernon, 1966; Caves, 1982). These are valid factors, but the political aspect is also important. As the leading economic and military power, the US has done its utmost to ensure American transnational corporations (TNCs) access to foreign markets. The United States' 1948 Marshall Plan served as the cornerstone for rebuilding Western Europe and keeping its economies open to the US and each other. Its economic goals were to maintain multilateralism, price stability and spark the recovery of production (Block, 1977: 89). By ensuring a favorable economic climate it was hoped that less liberal left-wing parties could be kept out of European governments. In general the plan was successful at providing a stable base for a relatively open system under US leadership. American efforts at assisting its transnationals in other jurisdictions did not end with the Marshall Plan, as intervention on behalf of ITT in Chile or opposition to Canada's National Energy Program demonstrate. TNCs took advantage of differing costs in territorial units to produce for a world market. Large transnational companies used techniques such as subcontracting, subsidiaries, joint ventures and takeovers to transnationalize their production.

The process was given added impetus by the internationalization and privatization of finance, which allowed companies to gather credit relatively free of national scrutiny.

The spread of TNCs through foreign direct investment (FDI) has formed an economic web binding OECD economies together. The vast majority of FDI originates in OECD countries (95 per cent) and over three-quarters of it goes to other OECD members (Spero, 1985: 134). While the 1950s and 1960s saw US investment flood into Europe and Canada, the 1980s has witnessed European, Canadian and Japanese investment penetrating the American market. This cross investment gives TNC owners, managers and workers a large stake in maintaining an open system. Of the 90 million manufacturing workers in the OECD during 1987, one-third, or about 30 million, were employed by transnationals (Gill and Law, 1988: 183–4). Another important effect of transnational production is that a vast amount of trade is undertaken within these companies. Estimates of the percentage of world trade dominated by transnational intra-firm trade vary from 30 to 40 per cent (Gill, 1990: 91).

Even when obstacles to globalization appear, such as in the case of trade protection, the process is rarely slowed. Protectionism will be examined in more detail later, but it should be pointed out that even this form of activity can result in further transnationalization. The Japanese, concerned about the restriction of their exports, have increased direct investment in North America and Western Europe by opening car plants. Rather than limiting economic exchange, trade restrictions may simply shift activity from exports to FDI.

Finance

As important as trade flows are to the global political economy, the vast flow of money between corporations, countries and financial institutions now surpasses the flow of goods 'by a factor of 50 to 1' (Spero, 1988–9: 114). Indeed, it can be argued that capital movements rather than trade have become the driving force behind the world economy (Drucker, 1986: 768). The mobility of capital creates a broad framework that sets the limits for domestic economic policy. To go beyond these limits risks economic disorder. In this way the structure of the financial system demands harmonization of national economic policies and punishes policies that restrict liberalization and globalization.

US government political and economic decisions have played a crucial role in the internationalization of the financial structure. The financial structure is 'the sum of all the arrangements governing the availability of credit plus all the factors determining the terms on which currencies are exchanged for one another' (Strange, 1988b: 88). Aspects of this structure are truly global, having little regard for obstacles of time or space (territoriality), while others are still governed by domestic authorities. For example, capital markets are global, operating around the clock at the speed of electronic messages, but the political responsibility for the value of individual currencies is fixed at the national level.

Central to the internationalization of the financial structure has been the emergence and dramatic growth of the Eurocurrency system (Hawley, 1987). This system is composed of financial institutions dealing in currencies other than their country of origin. An example would be banks operating in any currency other than pounds sterling in London, or using major currencies (dollar, pound, mark, yen) in the Bahamas. Financial institutions find this arrangement beneficial because they escape regulation by their home governments, the host government and international authorities. Host governments encourage this activity in order to strengthen the financial industry in their area (London is a good example).

In terms of economic policy capital mobility encourages states to pursue deflationary policies. Investment tends toward low inflation economies, as profits are greater. If most countries are following a monetarist policy it is nearly impossible for any single country to institute a Keynesian reflation. A Keynesian solution to unemployment would be increased spending, but this would result in rising levels of imports and increased inflation. Both Britain in 1976 and France in the early 1980s were forced to revise their left-leaning domestic economic policies because of pressure from international capital flows. The only exception to this trend has been the US whose position as the center of the financial and production structures has allowed it to stress domestic growth.

In the late twentieth century we are witness to and participants in a liberal globalization juggernaut. More and more areas of national life are open to global influences, the role of government is reduced and that of the market increased. If one were predisposed to functionalist arguments, it could be put forward that the global economic system demands liberalization and liberalization it will get, yet the system does not run on automatic pilot. Globalization in a neoliberal form benefits particular interests, is pushed along by those interests and requires political structures to facilitate its maintenance and implementation.

Social Forces

The globalization of production and finance and the internationalization of state have resulted in the strengthening of a group or bloc of people dedicated to further liberalizing the global economy. This social force is transnational capital and those who benefit from its activity. Social forces differ from interest groups in that they are broader organizations attempting to implement wide reaching social change. Globalization is creating, and being created by, a transnational managerial class attempting to manage and further liberalization (Cox, 1987: 355–91; Stopford and Strange, 1991: 21). The members of this social force include transnational companies that rely on the global market, the international financial industry that has profited from deregulated open markets, the working population dependent on these industries, and political and academic figures sharing the liberalization vision. Members of this social force are prominent in developed capitalist countries. Since many TNCs are American and the US plays a large role in the international financial structure, Americans are preeminent in this movement. Yet nationality is not a determining factor, as many Europeans, Japanese and Canadians are in similar economic positions and advocate similar policies. Members are influential in the political process through involvement in national business councils (chambers of commerce) or direct participation in political and bureaucratic offices.

Opposing liberal transnationalism are a range of groups stressing national development, local autonomy, or globalization based on principles other than those of the free market. They are not a unified group, although occasionally can cooperate. Resistance is based in: industry and labor that are nationally, but not internationally competitive; feminist movements stressing equality and local development; environmental movements advocating sustainable development and restrictions on corporate behavior; aboriginal societies demanding autonomy; social democrats trying to rebuild the welfare state; and right-wing nationalists arguing for the exclusion of foreigners and reassertion of national sovereignty

Ideas

The attempted transition to a transnational world order is accompanied by a shift in ideas concerning the appropriate nature of political and economic organization. The propositions put forward in conjunction with the transnational order are based on increased liberalism. Whereas the postwar international order combined domestic intervention in the economy with a more liberal international system, the new creed stipulates increasing liberalism domestically and internationally. Thus we see the erosion of what Samuel Bowles (1982) called the capital–labor accord, or what John Ruggie (1982) labeled 'embedded liberalism'. Liberal transnationalism preaches a reduced role for government, privatization, increased reliance on markets and the opening of national economies to world competition.

Before going further it is necessary to clarify a term that will be employed throughout this work – *liberalism*. When used here, it refers to a set of ideas for organizing society in both its economic and political dimensions that stress liberty in the form of individualism, the free market and private property (Gilpin, 1987: 27, n.1). The emphasis on liberty has two aspects. The first is economic liberty or being allowed to conduct commercial affairs with a minimum of state intervention. The second is political liberty from government oppression as articulated in legal protection through the courts from state agencies and the tyranny of the majority.

The revival of classical liberalism, as seen in the conservative governments of Britain, the US and Canada, tries to restore the economic foundation of liberalism – namely restricting government intervention in the economy (Friedmann, 1962; Hayek, 1960). As John Gray explains: 'Common to all contemporary classical liberalism is the goal of a form of limited government under the rule of law in which . . . the central economic powers of government – powers of taxation, spending and the issuance of money – are subject to rules no less stringent than those which protect the basic personal liberties' (1986: 79).

Using terms such as 'conservative' and 'liberal' can be confusing as their meaning varies from country to country and across time periods. In the US the word liberal is used to denote those who favor greater government intervention and conservatives are those who support less intervention. US conservatives support classical liberal principles with a dash of appeal to traditional values. This study will use the term 'neoliberal' for those who support a return to economic models grounded in nineteenth century classical liberalism. This includes most American, Canadian and British conservatives.

Liberal ideas and practice operate at the level of the international system or world order and domestically within states (Cox, 1987: 111–50). At the level of world order the US and its allies set up a postwar international liberal economic order (excluding Communist states) based on relatively free access to each other's economies. Individual states are liberal to the extent that they restrain government intervention in the market and use the rule of law to protect individuals from unjustified government coercion. It was not necessary, however, for a state participating in this order to be liberal in both its economic and political organization. Countries such as Chile and South Korea could protect private property and participate in the international free market, but violate the liberal legal rights of their citizens.

In the study and practice of international relations in Western countries during the postwar period liberalism failed at one level, yet succeeded at another. On the political and military levels, realism's power politics held sway, while in economic relations (excluding the Communist Bloc) it has been liberal principles that have dominated. The Idealist model of collective security had been demolished by the failure of the League of Nations to prevent the Second World War. Nuclear deterrence became the cornerstone of Western security following 1945. With the onset of the Cold War, security was viewed as a zero sum game as the superpowers struggled with each other through the use of proxy wars. The liberal doctrine of harmony of interests did not extend to Eastern Europe or most of the Third World. The interwar idealist approach to international relations was viewed as naive and impractical (Morgenthau, 1973).

In the realm of international economics, however, realist/neomercantilist policies were marginalized as Western countries experienced a tremendous opening and liberalization of their economies. Transnational companies extended around the world, capital mobility increased dramatically and significant progress was made towards reducing tariffs. Gradually industrialized economies became more exposed to each other and third world competition. The early 1980s saw Prime Minister Thatcher and President Reagan push for further liberalism both domestically and internationally.

These trends are not as contradictory as they might first appear. It was the realist security underpinning of US foreign policy that provided cover for the international liberal economic order. The United States' leadership propounded the principles of open trade and military strength in the face of Communism. Strong allied economies and integrated markets were seen as a key factor in holding the anti-Communist alliance together. The mixture of realist principles in foreign policy and liberal tenets in economics was pursued with idealist fervor. To use David Calleo's words about the Kennedy administration: 'Liberal faith in progress combined with Hobbesian faith in power' (1982: 11). While there were minor deviations during periods of US unilateral leadership starting with Nixon and culminating in President Ronald Reagan's first term, calls for a renewed commitment to liberal internationalism were once again gaining ground in the late 1980s. Liberal internationalism stresses cooperation with allies in economic and military fields, more effort in the United Nations while retaining the prerogative to act alone when necessary (Gardner, 1990).

Institutions

Liberal ideas are transmitted and sometimes enforced through informal channels and by formal institutions that serve the interests of those seeking a transnational liberal order. Effective institutions for articulating these interests can be intergovernmental economic organizations such as the General Agreement on Tariffs and Trade (GATT) and International Monetary Fund (IMF) or non-governmental such as bond rating agencies. In the area of trade, the GATT became the main agreement for trade liberalization after the early collapse of the International Trade Organization (ITO) in 1950. GATT's objective was to liberalize trade through the reduction of tariff and trade barriers. With the recent creation of the World Trade Organization (WTO) and a stricter dispute settlement mechanism it has expanded its liberalizing domain to include agriculture, investment, services and intellectual property rights. Its role is examined in more detail in Chapter 6.

The IMF was set up following the Second World War to stabilize the international monetary system. Its primary role was to provide liquidity to countries experiencing temporary balance of payments or currency problems. In the 1980s the Fund has helped to spread liberal economic policies by demanding concessions from indebted countries in return for helping them secure further credit from Western banks. IMF prescriptions usually include the reduction of government spending and subsidies of basic commodities, elimination of trade and investment barriers and tight monetary policies (Pauly, 1994; Carvounis, 1986: 1–19). Indebted states needing renewed private investment and loans from First World banks are likely to have great difficulty securing capital if they are unwilling to follow the IMF prescriptions. As such, the IMF's primary role is to provide information to private financial interests, signaling which states are following the 'correct' development path.

Another example of an influential non-governmental institutional structure shaping government policy is the organization of credit and the role played by bond rating agencies (Sinclair, 1994). These private, mainly US, credit rating agencies rank companies and governments according to their perceived credit worthiness. In preparing national and subnational budgets, finance officials are increasingly wary of the effect a negative evaluation or downgrading by a bond agency will have for financial management. A poor grading can shake investor confidence, increase the cost of borrowing and start a vicious circle of monetary difficulties. It is one more institution that governments must appease in the management of their expenditures, but is distinctive in that it is operated by private enterprise.

Resistance via (US) Protectionism

It should be noted that globalization in a liberal form is a disputed process. Policies to the advantage of transnational industry may be at the expense of national capital or labor. Just as some groups benefit from globalization, others suffer. Nationally based industry and labor press for protection from the world economy. Marginal groups in society may also seek relief, especially in so far as globalization is linked with monetarism and the reduction of welfare spending. States slashing welfare expenditures in response to a deteriorating international position are forced to deal with the backlash from the domestic victims. Social movements such as feminism and environmentalism also resist neoliberal globalization because they prioritize values other than economic efficiency. Environmentalists may put greater value on a clean, healthy living space than liberal economists, while feminists might stress the desperate need to promote equality rather than consumerism. The international alliance of central agencies, transnational corporations and international finance are usually more than a match for opposition groups.

The opposition groups that feature prominently in the opposition role in this study are those that lose out economically from increased liberalization and globalization. This may be because they work in industries that are not globally competitive, occupy a precarious position in competitive industry or operate in areas which would be undermined by the operation of unmitigated market forces. The size of these groups may increase with economic slowdown or increased competition.

Resistance has been strengthened by the simultaneous globalization of the world economy and universal slowdown of Western economies since the 1970s. This slowdown can be measured in rates of growth, productivity and real wages. It is possible that growth rates following the Second World War were abnormally high and the past twenty years has witnessed a return to average growth rates. This has meant that pieces of the economic pie have become thinner and thinner for many groups in society. The slowing of growth increases conflict and can fuel a backlash against increasing liberalization.

A number of scholars working under the rubric of the regulation school have located the cause of recent turbulence in a combination of worn out production techniques or technology, and intense international competition. Alain Lipietz (1987) labeled this a crisis of Fordism. Fordism is the name used for a method of organizing Western socioeconomic systems which coupled the techniques of mass production with a state commitment to mass consumption (Braverman, 1976: 85–123). Workers were paid enough money to buy the products being produced and governments undertook to support income in times of adversity through Keynesian economic policies such as unemployment insurance, welfare and pensions. The regulationists see the postwar labor–capital agreement undermined by the internationalization of Western economies (Bowles, 1982). Cheaper wage levels in Third World countries and resistance to lowering wages in industrial countries was seen to produce a squeeze on profits. Adding extra pressure was exhaustion of the mass production model in many industrial sectors and the emergence of new production processes, such as flexible specialization, to cater for diverse consumer tastes. A change between an economy based on one form of production (oil, petrochemicals and mass production) to another (microelectronics, flexible specialization) is also cited as contributing to systemic change and economic turbulence (Perez, 1985).

Economic slowdown can both hinder and aid globalization. The hindrance springs from the fact that people may become resistant to the process and challenge its underlying assumptions. Alternatively, it can add force to those demanding more liberalization to spur economic growth. In addition to the liberalization and harmonization demands of the transnational managerial class and the financial structure, pressure also comes from other groups within the US. It shares a similar cause, globalization of the economy, but emanates from different groups – labor in threatened industries, national business, uncompetitive industries and farmers. Their response to the challenge of globalization is to demand that others liberalize their economies!

Forcing other countries to liberalize is one area where some US free trade ideologues and protectionists seem to agree. Free traders want others to liberalize as a matter of principle, while protectionists believe it will aid their industries. This creates a curious alliance of forces pushing for fair trade and foreign liberalization. Robert Reich, President Clinton's Labor Secretary, has commented that 'Protection can be the sword of the free traders in their assault upon foreign trade practices, while it simultaneously serves as a shield for those anxious to preserve American jobs' (1983: 773). Despite the protectionist origin of US pressure for fair trade, free traders are quite willing to use it as a weapon forcing others to liberalize and restructure their societies. Where gentle persuasion fails to convince other governments to behave, the protectionist menace from Congress can be used as an effective threat.

Central to understanding the American push for harmonization emanating from domestic sources is the difference between relational and structural power (Strange, 1988: 24–9). Relational power is the ability of one actor to make another do something it would otherwise not do. It is often measured by analyzing the outcomes of struggles or by weighing potential resources before a conflict. Structural power, however, confers the ability to set the rules or frameworks in which actors must operate. The possessor of structural power is able to limit the choice of action available to others without overtly exercising force. It is this ability to set the rules that the US is exercising in its demand for new trade rules. In order to reinforce its structural power by changing the rules, however, the US will also make use of its relational power to coerce unwilling states.

THE STATE

Central to the argument of this book is the case that the state is going through a process of transition. Crucial decision-making powers are shifting from nationally accountable agencies to international or regional institutions. Decisions may be taken by regional courts, international bureaucracies, private actors or intergovernmental gatherings. This process has been building since shortly after the Second World War. Indeed, pivotal to the postwar order has been a process whereby 'national policies and practices have been adjusted to the exigencies of the world economy of international production' (Cox, 1987: 253). In recent years the tensions between the need for states to both maintain domestic support and conform to an international economic order have become more acute.

States have increasingly become more responsive to the commands of international economic institutions than to the needs of the domestic political economy, as articulated by the political leadership.[4] As the US aided Europe's reconstruction and the world economy expanded in the 1950s and 1960s, the tension between the domestic welfare of particular groups and the adjustment demanded by the international order was largely obscured. The slowing of the world economy in the mid-1970s and recessions in the early 1980s and the early 1990s have revealed the tensions. A good example is the need for governments to pursue deflationary policies because of the fear of capital flight and the domestic political turmoil caused by deflation and unemployment. In 1992–3 OECD governments set about cutting government deficits and reducing public spending in the midst of a lengthy system-wide recession and massive unemployment.

The internationalizing of the state results in state elites redefining their interests in terms of systemic priorities as articulated by transnational liberal interests. International economic institutions such as the IMF and OECD outline the appropriate monetary and fiscal policies for member states. State central agencies, such as central banks, finance ministries, presidential or prime minister's offices, coordinate their economic policies attempting to implement the expressed desires of the system. State internationalization is synonymous with increased liberalism. As states and economies are internationalized they become more open and liberal. Goods, services, and in some cases labor, are allowed to flow from one geographic area to another.

The EU is the most developed example of state internationalization, but it is indicative of the forces that are at work in all western states. Motivation for integration is provided by those seeking to gain economic advantages that cannot be had at a national level; those seeking a refuge if relations with the US and Japan deteriorate; and those seeking a larger entity in which social welfare can be protected from the forces of international competition. These are not necessarily compatible objectives. Britain's former Prime Minister, Margaret Thatcher, was a firm supporter of increased liberalization, but rejected the idea of a European social charter or political union.

In such an environment, traditional notions of state sovereignty, autonomy and democracy are altered. Sovereignty in the sense of F. H. Hinsley's definition of 'a final and absolute political authority in the political community . . . and no final and absolute authority exists elsewhere' is eroding at various speeds in selected issue areas (1986: 26). David Held has identified five gaps between the traditional theory of state sovereignty and present practice – the world economy, hegemonic powers and blocs, international organizations, international law and the end of domestic policy (1989: 214–42). The first four of these areas move decision-making to other actors (firms, hegemons, organizations, and international courts) while the final gap refers to the internationalization of all government policy because of its repercussions on neighboring states.

Sovereignty has been crucial to our understanding of both the state and the international system. Edward Morse identifies the concept and practice of sovereignty as one of the five central characteristics of the Westphalian state system dating back to seventeenth century Europe (1976: 22–46). It is the vision of people gathered into separate states, recognizing the leadership of those states as the legitimate and authoritative political voices of their community that has dominated traditional views of international relations. Political theory and the study of international relations have used the concept of sovereignty to divide and separate their disciplines. The study of politics and political theory was confined to activity within the state and international relations with activity outside or between states (Walker, 1993). States may never have had absolute sovereignty, but it was generally recognized that the appropriate decision-making body for the political community was the government of the state. Indeed, political communities were identified by the state boundaries that surrounded them. Outside the state anarchy reigned and relations between sovereign states were characterized by the struggle for power (Morgenthau, 1973).

State sovereignty is losing some of its relevance as a central practice and concept in international relations for two reasons. The first is the erosion of sovereignty by regional and international organizations and the second is its decreasing effectiveness in a world of reduced autonomy. States have gradually ceded sovereignty to regional organizations such as the EU and are subject to increased monitoring of internal affairs in economic and human rights matters. Indebted developing countries may have their economic sovereignty extinguished as international economic organizations set economic policy. The erosion of sovereignty is an uneven and gradual process which is transforming the role of states. The subsidy area is an example of this process.

Even where sovereignty formally exists it is more difficult to see its fruits because autonomy (the ability to pursue a course of action once chosen) is more circumspect. Governments are restrained by the liberalization of financial markets and transnationalization of production. The concept of diminishing autonomy, however, is slightly misleading in that even if one could establish that there was a greater degree of autonomy in previous eras, this autonomy was limited to powerful elites in the most powerful states. Autonomy for the majority of the world's citizens and political authorities has never existed. What is significant about the present environment is the limited autonomy of the most powerful state actors. Indeed, the issue of decreasing American autonomy has been at the forefront of US dominated international relations literature.

US scholarship has tended to view the loss of American governmental autonomy as the decline of hegemony (Gilpin, 1987). Hegemonic decline theorists drew attention to the fact that US military and economic power declined in the late 1960s and 1970s. By equating order with overwhelming power, it was a simple step to conclude that disorder was the result of a loss of power by the dominant actor (Krasner, 1976). Citing the decline of an international hierarchy and the growth in the number of issue areas and actors, Robert Keohane suggested that the concept of 'regimes' might be the answer to declining hegemony. Since US power has suffered a serious relative decline, the choice for the system is between no leadership or a different configuration of nonhegemonic leadership. The solution to chaos is some form of multiple leadership facilitated by international organizations. Keohane's 1984 work *After Hegemony* proposed that although US power had declined, regimes could still be maintained. Regimes are 'sets of implicit or explicit principles, norms, rules and decision-making procedures around which actors' expectations converge in a given area of international relations' (1984: 57). Assisted by institutions that facilitate cooperation and provide information to their members, regimes can serve states' national interests. Even though US hegemony is gone, regimes live on and offer hope for world order.

A purer liberal response has been that the hegemony debate is misguided. There has been no such thing as a real hegemony since the time of the Roman Empire. World order is indeed changing, but not in the way realists suggest. The change is from a system based on territoriality and military competition to one based on the rise of the trading state (Rosecrance, 1986). Due to the high cost of conflict (nuclear weapons), the tremendous gains available from trade and the fact that economic power and success no longer depends on control of territory, the world has the potential to move away from realist struggles. Taking this one step further, it is possible to argue that states themselves are losing power to an increasingly globalized economy. State autonomy is undermined by the global economy and state sovereignty must be reduced to facilitate the creation of institutions capable of managing the new environment.

The reduction of US autonomy has been noted in international relations, but there is often a failure to capture the dynamic of recent changes which involve the transnationalization of the international system. It is not simply that states cooperate to maintain mutually beneficial rules, but new centers of authority and decision-making are eroding the central position of the state. Among the new centers of authority are recently created or extended institutions to rule on subsidy disputes. These new areas of authority raise difficult questions about accountability and democratic control.

Similar to most sociological and political concepts, democracy has been associated with the state and not extended beyond its borders. If more and more decisions influencing the lives of communities are being taken in locations beyond the state (in international organizations, global firms or other states) the relevance of a concept of democracy confined to a national context is questionable. Examples of such far-flung decisions include terms for IMF loans (voting based on financial contributions), police actions by the United Nations (controlled by five permanent members of the Security Council) and the harvesting of the Brazilian rainforest (Brazilian state elite, foreign creditors). Liberal democratic mechanisms (parliaments, elections) may continue to function within states, but they have less and less of a role in securing popular interests. Representative democracy is less able to live up to its claims of fulfilling the democratic ideal of rule by the people.

Despite the alleged triumph of liberal democracy following the Cold War, the 1990s has seen widespread disillusionment with representative democracy in Western countries. 1992 was a particularly turbulent year for representative democracy in OECD states. In the EU many citizens informed their elites of opposition to the Maastricht Treaty and further integration. In North America, the Canadian population rejected an elite-brokered Constitutional package, while the US public experienced widespread disillusionment with the operation of Congress and many supported a third party candidate for President. In Japan, financial scandals and corruption caused a split in the ruling party, while Italian politics underwent a transformation following revelations of widespread corruption and disgust at Mafia murders of the judiciary. The first two years of the 1990s revealed a systemic division between representatives and their electorates in developed capitalist states (Dahl, 1994; Maier, 1994). Under pressure from increased globalization, many sensed that popular control was not being achieved through existing institutions and that it was time to reconsider democracy's original meaning and new forms of practice.

Are those decisions-makers operating beyond the confines of the national political community accountable to citizens in OECD states?

If democracy means popular control over important decisions, the general answer is no. The structures of national liberal democracy remain, but they are less capable of influencing the world we inhabit. Until recently the institutional structure of democracy and democratic theory have usually been confined to the national context (Held, 1991). Increasingly, decisions affecting citizens' lives are being made in distant, insulated political, economic, legal and bureaucratic forums. As decision-making slips away from state structures, so does accountability and with it the degree of democracy that has been achieved in the postwar period.

SUBSIDIES

Our present understanding of politics, the state and international relations is conditioned by the European experience dating back to the formation of the modern state system emerging out of the crisis of feudalism in the sixteenth and seventeenth centuries. The evolution from a European system of some five hundred fairly independent political units in 1500 to about twenty in 1900, was a bloody process requiring the exertion of considerable force and loss of life. Central to this story is the growth of military might in the hands of state structures. Indeed, Weber focused on this in his definition of the state as a human community that successfully claims the 'monopoly of the legitimate use of physical force within a given territory' (1958: 79). Essential for the centralization of physical force in state structures was the centralization of revenue or resource collection. Mercantilist economic practice erected economic barriers against foreign rivals, but liberalized domestic practice. States could not be molded, armies equipped, or imperial projects launched without the organization of credit and taxation. The first regular military units in Europe were financed by the first regular national tax, the French *taille royale* in the mid-fifteenth century, and by the mid-sixteenth century 80 per cent of Spanish state revenues went to military expenditures (Anderson, 1974: 32). Control over taxation figured prominently in both the French and American revolutions. The ability to tax and spend is fundamental to our understanding of the modern state (Tilly, 1975). A true state, in the traditional sense, must be able to collect revenues and spend them without recourse to outside powers.

Today, many forms of government expenditure have been labeled subsidies. Subsidies are grants or government expenditures that assist in the production of goods or services. Defined so broadly, they include just about every function that government undertakes from running a police force to providing tax breaks for corporations. This study suggests that international efforts to curb subsidy practices challenge our traditional understanding of the state because they restrict the ability of state leadership to disperse revenues. Governments are not as free as they were in the past to choose whatever method of economic intervention they desire. This does not mean that a state is no longer a state, but it does imply that states are changing. Attempts to move financial decisions to other areas of authority illuminate the evolution of political communities. Moreover, the international attempt to regulate subsidies highlights four general processes in the global political economy:

1. Liberalization of the state. Agreements to regulate subsidies move all states in a more liberal direction. They reduce government involvement in the economy or shift it into particular areas deemed legitimate by liberal thought. It is no longer legitimate for governments to direct financial assistance to those industries that export manufactured goods. Governments are not allowed to give special tax breaks to exporters, for example. Similarly, attempts to bring agriculture under increased subsidy discipline reflect a move to pry that industry away from government support. These steps demonstrate a shifting of power away from political authority to the market. Non-financial variables or motivations for government policy are undermined in favor of market mechanisms determining the structure and organization of more and more sectors.

In so far as a trend can be discerned, it is for states to reduce direct assistance to enterprises and concentrate on broad infrastructural expenditures. Expenditure for social support, education, welfare and basic research is more acceptable than grants to business. The trend is tempered by the reluctance of powerful actors such as the US and EU to suspend activity in certain crucial sectors such as agriculture, entertainment or cultural industries and aerospace. The subsidy tussle can be seen as part of a broader movement to reduce the role of the state as a direct economic manager.

2. Liberalization versus autonomy. Increasing liberalization has increased competition and insecurity amongst many groups. Those disadvantaged by increased competition have targeted others' economic practices as a cause for their plight. This is particularly true in the US, as domestic trade law encourages such activity. Recent cases have stressed that rivals are trading unfairly, cheating at the game of economic competition. Accusations of illegal subsidy practices have been a dominant theme in the targeting of unfair activity. It can be seen both as an attempt to restrict liberalization by increasing protection, and as an effort to force others to liberalize. There is pressure for protection at home and attack abroad.

Having reached the limits of growth from tariff reduction, the liberalization juggernaut turns its attention to other areas to fuel economic growth. The globalization and liberalization process is similar to peeling away the skins of an onion. The outer skin was tariffs on manufactured goods, interior skins could be subsidies, government procurement, agricultural protection, barriers to service trade or environmental regulations. Such peeling, however, encounters resistance from those who are being peeled, as well as governments subject to popular pressure requiring policy intervention tools. Subsidies are a particularly sensitive area because most of the controversial ones have been established to pursue domestic goals rather than achieve international competitive advantage. The attack on another government's domestic policies is an attack on its policy autonomy.

The subsidy issue also reveals the clash between societies based upon slightly different economic models. Although there is general elite consensus concerning liberalism, subsidy codes are one method whereby the US government presses others to restructure along hyperliberal lines. By defining 'fair trade' and 'legitimate' government intervention policies as those that are hyperliberal, the stage is set for the US government to either force weaker states, or assist embattled sympathetic state elites, to reorganize their economies and societies along the US pattern.

3. Transfer of decision making authority. Not only is the definition of legitimate government expenditure shifting, but so is the location of the decision itself. In the EU, the decision is made by the European Commission, subject to review by the European Court. In North America an unsuccessful attempt was made to shift the decision away from national governments to a bilateral or trilateral decision-making body. At the multilateral level, there has also been an attempt to empower GATT representatives to take decisions about the legality of particular national programs. Sovereignty, in the sense of denoting an ultimate legitimate decision-making body, is being internationalized in this vital issue area.

It is significant that the US has been the most reluctant to submit to this transfer of decision-making. The US Congress acts as a powerful brake on the internationalization of the American state. The notion of foreigners deciding upon the legitimacy of US expenditures strikes at the heart of the US system of government and representation. To turn a once powerful phrase, one could argue that there should be no expenditure regulation without representation. US eagerness to attack foreign subsidy practices combined with its reluctance to adhere to an international mechanism that might remedy such disputes highlights the tensions of a globalizing economy and the difficulties of transferring decision-making away from the state.

4. Erosion of democracy and accountability. The combined effect of the liberalization of the state and transfer of decision-making authority is to undermine the democratic process and exacerbate the liberalism/autonomy tension. The liberalization of the state removes more and more areas from government intervention and popular control. Entering into subsidy agreements restricts government policy makers, influences decisions in particular areas and eliminates the use of certain policy tools. Empowering international courts or bureaucracies to take decisions about the legitimate expenditure of national revenue raises large questions about control of those institutions. Who should determine the amount of national revenue that should be spent supporting rural communities? Is this a decision for the political community as a whole, exercising its will (however imperfectly) through its elected representatives? The trend in subsidy issues is that the decision should be taken by international bureaucrats and lawyers acting upon the authority of treaties. Once agreed, these treaties are not subject to popular review, nor can changes be made by popular representative institutions. In a sense they resemble a long-term constitution rather than legislation subject to review.

State elites have sought to create institutions which could depoliticize subsidy issues and turn decisions about tax expenditure into technical exercises. Such attempts are frustrated by fears within societies and some governing elites about turning such decisions over to unaccountable and unsympathetic neoliberal bodies.

2 The US Trade Law System

The character and operation of US trade law has had a major impact on the operation of the global trading system. Conflicts about subsidies, dumping and unfair trade cannot be adequately understood without reference to the operation of US law. This chapter gives the reader an overview of that system and some specific information about the way it approaches the subsidy issue. The first section reviews various approaches to thinking about trade and protectionism. This is followed by a brief review of key US institutions and laws. The last section details the operation of the countervailing duty (anti-subsidy) process and recounts a case from the Canada–US relationship: softwood lumber.

TRADE AND PROTECTIONISM

Commenting upon the persistence of protectionism in the face of economic models indicating its futility, a leading economist lamented 'rarely in the economics profession do we encounter greater dissonance between what we are taught in principle and what we observe in practice' (Cohen, 1990: 261). From a liberal perspective, government actions that restrict trade are illogical because they fail to maximize economic welfare.[1] To use more colorful language, 'if there is the equivalent of anti-Christ in economics, it is the proponent of trade restraint' (Goodwin, 1988: 211). Despite liberal enthusiasm for free trade, its effects vary according to the particular case in which actors attempt its implementation. Further, attempts at free trade are vulnerable to pressure from domestic groups harmed by moves that transfer power to markets from political authority. Labor is not simply a commodity – it is made up of individuals and, in liberal democratic countries, they vote. This tension between the imperatives of international economic liberalism and domestic political backlash is prominent in numerous approaches to international political economy (Strange, 1988b; Cox, 1987; Gilpin, 1987; Block, 1977; Polanyi, 1957).

'Trade is the stuff of domestic politics' a leading international political economy text book advises students (Spero, 1985: 91). Indeed, trade law is highly political, but it is not confined to domestic politics. Transnational or international politics intersect with domestic politics as economic theory and legal precedent are brought together in a melange of interests around trade issues. Forces working at the systemic, state and transnational level all have a role in influencing the trade law system (Lake, 1988; Milner 1988). The US trade law system is primarily an arena of conflict. It is not meant to produce economic efficiency, nor is it designed to operate in a legally coherent or consistent manner. It is the product of a conflictual process and represents the balance of forces influencing US institutions at the time of its introduction and is modified through time as forces within and upon American society fluctuate in strength.

Although discussion of protectionism is a staple of trade scholarship, it is helpful to consider the precise nature of the protectionist threat. The 1980s saw a multitude of warnings about the imminent protectionist threat and the risks of a breakdown of the trading system. The US, in particular, was identified as a major culprit by its trading allies and domestic liberal ideologues. Liberal economists, seeking to mold the world into their models of perfect free trade, were not comfortable with the system's trajectory nor calls for fair trade.[2] This section echoes the work of those who challenge the idea that protectionism *per se* threatens the health of the economic system.

Determining the threat of protectionism requires a decision about how important the export and import of goods is to the global economy. Many trade commentators put it at the center of their analysis. They see the effort at liberalizing trade as a nonstop struggle against the forces of protectionism. The bicycle theory of trade stipulates that unless you keep the bike in motion (liberalizing trade) you will fall off (protectionism). This view usually targets protectionism as the single largest threat to world growth.

A more accurate view is that trade-related disputes and protectionist pressures are secondary features of larger structures. The health of the monetary system and the structure of the production system is of greater importance to the global economy. From this viewpoint, the Great Depression was primarily caused by monetary collapse, with tariffs having a secondary effect (Strange, 1985: 239–40). If the monetary system is functioning well and the production system has created a web of contracts between countries and corporations, the protectionist threat is not a serious one.

An examination of the past two decades indicates that despite the emergence of a *new protectionism* and the worst economic downturn since the Great Depression, trade has continued to expand. New protectionism refers to the use of NTBs to support domestic industries.

The use of NTBs is not really new, they are just thought to be used more extensively since the source of 'old' protectionism (tariffs) have been effectively lowered by the GATT. The difficulty with dealing with many NTBs is that they are not easy to find, nor eliminate. Government health regulations, customs inspection or performance requirements may all be classified as NTBs. Despite recession and NTBs, the inflation adjusted increase in world trade during the decade from 1973–83 was between six and seven per cent (Strange, 1985: 242). Trade continues to grow faster than income and the ratio of trade to GNP has continued to grow in Canada, Japan, South Korea, the United States and the United Kingdom. One could claim, however, that without the growth of NTBs world trade would have grown even more (Bhagwati, 1988: 56).

The explanation for this apparent contradiction lies in the production structure. The global economy has progressed past the point where trade is simply the export of national products. The rise of intrafirm trade means that a vast volume of trade is done within companies. In addition, more and more products use components from other countries. Thus, the all-American car or Japanese VCR no longer exist. Similarly, corporate alliances across state boundaries against domestic rivals blur the nationalities of transnational corporations. In the car industry General Motors is working with Toyota and Isuzu while its rival, Ford, has linked up with Mazda and Kawasaki.

Companies find ways around protectionist barriers. A partial response has been an increase of FDI. This makes it far more difficult to halt parts imports as Honda or Toyota become *domestic* US manufacturers. Possible implications of this strategy for the operation of US trade law is illustrated by a recent case before American courts. A Japanese typewriter firm, Brother Industries Ltd, manufacturing in Tennessee, launched an antidumping suit against an American company, Smith Corona, manufacturing in Singapore. This case raises the question of whether the law is meant to protect US companies or companies employing US workers.

It would be more helpful to see protectionism not as an evil in itself, but as a symptom, a response to inadequate adjustment to globalizing economies. The inability of states to adhere to pure liberal policies should not be seen as failures of intelligence or movement towards closure, but as attempts to deal with intractable problems of adjustment and adaptation to changing economies of production, technology and trade (Clark, 1985). The threat to stability in OECD countries comes from liberalizing too quickly without adequate measures to compensate those disadvantaged by the process. As Ruggie suggested 'Ironically, then, the foremost force for discontinuity at present is not 'the new protectionism' in money and trade, but the resurgent ethos of liberal capitalism' (1982: 229). The links of the world economy are stronger than those slowly being frayed by the US Congress. They will not break as easily as some have suggested.

A major foreign complaint has been that US trade law is politicized. The system is seen to respond to domestic American industry seeking protection from competition rather than a decision on the effect of subsidies. Here we come across a major theme in much of the literature: messy politics getting in the way of economic and legal theory and reason. The operation of trade law should be taken out of the realm of politics. This was a principal goal of the Canadian negotiators of the Free Trade Agreement. However, Congress and the US President use trade laws as an escape valve for protectionist pressure. The Congress prefers to send industries through the legal process than deal with individual cases as it did in the Smoot-Hawley tariff. The President uses his (perhaps, one day, her) ability to negotiate voluntary export restraints as a tactic to respond to domestic cries of economic distress. This leads one to conclude that the purpose of US trade law in general and the 'unfair' trade remedies in particular is not to settle trade disputes in an even handed manner, but to offer limited protection to politically powerful domestic industry. Attempts to reform trade laws so that they are less protectionist collide with their primary political function. This is not to suggest that reform is impossible, but unless there is movement to resolve the cause of the distress (economic dislocation and lack of adjustment programs) the task will be arduous.

To gain a better understanding of the operation of the US system the following sections familiarize the reader with the primary institutions and laws that are at the heart of the system. This is followed by sections on the countervailing duty process and an illustrative case that was particularly controversial in US–Canadian relations.

Institutions

In a comparative study of the US, Japanese and European Community legal systems' interaction with international economic law, John H. Jackson urges readers to remember two crucial points (1984: 139). In the United States, the legislative arm of government has relatively more power over the executive than in other countries and the legal system is set up to give individuals, citizen groups and corporations numerous opportunities to challenge government policy. The institutional structure concerned with US trade law is decentralized and fragmented. Constitutionally, Congress is responsible for commercial policy, but the President is delegated power to negotiate and implement trade policy. A bureaucratic structure has emerged to manage trade laws and the conduct of commercial policy between the legislature and executive, but policy initiatives from the two branches of government can be contradictory. The primary institutional actors in US trade policy are the Congress, the President, the International Trade Commission, the Department of Commerce and the United States Trade Representative.

United States Congress. The United States constitution gives Congress (House of Representatives and Senate) the power to regulate commerce with other nations and the authority to levy duties and taxes on trade. Power over trade policy has swung back and forth between the Congress and the President for much of this century. Following the disastrous effects of the Smoot-Hawley tariff of 1930, the Congress used the Reciprocal Trade Agreements Act of 1934 to change its role from that of devising individual tariffs to regulating the degree of tariff-cutting authority it should give to the President and the access that should be given to industry for administered protection.[3] The main elements of this system were using the tariff as an international bargaining tool, relying on the executive to broker deals, special deals for the most powerful industries (textiles and steel), strong congressional committees that could sidetrack protectionist legislation, and trade remedies for cases that were *deserving* of protection (Destler, 1986: 9–26).

The postwar era has seen a gradual shift back to Congressional influence as the use of trade remedies expanded. In return for granting succeeding Presidents the ability to negotiate tariff reductions with other countries, Congress modified the implementation of trade laws governing import policy to allow slightly more protection for domestic industries (Baldwin, 1985: 33–77). Examples of this include setting shorter time limits for investigations of subsidy and antidumping in the Trade Act of 1974 and shifting the determination of injury in subsidy cases away from the Treasury Department to the International Trade Commission (perceived to be a more sympathetic body) under the Trade Agreements Act of 1979.

President. Being responsible for the health of the economy as a whole and less susceptible to the pressure from any particular industry, the institution of the Presidency is often deemed to have a pro-free trade bias. This commitment to ensuring the free flow of goods and services often varies with the arrival of Congressional or Presidential elections when there is a need to show that the President is concerned about trade issues. In such a case the President usually reacts to a general feeling that some action should be taken rather than selecting a particular industry for protection (Baldwin, 1985: 115–74).

The President's role can be crucial in both broad and narrow policy areas. The head of the executive can set the tone of trade policy and launch large initiatives such as pursuing trade deals with Canada and Mexico or pushing for the start of a new GATT round of negotiations. More narrowly, the President can reject the International Trade Commission's recommendations for import restrictive actions or negotiate orderly marketing arrangements such as voluntary export restraints. In times of economic difficulty even ideologically liberal presidents resort to protectionist policies for political advantage. A review of President Reagan's record concluded that even his ability to resist import restrictions was weak (Pearson, 1989: 36).

The International Trade Commission (ITC). Established in 1916 as the US Tariff Commission, this organization was refashioned into the US International Trade Commission in 1975. The ITC conducts investigations to determine if American industry has suffered material injury from imports and can recommend relief for producers harmed by both fairly and unfairly traded imports. It is responsible for administering Section 201 escape clause actions and submitting a yearly review of this activity to the President. Investigations of foreign activity that infringe upon agriculture programs or patents (Section 337) are also in this organization's domain. The ITC plays an important role in the administration of countervailing duty (CVD) and antidumping laws as it is responsible for making preliminary and final determinations of injury.

Members of the ITC are appointed for nonrenewable nine-year terms in the hope that they will not be influenced by political pressures. Yet, the ITC is influenced by Congress in two ways. Firstly, Congress controls the Commission's budget. A Commission that continuously took decisions against Congress' wishes could find itself short of funds. Secondly, since 1973, Congress has insisted that more Commission appointments have Congressional work experience so that they are sensitive to its concerns. The ITC has been more likely to grant positive decisions of import injury since the Trade Act of 1974. While the 1963–74 period saw only 28 per cent of cases succeed in their injury claim, this jumped to 60 per cent between 1975 and 1983 (Baldwin, 1985: 102). It is difficult to conclude whether the change is due to the modification of trade laws or composition of the commission's members, but it is not unreasonable to suggest that the ITC now tilts further towards protectionism than it once did.

International Trade Administration (Department of Commerce). The Department of Commerce (DOC) has broad responsibility for the operation of nonagricultural international trade. Within the DOC, the International Trade Administration (ITA) determines whether a foreign product has been subsidized or is being sold for less than its value. In CVD cases, the ITA has the crucial role of deciding what is or is not a countervailable subsidy. Some analysts have suggested that the ITA's decisions are influenced by the mood of Congress (Percy and Yoder, 1987: 13). The Department of Commerce may interpret particular sections of the law in a protectionist manner so that Congress does not legislate even more detailed and protectionist measures. This is the charge with regard to the issue of specificity which will be dealt with in more depth in the discussion of the softwood lumber case.

United States Trade Representative (USTR). In order to balance domestic and international concerns in the trade area, Congress created the position of the President's Special Representative for Trade Negotiations (STR) through the Trade Expansion Act of 1962. In 1979 the office was reorganized and renamed the USTR. The role of the USTR was to be a representative of the United States in international negotiations and chair of an interagency trade organization for the President. I. M. Destler describes its function as that of an 'executive broker' mediating deals between government agencies, domestic and international interests, and the executive and Congress (1986: 89).

Trade Laws

Canada's Trade Ambassador to the Tokyo Round of GATT, Rodney de C. Grey, aptly described the use of a variety of US domestic laws to restrict trade as 'contingent protection' (1982: 8) The system provides relief from competition on a case by case basis, usually at the request of industry. Those pressing for protection use whichever law is most likely to further their objectives. Two or more statutes may be employed in an effort to restrict competition by whatever means are possible. Because separate laws cover different aspects of trade, a number of laws can be employed for a similar purpose, such as the exclusion of particular imports.[4] It is more helpful to speak of a system of trade law rather than individual protectionist laws if one is to understand the legal maneuvering of trade disputes. The following sections are the most important (Vakerics, Wilson and Weigel, 1987):

Section 201 – Escape Clause (Safeguards). Section 201 of the Trade Act of 1974, known as the escape clause or safeguard action, allows industries suffering from *fairly* traded imports to seek temporary relief via tariffs, quotas or domestic adjustment assistance. Because safeguard actions require a substantial degree of injury, are limited in time and may be matched by other states, they are generally seen as being less protectionist than unfair trade laws such as countervailing or antidumping duties.

Section 232 – National Security Protection. Section 232 of the Trade Expansion Act of 1962 allows the Secretary of Commerce to determine if certain articles are imported into the United States in such quantities that they could threaten national security. If a threat is found, imports in strategic materials will be curtailed to ensure sufficient domestic production. This tool is mainly used for petroleum products but efforts have been made to apply it to strategic minerals and machine tools.

Section 301 – Removing Foreign Barriers. Rather than protecting the domestic market, Section 301 of The Trade Act of 1974 attacks foreign barriers to trade (Bhagwati and Patrick, 1990). Its purpose is to pry open markets that restrict American exports. It targets other countries' practices seen to harm American exports and authorizes the President to take retaliatory action. Foreign barriers are catalogued in the annual Trade Barriers Report issued by the office of the USTR. When the first report was released in 1985, the USTR, Clayton Yeutter, made American goals explicit: 'In short, we are seeking to eliminate all of the unfair barriers listed in the report.' Many of the barriers, he admitted, are not 'unfair in a legal sense. They are, nevertheless, practices that impede US exports and we ought to seek to eliminate them.'[5] Essentially, *unfair* is interpreted as anything that might restrict American access. If other countries fail to eliminate their barriers the President may withdraw trade concessions, impose tariffs or quotas, and deny licenses issued by federal regulators to foreign suppliers of services.

Sections 701 to 707 and 303 – Countervailing Duty Laws. This is the section that is of primary concern when discussing the subsidy issue. A duty may be levied against imports if it is found that they have benefited from a subsidy and cause or threaten material injury to US industry or may materially retard its establishment. If these conditions are met, a CVD equal to the amount of the subsidy is imposed on the imported goods.

The CVD law originated in the United States in the 1890s.[6] In the 1890 McKinley Tariff the United States instituted a countervailing duty on refined sugar from countries that supported their own sugar industry with an export bounty or subsidy. The Americans were subsidizing their sugar industry and were determined to protect it from those countries giving subsidies to help exports jump the US tariff barrier. In 1897 the US Congress extended the CVD law to cover all imports subject to duties. There was no requirement that domestic production be injured for the duties to take effect because the clear intention was to protect US production and the tariff system (Barcelo, 1991: 321–2; Viner, 1986: 168–9). The law was amended in 1922 to include domestic production subsidies as well as export subsidies, but this was not utilized until 50 years later.

The CVD law was instituted for a specific purpose – the protection of domestic industry from foreign government policies that assisted exports into the US market. Its sole task was to provide protection. From a purely liberal economic perspective, instituting countervailing duties against subsidized imports is counterproductive as they only raise the cost of products to domestic consumers and producers (Rugman, 1986: 372). They are as inefficient for the country levying them as subsidies are for the exporting country. A consistent liberal would argue that 'there is no countermeasure that one nation can take against another nation's protectionist policies that will not hurt the first nation still further' (Stone, 1988: 119).

Sections 731 to 740 – Antidumping. The Trade Agreements Act of 1979 repealed the Antidumping Act of 1922, but kept most of its basic principles. The practice of selling goods for less than the cost of production is known as dumping. An antidumping duty can be applied against imports that have been sold at less than a 'fair market value'. There are three different methods for determining if an import is being sold at a less than fair market value. The price of the import may be compared to the price of a similar product in the home market, in a third country or a constructed price determined by the Department of Commerce. If the import is being sold at a discount of more than 0.5 per cent of the fair market value, an antidumping duty is applied.[7]

Similar to CVD cases, imports must be found to cause or threaten material injury to American industry or materially retard its establishment. Unlike the original law of 1916, however, there is no requirement to show that the products were dumped in an attempt at predatory pricing. Predatory pricing occurs when companies charge artificially low prices to drive competitors out of business. The company that engaged in predatory pricing then steps forward to reap the benefits of being a monopoly supplier.

For those interested in minimizing the distortions of antidumping laws in Canada–US trade the preferred solution seems to be an elimination of this device completely. Present competition laws in Canada and antitrust laws in the US target the same activity that was the original goal of antidumping laws – namely the prevention of predatory pricing. The Canadian and US Chambers of Commerce have stated that domestic laws are sufficient to deal with the problem and that antidumping laws aimed across the border only hinder trade (Feltham et al., 1991).

The antidumping and countervailing duty laws share a couple of common features. Administratively, they follow a similar path through the ITA and ITC. Politically, they limit the President's ability to use discretion in rejecting punitive measures against foreigners. Both laws originate before the Great Depression and are based upon economic theories inspired by mercantilists such as Alexander Hamilton. The protectionist notions of pursuing *fair* trade have been encased in these laws and continue to exercise influence in modern trading relationships (Goldstein, 1988). It is often the case that a firm will launch both CVD and Antidumping cases against a rival. The primary difference in the approaches is that antidumping is aimed against the practice of foreign companies while countervail takes government spending as its main target. One is trying to change the practice of firms while the other tries to change the practice of governments. Since this study is concerned with the role of government, the concentration is on the countervailing duty law.[8]

Informal Protection. In addition to the above mentioned legal devices, imports are restricted by a number of informal understandings known as voluntary export restraints (VERs) or orderly marketing arrangements (OMAs).[9] This is an agreement by a foreign industry to limit the volume of exports to a particular country. For example, Japanese automakers could agree to limit exports to 30 per cent of the North American market. VERs are not actually voluntary. Industries usually adopt such arrangements because of the threat of more serious trade action. They are often undertaken to persuade US industry to drop its antidumping or countervailing petition or as a reaction to a more general protectionist attitude of the Congress. In some cases the President proposes VERs as an alternative to tariffs or quotas. This was the solution offered by President Reagan to the US steel industry crisis in 1984 (Wolf, 1989; Hufbauer et al., 1986).

VERs have proved useful to the United States executive for three reasons. Firstly, they are a signal to the Congress and the American people that the President is willing to do something about the trade deficit. This deflects political charges that the welfare of US industries and workers is being ignored. Secondly, in the ongoing battle between the President and Congress over trade policy, VERs are a method of ensuring that the executive retains some discretion (Stern and London, 1990; Destler, 1986). Thirdly, it is seen as a less serious violation of free trade principles than visible tariffs and quotas. Some have suggested that VERs are less threatening to the liberal trade system than legislated measures (Bhagwati, 1988: 58).

Section 301, meant to pry open foreign markets and liberalize trade, can also have the effect of creating *voluntary import expansions* (VIEs) which restrict trade. A country being threatened with Section 301 retaliation unless it allows increases in US imports may simply transfer its sourcing of imports from other countries to the US. There is some evidence to suggest that South Korea has shifted it imports in agricultural products from China and Argentina to the United States for just such reasons (Bhagwati, 1988: 84). Trade diversion replaces the goal of liberalization. The result of unilateral action can be increased emphasis on the quantity of US imports rather than the openness of the market. This signals a move from a system based on rules to one based on quantitative outcomes for the strongest members and raises the prospect of the most powerful countries gaining export markets at the expense of less powerful and more efficient rivals. To use Bhagwati's (1989: 467) terms it is a change from a fixed rule to a fixed quantity regime.

THE CVD PROCESS

A countervailing duty investigation can be self-initiated by the Department of Commerce, but is usually launched by a petition from an American industry. Any 'interested party' such as an industry, union or trade association that is in competition with the product in question may file the petition. Petitions filed against countries such as Canada that are signatories of the 1979 Tokyo Round GATT Agreement on Subsidies and Countervailing Measures, follow a two-track process before the Department of Commerce's ITA and the ITC.[10] Figure 2.1 is attached to give a visual demonstration of the process. The ITA begins its investigation to determine whether a countervailable subsidy has been given while the ITC must investigate whether the domestic industry has or will suffer injury. Within twenty days of filing it must determine if the petition contains sufficient information to proceed. Since the pre-filing period is marked by consultation between the DOC and the petitioner, it is rare that a petition is thrown out at this point.

Generally, the ITA has 85 days from the date of filing to deliver a

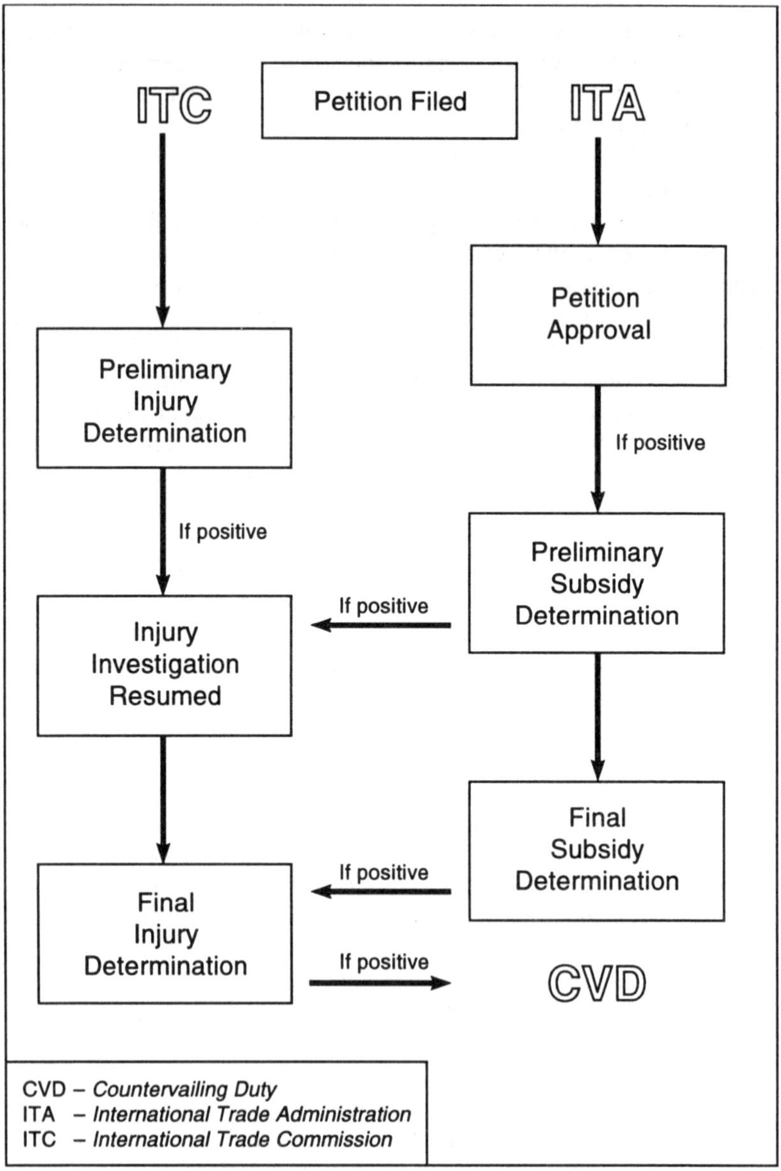

Figure 2.1 The CVD process

preliminary determination of subsidy. If the case is deemed to be extraordinarily complicated the time period is extended to 150 days or if an 'upstream subsidy' is involved 250 days is allowed.[11] Three hundred and ten days are provided if the case involves upstream subsidies and is extraordinarily complicated. If the preliminary subsidy decision is affirmative, a bond must be posted for entry of the product into the American market. If the preliminary decision is negative, the ITA continues with its final investigation, but the ITC injury process comes to a halt until the final subsidy determination. A final determination of subsidization should be made within 75 days of the preliminary determination. This can be extended if the case involves upstream subsidies. If the final determination is negative, the case is dropped. If the verdict is positive, an estimate of net subsidy is given. Pending an affirmative ruling of injury from the ITC, a countervailing duty equal to the subsidy is imposed.

In order for the CVD to be instituted the value of the subsidy must reach a certain minimum level or *de minimis*. The *de minimis* level is 0.5 per cent of the merchandise in question. If the subsidy is calculated to be 0.5 per cent or above, the CVD is applicable. Since a number of subsidy programs can be added together to reach *de minimis*, any particular subsidy need only be a fraction of the total production cost to contribute to a CVD ruling. This leads to an investigation of as many subsidy practices as possible in order to reach or exceed the 0.5 per cent hurdle.

As noted above, the ITC begins its investigation of injury following the filing of the petition. A preliminary ruling must be given within 45 days of filing of petitions. If this injury investigation is negative, the process comes to a halt. If it is affirmative, the ITC simply notifies the ITA and both continue with their investigations. If the ITA's preliminary determination of subsidy is positive, the ITC must then give a final injury determination within 120 days. As mentioned above, if the ITA preliminary determination is negative the ITC suspends its investigation until a final ITA positive subsidy determination. If the ITA's final determination is positive, the ITC has 75 days to give its final word.

The ITC's final determination imposes a stricter definition of injury than in the preliminary investigation. It must be shown that the industry faces material injury, the threat of material injury or that the establishment of domestic industry is being materially retarded. If ITC's final determination is of material injury the Department of Commerce will impose a CVD within seven days. Usually, the CVD order is placed on all companies exporting the product from the offending country.

The President does not have any authority to overturn CVD decisions.

Since the early 1970s the CVD law, similar to other trade laws, has been amended to make it easier for petitioners to gain relief from imports. The 1974 Trade Act outlined strict time limits for action on CVD cases and required the President to take action on cases within 60 days of relief being recommended by the ITC. This resulted in an immediate jump in the number of CVD cases being filed. Investigations rose from one in 1973 and five in 1974 to 38 in 1975 (Destler, 1986: 117). Industries did not receive the protection they were seeking, however, because the administration made broad use of authority to ignore decisions so trading partners would not pull out of the Tokyo GATT round which was dealing with the subsidy issue.

The Trade Agreement Act of 1979 was required to make US law conform to the recently concluded Tokyo Round results. Congress was instrumental in drafting this legislation and used the opportunity to bolster its trade remedy laws. As part of the Tokyo agreements the United States was required to change their CVD law so that 'material injury' would have to be proven before a duty was levied on countries that subscribed to the Tokyo Round subsidies code. Congressional pressure ensured that material injury was defined as harm which is not 'inconsequential, immaterial or unimportant' rather than a more strict interpretation of 'a substantial cause' as in escape clause action. Although demanding proof of material injury was meant to reduce the frivolousness of CVD cases, its loose definition made them more appealing for industries seeking protection. Once again, the time limits for the CVD process were tightened.

Another important change was the shifting of administrative responsibility for unfair trade remedies from the Secretary of the Treasury (since 1897) to the Secretary of Commerce. Many members of Congress felt that the Treasury did not take its trade responsibilities seriously enough. Senator Danforth accused the Treasury of 'Lax enforcement after the investigation was completed, permitting lengthy postponement of antidumping duties, or an outright waiver of the duty in some countervailing duty cases . . .' (Bello and Holmer, 1987: 126). The result of strengthening the CVD and antidumping laws was a shift away from using Section 201 (escape clause) to unfair trade laws for protection. Increasingly, industries seeking relief were claiming that their rivals traded unfairly rather than more efficiently. The 1980s saw a sharp jump in the number of cases being investigated and the duties in effect, relative to the late 1960s and early 1970s. Whereas there was only one investigation in 1973 and five in 1974, this rose to 10 in

1980, 27 in 1981, 146 in 1982, 30 in 1983, 55 in 1984, and 43 in 1985. In 1983 there were 56 countervailing duties in effect compared to 13 in 1968 (Destler, 1986: 125). Another reason for making CVD and antidumping laws the weapon of choice is that in comparison with safeguard actions, the President has less discretion in applying sanctions. Once subsidies and injury have been found, the duty kicks in whereas the President can delay relief in safeguard actions.

Further, less far reaching, steps were taken to strengthen the antidumping and countervailing duties law in 1984 and 1988. The Trade and Tariff Act of 1984 refined the test for an upstream subsidy, and took a number of steps to allow small businesses greater access to unfair trade remedies by streamlining procedures and providing more information (Bello and Holmer, 1987: 83–117). The Omnibus Trade and Competitiveness Act of 1988 clarified a number of provisions including the order that the Commerce Department must examine whether or not a subsidy is specific by looking at actual practice rather than intent. In other words, if a subsidy was generally available, but used by only one industry, it should be considered a specific subsidy.

A definite pattern has emerged in the Congressional trade bills of 1974, 1979, 1984, and 1988. At each stage industries that are feeling competitive pressure or have been unsuccessful in previous trade remedy cases go to Congress with specific complaints and advice about how the laws could be tightened. In fact, 'revisions have been an *ad hoc* series of amendments derived from specific proposals from domestic companies involved in recent or anticipated cases' (Horlick and Oliver, 1989: 5). Changes to the law are driven by companies seeking protection, not liberalization. Individual industries concentrate on how they can get an edge on imports rather than whether the system is liberal. The administration and large business lobbies, such as the Chamber of Commerce, American Association of Exporters and Importers (which includes Mobil, Occidental and Union Carbide), the Coalition to Promote America's Trade, and the National Foreign Trade Council usually fight against the more protectionist positions (Bello and Holmer, 1987: 49–82). A compromise is reached that tightens the laws, but leaves out the most threatening elements. Unhappy industry representatives start preparing for the next round.

From a liberal perspective the administration of US trade law is highly protectionist, harmful to the United States and its trading partners. The process is tilted in such a manner as to favor petitioning domestic industries. It has come under blistering attacks such as the decrying of the ITC as a 'monster created by the protectionist lobby in

Congress' (Rugman, 1986: 373). The application of US fair trade law is seen by critics as a nontariff barrier to trade, as effective as any tariff. At least six major objections have been raised about the administration of the CVD law:

1. It is quite easy for petitioners to demonstrate 'material injury' or the 'threat of material injury' at the ITC's preliminary hearing. This is because the ITC finds material injury simply if there has been an increase in imports. Other factors such as the domestic industry's own competitiveness are not examined. Thus, approximately 75 per cent of ITC preliminary votes rule that there has been injury (Rugman and Anderson, 1987: 42).
2. Once material injury has been found (more often than not) in the preliminary ruling, the burden of proof falls on the foreign firm to demonstrate that the ruling is incorrect. This requires the employment of expensive Washington legal counsel and a great deal of executive time. Only large industries are able to afford these expensive legal battles. For a relatively minor cost US petitioners are able to get a ruling against foreign industries which require far more effort and money to fight.
3. The competence of the six politically appointed ITC commissioners has been questioned. Alan Rugman points out that in 1985, with the exception of the Chair, Dr Paula Stern, few of the other commissioners had any 'intellectual, business or academic qualifications for the job' (Rugman, 1986: 367). Interestingly, Chairperson Stern has expressed a minority dissenting opinion that the degree of injury should be determined by how much aid a subsidy has given a particular product rather than the import effect of the product as a whole. Her fellow commissioners preferred a looser standard (Bello and Holmer, 1987: 162–67). The practice of appointing qualified academics or subject-matter experts ended in 1968. Appointing out-of-office party officials may increase the potential for decisions to be made on political rather than economic grounds.
4. ITC reports and ITA investigations have been criticized for being one sided and superficial. Rather than being caused by incompetence, this results from the brief amount of time allowed for preliminary rulings. The ITC and the ITA tend to rely on evidence supplied by the petitioners themselves and fail to thoroughly examine the case of foreign exporting firms. Foreign firms are often unable or unwilling to provide the information requested. Commenting on this practice at the Department of Commerce one CVD manual

concluded that 'Relying upon the petition as the basis for its determination will inevitably lead to affirmative subsidies determination' (Vakerics, Wilson, and Weigel, 1987: 203).

5. There is no need for the petitioner to demonstrate that it is the alleged foreign subsidy which is the major cause of injury. The ITA finds subsidies, but does not test for injury. Rising imports could cause material injury largely due to an overvalued US dollar, but because the exporting firm was found to have used a subsidy, the blame is placed in that area.

6. When examining subsidy practices the ITA makes no provision for calculating domestic American subsidies. A US industry receiving domestic subsidies can still launch a complaint against foreign practices. If the purpose is to liberalize trade or ensure competition, looking at the practices of foreign firms alone is not astute.

Complaints about US unfair trade laws usually concentrate on two points. The first is that because of their structure, US laws allow domestic industries to harass imports by imposing large financial costs. The second is that US industries use the law in order to force competitors to the bargaining table. The question of cost will be dealt with in later sections, but it does appear that American industry uses unfair trade laws to bully other nations into adopting VERs.

The case of the US steel industry is illustrative. When American steel producers decided to target foreign competition in 1982 they filed over 150 unfair trade petitions! The Europeans sought a deal restricting their exports rather than fight the cases. In adopting similar tactics against Newly Industrializing Countries in 1984, US steel officials admitted the aim was to make the burden of fighting legal cases so great that foreign producers would be forced to enter into negotiated trading practices (Destler, 1986: 130). The result is that the American steel industry receives blanket protection, punishing foreign countries with specific market shares oblivious to varying levels of subsidy or efficiency.

Fair Trade and Domestic Subsidies

The purpose of US trade remedy laws is to get other countries and economic actors to trade *fairly*. Determination of what is or is not fair is crucial. The use of the terms 'fair trade' and 'level playing field' is highly subjective and loaded with political meaning. Their origin lies with those seeking increased American protectionism citing any foreign practices that might aid competition. Both terms are used in debate as shorthand for the American way of doing things. One critic of the concept commented that 'in recent years it has become virtual gospel for the administration, Congress, and the general public, that US trade practice is fair; that foreigners engage in a host of covert and overt unfair trade practices; and that this cripples our ability to compete' (Pearson, 1989: 73).

To establish a level playing field is to ensure that others play by the same (US) rules. American negotiators can score a considerable tactical victory if they can get others to accept such a discourse. With reference to Canada's attempt to limit US trade law under the Free Trade Agreement, one of Canada's leading economists declared: 'What one can hope for is piecemeal modification of the substance, and application, of these laws. The purpose is to allow them to fulfill their legitimate function of *levelling the playing field* while preventing them from acting as concealed trade barriers' (Lipsey and York, 1988: 18) (emphasis added).

The divergence of American and Canadian perceptions about the issue of legitimate trade practices can also be seen in their characterization of US trade law. Canadians term the system 'contingent protection', emphasizing their protectionist nature. Americans usually speak of the system as 'trade remedy' laws, implying that their prime function is to redress a wrong (Smith, 1987: 5). These two terms demonstrate that participants are addressing two different problems – US protectionism and Canadian subsidization.

The countervailing of *domestic* subsidies is a highly controversial act which results in much of the political debate about the appropriate use of subsidies and countervailing duties. Domestic subsidies are expenditures undertaken by governments in order to achieve some domestic goal. Export subsidies are seen to be a hostile economic policy because they aid one country's producers at the expense of another's and shift employment from one country to another. In contrast, domestic subsidies are often overlooked because any influence on trade is a byproduct of other priorities. Yet, as OECD economies continue to globalize, domestic activity increasingly impacts on trade policy. Attempts to countervail domestic subsidies strike at the heart of a state's ability to set priorities for domestic management. Because of this, it is usually seen as threatening political interference in domestic affairs.

Canadian Softwood Lumber

As will be outlined in a later chapter, Canada was one state that became increasingly worried about the operation of US trade law in the 1980s and took far-reaching steps to ease the problem. The most prominent US–Canadian subsidy dispute was over softwood lumber and serves as an excellent example of the operation and effects of US trade law.

In May of 1986, the US Coalition for Fair Lumber Imports filed a petition at the ITC alleging that timber harvested on Canadian Crown lands was priced so low that it constituted a subsidy to the Canadian softwood lumber industry. The same complaint had been filed by the same group in October 1982. At that time, the ITA ruled that stumpage fees (the amount firms paid to cut down trees on government land) could not be classified as a countervailable subsidy:

> In conclusion, based on information in the record, we determine that Canadian stumpage programs . . . do not confer a subsidy within the meaning of the Act because they are not offered contingent upon export performance, because they are not provided to a "specific enterprise or industry, or group of enterprises," and because they do not confer a domestic subsidy within the meaning of subsection 771(5)(B).[12]

Despite the fact that there had been no change to the law or underlying facts of the case, the Commerce Department 1986 preliminary ruling reversed its earlier decision by declaring stumpage fees a subsidy. Canadians denied the subsidy allegation claiming their market share was due primarily to market forces rather than unfair trade practices. They saw the softwood lumber case as evidence of blatant political interference in the application of US trade laws.

While it is true that the law had not changed, the Department of Commerce (ITA) was taking a different interpretation of the sections dealing with 'specificity' and 'preferentially'. In determining whether or not a subsidy is liable to countervail the ITA must determine whether or not it is generally available to all users or is specifically available to some users.[13] Similarly, it must determine if the subsidy gives goods to specific firms at preferential rates. In 1983 the ITA found that stumpage fees were not reserved for specific industries or enterprises, nor did they offer preferential rates.

At the same time that the US was dealing with the softwood issue, considerable attention was focused on Mexico's use of lower priced energy to give exports a boost. Pressure from higher levels of judicial review (US Court of Judicial Review) and the desire of Congress and industry to do something about the way that foreign countries priced their natural resources resulted in the ITA applying its definitions more strictly. In a June 1983 decision Commerce found that cheap rates for natural gas and electricity inputs bestowed preferential treatment to the Mexican carbon black industry.[14] The reduced power rates were part of a regional development program which carbon black producers utilized. Although the program was not aimed specifically at carbon black producers, they benefited greatly from its existence.

The Mexican precedent allowed a shift in the ITA's position. Whereas in 1983 Commerce found that the stumpage fees were generally available to a number of industries such as furniture, pulp and paper, and softwood lumber, it now grouped them as a single industry and found the fees to be 'specific'. Subtracting the government's cost of running Crown lands from the revenue generated from stumpage fees the ITA found that the government spent more than it gained in revenue and thus offered preferential rates.[15] It should be noted that the US Forest Service would not be able to pass this test either.

Before the ITA could give a final determination of subsidy and the ITC ruled on a CVD, Canada and the United States signed a Memorandum of Understanding. Canada agreed to impose a 15 per cent export tax on softwood products and the American petitioners dropped their case. A number of considerations may have influenced the Canadian government's retreat. They could have been afraid of the legal precedent that would have been set if the final determination had gone against them. Imposing an export tax at least keeps the revenue within Canada whereas a CVD would have given the money to the American government. A further consideration was the threat of American Senators on the Finance Committee not to give the go-ahead for fast track negotiations for the Free Trade Agreement unless a deal was reached on lumber.

A number of troubling lessons have been drawn from this incident by Michael Percy and Christian Yoder (1987: 101, 136–7). Firstly, if US resource industries are feeling the pinch of economic competition they can target foreign products that use government owned inputs. Other Canadian industries that could fall into this category are pulp and paper, uranium, and potash. Secondly, any thought that the quasi-judicial process of resolving trade disputes is not subject to political and protectionist pressure should be eliminated. Thirdly, Canadian industry should budget the expense of legal measures to fight protectionism as a cost of doing business in the United States. Finally, even if a US market share is due to market forces, Canadian companies should consider limiting their expansion or prepare for a protectionist backlash.

It was the increasing threat of protectionism and the difficulties highlighted by the Softwood Lumber case which prodded the Canadian government into seeking a refuge from US anti-subsidy practices and a comprehensive free trade agreement. The relationship between subsidy regulation and the Canada–US Free Trade Agreement is the subject of Chapter 4. Before looking at that agreement it is helpful to understand the national origins of distinctive public policies in Canada and the US which contributed to the conflict over subsidy regulation.

3 National Origins of Canada–US Subsidy Conflicts

This chapter considers the historical roots of selected Canadian and US government policies that became the subject of conflict during the subsidy disputes of the 1980s. The purpose is not to determine whether practices in a particular field constitute a subsidy for trade purposes, but to briefly explain the evolution of these different practices. Rather than grounding Canadian–US subsidy conflict in a vague notion of political culture or equally imprecise 'histories, geographies and immigrant experiences' (Lipsey and York, 1988: 123), this chapter gives substance to the differences by examining a number of public policies in key issue areas. These public policies are the result of previous conflicts in the political economy of each state and lay the foundation for present disputes. Today's issues of contention have their origins in steps taken to resolve previous political and economic conflict.

LIBERAL BY DEGREE

Those unfamiliar with Canada and the United States might imagine that they have almost identical political economies, but they would be mistaken. The US leans towards a hyperliberal model while Canada exhibits state capitalist tendencies. Interestingly, the national governments in both federations seem to be more committed to liberal development strategies than subnational units. The contest between hyperliberalism and state capitalism is a continuation of a long debate about the relationship between the individual and the state. Throughout North America, liberalism dominates in both practice and ideology limiting discussion to what forms of liberalism should be implemented. Since its creation Canada has been less liberal than the US. On the narrowly political side, Canada has given fewer legal freedoms to individuals and more protection for group rights than the US. On the economic side, the Canadian state has played an active role in supporting business in its struggle to survive on the North American continent. Government initiatives to deal with the power of US business led one economic historian to characterize the Canadian state's role as 'defensive expansion' (Aitken, 1988). Another Canadian commentator suggested that 'We did not choose public enterprise freely. It was forced upon us by American expansionism' (Hardin, 1974: 55). Although this discussion can be framed in numerous ways, there seem to be two primary approaches – political culture and economic history.

Those who study political culture examine the 'beliefs and values related to politics, attitudes to the political system and to political issues, and commonly accepted standards of political behaviour' (Bell, 1990: 137). Attitudes of interest include deference toward authority, resistance to taxation, entrepreneurship, and responsibility towards others. The relative strength of socialism in Canada and its absence in the United States attracted the attention of the early scholars studying political culture. Gad Horowitz (1978, 1966) and Seymour Martin Lipset (1990; 1970) claimed the answer lay in the different political cultures of the two countries, but they differed on what was responsible for creating these cultures. Horowitz adopted Louis Hartz's (1964, 1955) fragment theory linking present political culture to the ideologies of the first European settlers in North America. Lipset rested his analysis on the major formative event in Canadian and US history – the American Revolution (or War of Independence depending on your political culture).[1]

A different path has been taken by economic historians and Marxists who focus on the state's role in organizing the economy (Innis, 1956; Whitaker, 1977). They stress the use of crown corporations and government intervention as the basis for explaining the differences between political attitudes in Canada and the United States. Emphasis is laid on the structure of the economy as the primary determinant of political culture.

This study pays greater attention to the form of state in Canada rather than political culture as a separate variable. Political culture is seen as a product of the intermingling of ideas, material capabilities and institutions which shape the attitudes of a country's citizens. Subsidy negotiations are of relevance in that the binational structure emerging from these negotiations will influence ideas, capabilities and institutions. Ideas will be influenced by the determination of what is the acceptable role of government financial intervention in the economy. Material capabilities or the structure of the economy will be changed according to the degree to which some businesses or activities are detached from government funding while others are encouraged. This will have a ripple effect throughout the political economy.

Steps towards liberalizing Canadian society have run into opposition. The primary objection is to losing a way of organizing society that puts more stress on the wellbeing of the group than US liberalism. Canadian philosopher George Grant described the *raison d'être* for a separate Canadian state as being 'the belief that on the northern half of this continent we could build a community which had a stronger sense of the common good and of public order than was possible under the individualism of the American capitalist dream' (1986: x). This desire for a tempered liberalism also has a strong economic element, the social wage. The social wage is comprised of the percentage of government expenditures that directly support the income and consumption of people who work for wages (as opposed to those who gain income from investment or property). Applicable areas of government expenditure include education, health services, public transportation, postal services, labor training, and income support such as social security, unemployment insurance and welfare. Not all of the money spent in these areas goes to workers and is part of the social wage, but since wage earners make up the majority of the population, they use the bulk of these public services.

The amount of work done in this is limited, but one analysis suggests that the social wage in the US in 1980 was 16.2 per cent of Gross Domestic Product while it was 25.7 per cent in Canada (Bakker, 1988: 411). This means that a higher percentage of Canadian government spending goes to services that are of direct benefit to lower and middle income groups in Canada than the US. When one broadens the definition of the social wage so that it takes into account the taxes paid by those who benefit from government services, the distinction between Canada and the US becomes more clear. Since the 1970s, the net social wage (value of workers' benefits less the value of workers' tax contributions) has tended to be negative in the US and positive in Canada (Bakker, 1991). In other words, a greater percentage of taxes paid by Canadian workers are returned as benefits than in the US. American spending preferences lean more to supporting business (for example, defense spending) than redistributing wealth to its poorer citizens through social programs. This dissimilarity is a good example of the variation in liberal models and is a concrete difference in the way the two countries are organized.

The complete triumph of a US form of liberalism could spell the end of Canada as a state. If markets were entirely open and there was little difference in the organizing principles of the US and Canada, the existence of separate countries would no longer be required. Indeed,

Canadians would at least want a political voice at the center of power if there was complete economic integration and no political differences between domestic societies. In Canada, the consummate proponents of economic liberalism and assimilation of US liberalism are the continentalists. As George Grant remarked over thirty years ago: 'In its simplest form, continentalism is the view of those who do not see what all the fuss is about. The purpose in life is consumption and therefore the border is an anachronism' (1986: 90).

In case one doubts that prominent individuals and organizations favor increasing harmonization to the US standard, or at the very least, are unconcerned about such a transformation, we have the excellent example of one of Canada's leading corporate leaders and media owners, Conrad Black. Mr Black, personal friend of conservative Presidents and Prime Ministers, has offered his view of Canada's future. Calling for a *desocialized* state Mr Black decries Canada's 'uncompetitive, slothful, self-righteous, spiteful, and envious nanny-state, now hovering on the verge of dissolution and bankruptcy. We can do better than that, and we will, with Quebec or without it, in the US or outside it' (*Financial Post,* 6 February 1991).

The five policy areas chosen for review illustrate many of the differences in economic and social organization of Canada and the US. In comparative perspective, the US spends more on defense and uses military/space expenditure to bolster research and support regional economies to a greater degree than Canada. Subnational governments (states, provinces and municipalities) are increasingly playing a large economic role in both countries, but US activity seems to be a more recent trend. Canada relies on an explicit regional development strategy, gives support to cultural industries and finances a public health care system. The US has chosen to not support similar activities, relying on the market to provide those goods. While Americans might argue that defense spending is meant primarily for security and Canadians would insist that cultural industry protection is designed solely to bolster Canadian identity, these policies have trade consequences and are not as sympathetically received on the other side of the border. Each section looks at policy in Canada and the US, beginning with the country in which it plays a more crucial role. More space is devoted to the country whose policies are a source of concern to the other.

NATIONAL SECURITY

The preparation for and prosecution of warfare has played a crucial role in twentieth century economic development (Buzan and Sen, 1990). Interaction between military industry and the rest of the economy is especially complex in the leading postwar economic and military power, the US. Because of the size of the US economy and the role of the defense establishment within it, economic policies implemented for national security motives have a trade impact on allies, as well as enemies.

United States

Vast defense expenditures allow the US government to play a leading role in the economy that is ideologically consistent with hyperliberal principles. Since money is funneled to private firms, it is more acceptable than intervention by state enterprises. The exception to letting the market operate freely is justified in terms of protecting the United States from military threat, rather than as a need for an industrial policy. In the early 1980s, Ronald Reagan used a combination of military Keynesianism and supply-side tax cuts to pull the economy out of recession. Adjusted for inflation, the 1989 defense budget was as large as at the peak of the Vietnam War in 1969 (Haglund 1989: 245). The increased level of spending prompted a jump in the military's share of research and development (R&D) money from 50 per cent of federal research outlays to 70 per cent ($35 billion) over the course of the 1980s (Markusen, 1990: 152). While this form of government intervention is ideologically acceptable to conservatives, it is not universally supported. Individuals to the left of the Republican party often decry the effects of bloated military spending, while more consistent anti-government neoliberals have lamented the fact that the 'Department of Defense is the third largest planned economy in the world, led only by the total economies of the Soviet Union and the People's Republic of China' (Niskanen, 1990: ix).

Two aspects of policy are worthy of consideration. The first deals with government support and protection of industry channeled through national security institutions. The second area is the tremendous impact that spending has had in developing regional economies. The latter will be considered below, under the regional development section.

An illustrative, rather than exhaustive, list of programs that assisted military related industry in the 1980s is the Independent Research and Development Program (IR&D), the Strategic Defense Initiative Organization (SDIO) and the Defense Advanced Research Projects Agency (DARPA). If a company undertakes research and development (R&D) spending on a project, subsequently of interest to the Department of Defense (DOD), they may recoup some of that cost through IR&D funds. Firms begin R&D expecting to be partially reimbursed if they can sell it to the military. From 1976 until 1988, $18 billion or 5 per cent of military related R&D was accounted for in this manner. A further $10.5 billion was distributed between 1980 and 1988 through a supplementary program which covered firms' bid and proposal costs (Difilippo, 1990: 93–4).

Ronald Reagan's pursuit of a defense against ballistic weapons through the Strategic Defense Initiative (SDI) gave a boost to military funds for pure research. When it was clear that large amounts of money would be made available for private industry, there was no shortage of military bureaucrats, academics or business people willing to trumpet the economic benefits of pursuing Star Wars. The SDIO was set up to distribute funds to companies engaging in experiments designed to test the feasibility of lasers, X-rays and computer systems. Major companies that signed up for funds included Boeing, General Dynamics, General Electric, Lockheed, McDonnell Douglas, Westinghouse, Eastman Kodak, Honeywell, and Texas Instruments (Nozette and Kuhn, 1987).

DARPA is a government agency that fulfills the requirements of more blatant industrial policies. It funnels money to a select number of high technology companies, purchases their products in early commercialization stage by following a Buy American policy, builds, leases and sells plants at bargain prices and assists in worker adjustment and training programs (Markusen, 1990: 152). Some of its projects are aimed at areas that have a primarily civilian purpose. A good example is the race by Europe, Japan and the United States to develop high definition television (HDTV). HDTV is the next generation of television technology that delivers a much clearer picture. While Europeans pursue the project through their own forms of industrial policy, the United States turns to its primary means of helping industry. The Commerce Department relaxed its antitrust laws so that US firms could form a consortium and DARPA committed itself to spend $30 million annually to assist in technological development (Difilippo, 1990: 1).

Massive government intervention in the defense industry creates a market structure highly beneficial to large US contractors. The government has a virtual monopoly on the demand side while there are a few privileged sellers forming an oligopoly. Unlike other monopoly buyers, however, the defense department does not use its market power to lower product prices. Being more concerned with performance and delivery schedules, the defense department hands over large profits to favored supplier's. Cost overruns of 100 per cent on major equipment purchases are not unusual (Markusen, Hall and Glasmeier, 1986: 45).

From a supplier's point of view, large contracts providing steady cash flow are often awarded with a minimum of competition. By dollar value only 5 per cent are awarded on a closed bid value, 60 per cent go through a process of competitive negotiations with companies the Pentagon feels are qualified, while the remaining 35 per cent are not subject to any bids at all (Smith 1988: 10). A number of large firms rely heavily upon defense department funding to drive their R&D work. In 1987, the percentage of total R&D expenditures accounted for by military work for major companies was: McDonnell Douglas 72 per cent, Lockheed 75 per cent, Boeing 60 per cent, Honeywell 54 per cent, and General Electric 40 per cent (Difilippo, 1990: 139–40). Some firms are extremely dependent on government contracts. General Dynamics, which produces the Trident nuclear submarine, F-16 fighter aircraft, M-1 battle tank, and Tomahawk cruise missile, relies on the government for 96 per cent of its sales (Smith, 1988: 11).

US activism in the defense industry field has led some to suggest that it is pursuing a policy of 'Techno-Nationalism' by limiting the export of technology and protecting domestic markets (Haglund, 1989: 234–77). Military R&D supports high technology manufacturing jobs under increasing attack from foreign competition. Under Section 232 of the 1962 Trade Expansion Act the US may restrict the imports of products that might undermine national security. Dependence upon foreign supplies for products that are needed to run the war machine could threaten security in times of conflict. Trade restrictions have been aimed at oil products and machine tools. Other product sectors that have been protected for security reasons include ball-bearings, precision gears and semiconductors. The dispute with Japan concerning semiconductors reflects the Pentagon's concern with preserving a domestic high-tech industry. Due to increasingly sophisticated weapon systems, electronics that support advanced weapons are now deemed indispensable for national security.

As the world's most potent military power, the US has a requirement to spend a large amount of money upon defense. This expenditure is reinforced by the interests of some large industries and conservative interests. The military industrial complex allows conservatives to prime the economic pump, sheltered behind an acceptable explanation – military security. Defense contractors back military funding as a source of almost guaranteed income. Nine of the top ten contractors are among the largest 100 US companies and these giants account for almost 50 per cent of Defense R&D contracts (Difilippo, 1990: 139). Clearly, one way for a US company to secure government funds has been to tap the national security money pipeline.

Canada

Although Canadian defense expenditures have been high during times of conflict, they fall drastically during peacetime. Whereas the percentage of military research and development as total R&D in the economy is over 30 per cent in the United States, it is less than 6 per cent in Canada (Treddenick, 1989: 33). With the 1959 cancellation of the Canadian designed fighter Avro Arrow, Canadian companies abandoned the attempt to produce large integrated defense systems. Most of the defense industry based in Canada relies on exporting components to the United States under the 1959 Defense Production Sharing Agreement. A 1963 addition to this agreement requires Canada to purchase an equivalent amount of American hardware to its sales in the US. Recent Canadian activity has concentrated on further integration through the creation of a North American Defense Industrial Base (NADIB) (Avery, 1989; Haglund, 1989: 189–237).

With the election of a Canadian Conservative government in 1984, momentum built for an US styled military/economic development strategy (Langille, 1990: 81–125). Its apex was reached in the 1987 defense policy paper, *Challenge and Commitment.* With the backing of the Business Council on National Issues (BCNI) an ambitious Defence Minister, Perrin Beaty, called for increased commitment to a defense industrial base. Economic benefits were a prime justification for funneling money to defense industries: 'By enhancing Canadian international competitiveness, defence expenditures allow us to take advantage of economic opportunities abroad in both defence and parallel non-defence industries' (Department of National Defence 1989).

Despite high level support in the business community and in the military, the attempt to pursue military Keynesianism was not successful. The greatest obstacle was the government's debt load and its fight against the deficit. The government found it difficult to advocate deficit cutting and justify large expenditures on programs such as nuclear powered submarines and tanks. It was not the first time that a Canadian Minister of Defence would have his wings clipped by the Finance Minister. A second 'problem' was the end of the Cold War. The anti-Soviet rhetoric that was used to sell a military build up had less and less resonance as it came closer to the point where budget decisions had to be taken. The 1987 commitments were abandoned and the plan for a defense industrial structure was left floundering. With a wavering defense policy, the attempt to cash in on the military side of hyperliberalism also collapsed.

REGIONAL DEVELOPMENT

A prominent scholar once observed that Canadian federalism revolved around three axes: French–English, Canada–US and heartland–peripheries (Smiley, 1980). This section considers the heavy federal Canadian involvement in, and commitment to, regional development in contrast to the US government's lack of presence. Regionalism is a much more powerful force in Canada than in the US and regional development policy is one method federal officials use to accommodate regional and provincial demands.

Canada

The Canadian government has addressed the problem of regional economic disparities through three sets of policies – equalization payments, federal income support programs and regional development programs (Smiley, 1987: 171). Equalization payments refer to the transfer of tax revenue to poorer provinces so that their citizens may enjoy public services similar to those in wealthier provinces. The political support for such measures was demonstrated when equalization payments were inserted into the Canadian constitution in 1982.[2] Federal income support programs assist individuals in poorer provinces by providing income through old age pensions and unemployment insurance.

Prior to the Great Depression of the 1930s, regional disparities were not considered to be a problem separate from national economic growth. The 1940 Rowell-Sirois Commission examined the impact of the Depression on provincial finances and found that Canadians could not expect the same level of government services because of disparities in provincial tax bases. People living in poorer provinces (especially the prairies and Atlantic Canada) had suffered the ravages of the economic downturn to a greater extent than individuals residing in wealthier areas. In an attempt to equalize access to government services, the commission suggested that funds be transferred from richer provinces to poorer ones through the federal government. Following the war, the federal government negotiated a system of equalization payments with the provinces.

In 1957, the Royal Commission on Canada's Economic Prospects (Gordon Commission) detailed the difference in growth potential between provinces. These disparity gaps fluctuated slightly over time, but did not disappear. In order for the gaps to be eliminated or reduced, the disadvantaged areas would have to grow faster than the advantaged areas. Recession in the late 1950s forced the government into a number of policy initiatives to address economic difficulties. Major programs included winter works, occupational training, and rural economic development. These were *ad hoc* initiatives with different departments administering each program.

Regional development was elevated to a principal policy goal with the 1968 election of a Liberal government. Prime Minister Pierre Elliot Trudeau's prime preoccupation was with the issue of national unity and he made it clear that regional development was a means of bolstering that unity: 'Economic equality . . . [is] just as important as equality of language rights . . . If the underdevelopment of the Atlantic provinces is not corrected, not by charity or subsidy, but by helping them become areas of economic growth, then the unity of the country is almost as surely destroyed as it would be by the French–English confrontation' (Savoie, 1986: 28). Although most of his attention was focused upon Quebec's place in Canada, programs that assisted the poorer Atlantic provinces also played a critical role.

In order to take a rational planning approach to promote economic expansion in disadvantaged areas the federal government established the Department of Regional Economic Expansion (DREE) in 1969. The department targeted growth poles and provided assistance for infrastructure, social adjustment and encouraged private investment in specific sectors. Eighty per cent of DREE's funds were to be spent east of Trois-Rivièrs, Quebec (Beaumier, 1990: 9). In other words, funds would be aimed at the Atlantic provinces and poorer areas of Quebec. After experimenting with the growth poles approach, the government moved to a cooperative arrangement with the provinces known as Economic and Regional Development Agreements (ERDA).[3] Provinces were given a role in articulating project objectives under the ERDA.

In 1982, DREE was replaced by the Department of Regional Industrial Expansion (DRIE) which was a combination of DREE and the Department of Industry Trade and Commerce. In 1987, the system was overhauled when the federal government carved DREE up into regional organizations. Responsibility for southern Ontario and Quebec was given to the Department of Industry, Science and Technology (DIST) while northern Ontario was under the care of NORFED, a DIST sub-agency. Separate federal departments were created to look after the interests of eastern and western Canada. Federal policies for regional development in Atlantic Canada were coordinated by the Atlantic Canada Opportunities Agency (ACOA). ACOA was also responsible for providing the government with a regional perspective on national policies and programs. The four western provinces were also given their own federal department, the Department of Western Diversification.

Regional development initiatives are usually undertaken in conjunction with provincial governments so that federal expenditures supplement or subsidize provincial initiatives. For example, the federal and Quebec governments made a joint interest-free loan of $220 million dollars so that General Motors would locate a plant in Ste Thérèse, Quebec, in 1987 (Stevenson, 1989: 191). These programs tend to respond to areas of the country where economic and political discontent is the greatest. In 1969, 51 per cent of DREE spending was distributed to Atlantic Canada with 12 per cent given to Quebec. Following the upswing in support for independence in Quebec, more money was transferred to that province as its share of DREE funding rose to 39 per cent and Atlantic Canada's fell to 38 per cent (Lithwick, 1986: 128). A similar trend can be seen in western Canada in the 1980s. The Liberal government offered a Western Development Fund in order to salvage some support west of the Ontario border, while the Conservative government's western diversification efforts were also meant to cement support.

Regional development initiatives are an attempt to parcel out the country's wealth so that all areas receive some benefit. To some extent, Canadian politics is regional politics, pitting the interests of groups in provinces against each other (Stevenson, 1989; Brym, 1986; Gibbons, 1982). Some accommodation of regional interests is required to maintain political power at the federal level. Federal political parties tend to have strong regional bases and one key to success is to forge an electoral alliance of regional interests. The Conservative government reign from 1984 until 1993 was anchored in the provinces of Alberta and Quebec. The rise of regional parties in these provinces in the early 1990s led to the electoral obliteration of the Conservative government in 1993.

United States

While the United States does have large regional economic disparities, it lacks an extensive regional development program similar to Canada. Defense spending is the area of federal expenditure that probably has the greatest regional impact. In contrast to Canada, the US system promotes mobility and encourages people to move to jobs in other parts of the country.

As the emphasis of military procurement has shifted from relatively simple mass production items to high tech products, such as aviation and missiles, military expenditure has accelerated the migration of individuals and jobs from the rustbelt to the sunbelt. While there has been some variation over time, since the early 1940s California, Washington, Connecticut and New York have been able to hold onto military spending. The Reagan boom benefited these states as well as adding to the fortunes of Massachusetts, Virginia, New Hampshire, New Mexico and Maine. The trend has been towards an abandonment of the industrial heartland to a defense perimeter of coastal states.

The one area where US defense spending does resemble Canadian regional development is that of locating military bases. Bases play a key economic role in a number of poorer regions. The southern states receive few large scale contracts, picking up orders for nonweapon supplies such as food, tobacco, coal and oil. As a result, they rely far more heavily on military bases to support local economies. Unfortunately, a base employing a thousand people brings fewer benefits than an advanced weapons project employing the same number of people because base employees spend less money in the local community and the jobs may not be as highly paid. The effect in many southern states has been to buttress the low wage nature of their economies (Crump, 1989).

With the exception of American defense spending, federal regional development initiatives are not of much importance in the United States. Casting an eye northwards, some Americans view Canadian use of the term regional development as nothing more than a code word for harmful subsidy practices. Such an opinion was clearly expressed by Robert J. Muth, (1988) President of the Non-Ferrous Metals Producers Committee during Congressional hearings of the 1988 Canada–United States Free Trade Agreement.

SUBNATIONAL ECONOMIC POLICIES

In reviewing the role that government has played in specific areas of the Canadian and US economies, some attention should be given to government activity at levels other than federal. Subnational governments are unwilling to allow either unrestrained market forces or federal policies to determine the economic fate of their citizens. As a result, numerous US states and Canadian provinces are large economic actors in their own right and play an important economic development role (Fry, 1985). For example, California's population is three million larger than Canada's and with $600 billion in gross state product would rank as the seventh largest country by this standard (Fry, 1990: 44). New York State would also rank in the top ten of geographic economic entities, while Texas produces more than Mexico. State and provincial policies cannot avoid having some impact on Canada–US trade flows. The primary difference in policy between the two countries at the subnational level is the higher extent of public ownership north of the border.

United States

US states were instrumental in assisting economic projects following the break with Britain, but this activism abated in the middle of the nineteenth century. In the first 30 years of the present century states confined their activities to providing transportation infrastructure and some education services. With the onset of the Great Depression states tried to stimulate industry by influencing supply-side factors such as providing cheap land, labor or capital. It was not until the 1970s that states became actively involved in trying to influence demand by creating new markets and products. The 1980s saw state and local level activity increase, partially in response to cutbacks under the Reagan administration. State governments now play a leading economic role:

> In 1986, total state and local government personal income, sales and property tax receipts were greater than the federal government's personal income tax revenues, and state and local government purchases of goods and services amounted to 85 percent of non-defence purchases by all levels of government in the United States. (Fry 1990: 43).

Supply-side initiatives to attract business are accomplished primarily through tax breaks or tax expenditures, but low interest loans, grants of money or land, job training subsidies and enterprise zones are also common. Companies are given credits or forgiven taxes in the range of hundreds of millions of dollars to invest or remain in a particular area. Prime examples of this form of activity is the frenzied chase for automotive investment. In recent years, Ohio offered Honda $70 million dollars in incentives, Tennessee dangled $66 million in front of Nissan, Michigan put up $120 million for Mazda and Kentucky is distributing $325 million to Toyota over a 20-year period (Fry, 1990: 47). This sort of activity is extremely destructive, however, as it spends a large amount of taxpayers money to influence location from one state to another.

Numerous states (primarily the southern and plains states) also try to cut labor costs by making unionization more difficult. 'Right-to-work' laws stipulate that no individual is required to join a union even if a majority of workers have decided to pursue collective bargaining. By preventing closed shops, the power of unions is diminished because their membership is reduced and the threat to strike is not as serious.

Peter Eisinger (1988) argues that since the 1970s states have become increasingly involved in addressing the demand side of economic development. They are trying to assist private business develop new markets and new products. This is done through the provision of venture capital, support of high technology ventures, and export promotion activities. As one aspect of finding new markets for local products, states are increasingly involved in international trade relations. The actions of state governors are growing in importance as they seek out trade opportunities and take part in international trade disputes.

State development policies have become such big business that a US research institute now publishes a 700-page user guide for investors seeking financial assistance for their industries (Urban Institute, 1986). Direct financial assistance is listed under the following categories: customized industrial training; direct state loans; enterprise zones; industrial development bonds; and state grants. A handy index also provides information about state tax rates and rebates.

The result of all this activity has been an increasing divergence between federal and state level economic development strategies:

> At the national level . . . the critical ideas were deregulation, privatization, the free market, voluntarism, and the supply-side macroeconomic doctrine. Yet, the entrepreneurial state is based on a strategy of intervention, guidance, and initiative in the economy. The 50 states and many of their communities are in the process of fashioning, with varying degrees of vigor and coherence, separate little industrial

policies, self-conscious attempts to foster selected industries judged to provide comparative local advantage or to be critical to the local economic future. (Eisinger, 1988: 6)

Canada

In Canada, provincial economic activity is so prominent that some have described a process of *province building*, similar to state building (Black and Cairns, 1966; Young, Faucher and Blais, 1984). Moving to fill a void left by federal inaction, provinces have created public utilities and crown corporations in the resource, insurance and financial industries. In 1906 Ontario created Ontario Hydro (Nelles, 1974) to provide cheap power for industrialization, while Manitoba, Saskatchewan and Alberta put the telephone systems under public control before 1914. Following the Second World War, most provincial governments focused on resource development as the key to economic success. The province of Quebec moved vigorously to further economic development by following a strategy based upon massive hydroelectric projects, while the government of Saskatchewan nationalized the potash industry and the government of Alberta did its utmost to support the growing oil industry (Richards and Pratt, 1981). By 1985 sixteen of Canada's top 500 industrial companies were wholly owned by provinces (Laux and Molot, 1988: 61).

Provinces also compete to attract industries in a manner similar to the contest between US states. Buoyed by increased provincial revenues and transfer payments from the federal government, provinces have been able to offer companies loans, grants and direct equity participation. Action may also be taken to reduce labor costs, similar to US states that follow anti-union policies. In order to encourage the expansion of Michelin Tire in Canada, the province of Nova Scotia introduced special legislation effectively barring unions from organizing in Michelin factories.[4]

Another aspect of provincial development strategy has been discrimination against products and labor from other provinces. Barriers include procurement policies, differing product and technical standards, trucking regulations, hiring restrictions, restrictions on extra-provincial takeovers and real estate purchases and tax breaks for provincial companies (Leslie, 1987). In some cases the barriers between provinces are as great or greater than between Canada and the United States. Recent provincial conferences have pledged to remove most of these barriers, but the process has a long way to go before there is a true common market.

CULTURE

The issue of culture offers a point of sharp disagreement between Canada and the US reflecting disparate approaches to the role of the state. To put it quite simply, Canadians regard cultural issues as dealing with identity while Americans view it as a business concern. This has created an acrimonious debate. It is one area where it is almost impossible for Canadians to accede to US demands.

From a Canadian perspective, many of the disputed policies are not export oriented, they do not assist the conquering of foreign markets. Nor are these policies seen to impose great economic costs on their southern neighbors. The goal is simply for Canadian products to have access to their own market. Americans do not condemn Canadians for supporting culture by helping artists. The objection is to government activity that assists in communicating the fruit of their work to other Canadians on a mass basis. The conflict is a battle over the means of distribution – book and music publishing, film distribution and television content.

Canada

In contrast to the United States, the Canadian state has been active in supporting culture. It intervenes in four ways to moderate market forces (Magder, 1989). The first is the ownership and control of production activities such as the Canadian Broadcasting Corporation, the National Film Board or the National Arts Centre. The state is also the patron of official culture through the Canada Council granting body and its financial support of institutions such as the National Ballet, the Canadian Opera Company and the Stratford Festival. A third method is the use of tax expenditures to encourage private individuals or corporations to support the film industry or official culture. Finally, the state regulates ownership and content requirements of cultural industries to ensure some Canadian content.

With varying degrees of commitment and seriousness the Canadian government has enacted policy measures in the fields of publishing, broadcasting and film to assist Canadian culture. Although hyperliberal ideas have undermined the justification for some of these measures amongst the Canadian elite, the belief lingers that unrestricted market forces in the cultural field would lead to the extinction of a distinct Canadian culture and possibly the Canadian state itself.

Canadian broadcasting policy originated in the 1920s when a Royal Commission on Radio Broadcasting determined that a public broadcasting system similar to that of the United Kingdom, rather than the US private enterprise model, would be most appropriate for Canada. Canada was faced with two principal problems. Firstly, many areas were swamped with US programs and lacked a distinct Canadian alternative. Secondly, many parts of the country did not receive Canadian broadcasting at all because the profit criteria concentrated stations in urban areas.[5] In May 1932, the Conservative government of Prime Minister Bennett introduced the Radio Broadcasting Act, creating the Canadian Radio Broadcasting Commission which later became the Canadian Broadcasting Company (CBC). Only one Member of Parliament opposed the principle of public ownership.

Powerful business interests (railways, Canadian Manufacturers Association) opposed a public broadcasting system because it interfered with private enterprise. They favored a private system such as the monopoly proposed by the Canadian Pacific Railway. Their desires were overruled by a coalition of urban nationalist forces that felt a public broadcasting system was essential to the survival of a separate state and by social movements (labor, western populist) fearing that a private system chasing the advertising dollar would cut them off from the airwaves. As one persuasive advocate outlined the dilemma '. . . it is a choice between commercial interests and the people's interests. It is a choice between the State and the United States.'[6] Thus, a conservative Prime Minister with close business ties allied his party with worker and cooperative groups. He declared that public ownership was necessary so that 'national consciousness may be fostered and sustained and national unity still further strengthened' (Bird, 1988: 111–14).

Since that time public broadcasting has been used to deal with two political threats. In the early years the primary threat was external, coming from broadcasters in the US. In the 1960s and 1970s the threat of Quebec nationalism was also targeted by the public system. Integral to the establishment and continuation of the public service has been the political objective of bolstering unity against fragmentation.

In 1968 the Canadian Radio and Television Commission (CRTC) was set up as an independent regulatory body to supervise Canadian broadcasting and grant licenses. The CRTC pushed Canada's private network, CTV, to extend its broadcasts into many of the outlying areas that CBC was forced to serve. A second priority was to deal with the flood of US programming coming into Canada. In areas such as Bellingham, Washington; Buffalo, New York; and Burlington, Vermont US stations beamed signals into Canada to secure advertising revenues from Canada's major metropolitan centers of Vancouver, Toronto and

Montreal. Windsor, Ontario could try to do the same to Detroit, but US network stations ensured that American shows sold in Canada were excluded from the Detroit market. Another difficulty was that US programming was often bought by Canadian networks because its costs were already covered in the US market:

> An episode of a television programme costs about $350 000 to produce in Hollywood. Production costs are basically the same in Canada, but the English-speaking market is only 16½ million people and no one in Canada can spend $350 000 on one programme. Canadian rights to a Hollywood programme cost between $7000 and $10 000. Thus it tends to be much more advantageous to import programmes than produce them. (Webster, 1977: 38).

In order to deal with the saturation of Canadian airwaves due to US broadcasts and cheap sales, the CRTC has tried to legislate more Canadian content. Once again, the justification for such measures was to support Canadian identity. As with the founding of the CBC, private industry generally resisted such moves.[7] Sixty per cent of all programming must be of Canadian content, while from six in the evening until midnight CBC must meet the same standard while private networks are allowed to slip to 50 per cent. This rule is not always respected and rarely enforced.

The Canadian motion picture industry was also of great concern. Since its origin, the Canadian market for feature films had essentially been a dumping ground for British and later US movies. In the 1970s for example, box office receipts averaged $200 million a year, but only $1.7 million or less than one per cent, would go back into making Canadian films (Webster, 1977: 36). The Canadian government has been extremely responsive to the lobbying of US administrations and the Motion Picture Export Association of America (MPEAA). In the 1950s the Canadian government worked out a cooperative agreement with Hollywood called the Canadian Cooperation Project, which was meant to bolster the Canadian film industry by relying on market forces and the goodwill of US companies. It did not succeed. Recognizing that the feature film industry in Canada was lagging, the Canadian Film Development Corporation (CFDC) was formed in 1967 to assist in the manufacture of feature length films. Its purpose was to pump money into the Canadian industry through loans, grants and investments. The CFDC had some positive impact, but it soon became apparent that the major obstacle was not in the production, but in the distribution of films.

There are three players in the feature film industry, the producers (movie studios), the distributors and the circuits or movie houses. Distributors rent films to movie theaters, because no single producer or studio would be able to supply enough movies for the year. The major studios generally distribute their own films, while a number of independents distribute the films of other producers or foreign films. Large US producers rarely distribute Canadian films. In Canada, between 1967 and 1977 eight independents distributed a hundred domestic films while eight large American distributors (Paramount, Universal, MGM, Columbia, Fox, Warners, United Artists and American International Pictures) only distributed 14 between 1970 and 1978 (Pendakur, 1990: 153). In the United States, the major studios are reluctant to distribute Canadian films and rarely give them much publicity. When *The Apprenticeship of Duddy Kravitz* was offered to Paramount Pictures for US distribution, the studio demanded that it not be billed as a Canadian film because it was thought the label would be a liability (Webster, 1977: 36).

Movie theater chains reserve peak playing dates such as Christmas, Thanksgiving, Easter and the summer for major US distributors. To secure the high budget blockbusters from the major studios, chains must agree to take a package of movies, including known bombs, filling up their schedule a year in advance. Independents (Canadian films) are reduced to waiting for gaps in the schedule. If they do get a turn, they are released *cold* – without the required publicity, planning and timing. Canadian pictures may sneak into limited runs in theaters if they are recognized internationally at film festivals beforehand!

The latest attempt to address this problem was the Conservative Government's Film Distribution Bill. It tried to create a separate Canadian market by allowing Canadian companies to import any foreign film and foreign distributors to import any film to which they had the world rights (as opposed to American rights). This would free up more films and increased revenue for Canadian distributors. Jack Valenti, President of the MPEAA, lobbied vigorously against the bill in Canada and the US. Former actor and then President of the United States, Ronald Reagan expressed his displeasure with the moves in April of 1987. Eventually the bill foundered on the shoals of the Free Trade Negotiations in 1987–8.

United States

It has been estimated that US federal, state and local governments assisted cultural programs to the tune of $5 billion (US) in 1985 (Carr, 1991: 14–15). Using a combination of grants and tax expenditures politicians acted to mitigate market forces. In comparison to Canada, however, the United States does give greater rein to private industry and offers far less assistance in the mass distribution of cultural products. The three major American TV networks are private and Hollywood dominates the world film market.

US films, TV shows, and books are viewed as entertainment rather than cultural products. Their primary purpose is to generate revenue for their creators. Because US exports in the entertainment business generate a trade surplus of over $1.5 billion (US) they are seen as an area where further progress could be made. Canadian policies are part of an irritant that is also found with the EU. Any foreign policies that interfere with the goal of increasing export surpluses are unfair trading practices and need to be eliminated. Even relatively sympathetic US work in this area minimizes the validity of Canadian concerns. For example, Charles Doran (1990) acknowledges the principle that Canada has an interest in preserving its culture, but objects to most methods of protection. California's Governor Pete Wilson is blunter: 'Canada's claim of cultural sovereignty frankly strikes me as little more than thinly disguised protectionism' (*Financial Post*, 22 August 1991).

SOCIAL PROGRAMS – HEALTH CARE

Because American provision of welfare services has lagged behind West European efforts, the US has sometimes been described as the 'reluctant welfare state' (Wilson, 1987). Canada has followed a system that combines elements of the European and American systems. Similarly to the US, Canada was never committed to full employment policies to the same degree as the Europeans, but has had more extensive income maintenance and health care services than her southern neighbor. In general, Canadian programs are not as extensive as most of Western Europe's, but more developed than the United States' system.

This section focuses on the area of greatest difference between the provision of social welfare in Canada and the US, health care. The US system is dominated by private health insurance, private enterprise and selective government assistance while the Canadian system is publicly administered and offers universal coverage. Medical coverage in both Canada and the US accounts for large portions in each country's budget. In Canada, the total public expenditure for hospital services alone (not including buildings and equipment) is over $5 billion – more than is spent on national defense (McGilly, 1990: 247).

Canada

In Canada, use of the term health care or health care system usually refers to arrangements covering hospital and medical care services. Canadians' hospital bills and fees for visiting a doctor are paid through government programs funded primarily by general tax revenue and payroll deductions. Each province administers its own hospital and medicare services, but must meet certain federal guidelines in order to receive a substantial portion of their funding.

Public hospital insurance was brought in by the provincial government of Saskatchewan in 1946. Other provincial governments followed suit (British Columbia in 1948, Alberta in 1950) with the federal government committing funds in the 1957 Hospital Insurance and Diagnostic Services Act. By 1961 coverage had spread to all provinces. In order for provincial programs to be eligible for federal cost sharing they were required to provide a minimum package of services, offer universal coverage, abstain from levying charges on users, and facilitate portability of coverage from province to province. Although there is some variation between provinces, most services provided by hospitals are covered. Private insurers have not completely left the market, however. They concentrate on insuring for higher standards of comfort in rooms, extra nursing and provision of income while hospitalized.

Saskatchewan was also the first province to introduce medicare in 1961. Other provinces followed their lead, the last being New Brunswick in 1971. The federal cost-sharing conditions were set out in the Canadian Medical Care Insurance Act of 1966. As in the field of hospital insurance, it required that provincial programs be publicly administered, make specific services universally available and extend coverage to residents of other provinces that had similar plans. Although the federal government does not have jurisdiction over health care, it can use its contribution of about half the revenue to hospital and medical care as a lever to ensure its standards are met. Private insurers have some role in the health field insuring individuals for dental services, eyeglasses, physiotherapy and some drug costs.

The introduction of universal medicare coverage sparked a severe political conflict that pitted labor and agriculture interests against doctors, insurance companies and chambers of commerce. Breakthroughs in hospital insurance and medicare were the product of the socialist Cooperative Commonwealth Federation (CCF) government of Saskatchewan. Reacting to the ravages of the Depression and trying to assist farmers who could not pay for medical care, and hospital stays in particular, the government moved to a public system. The position of the government was that the private system of health care provision was unable to deliver universal health care.

Rather than a universal system, the Canadian Medical Association (CMA) favored government subsidization of low income individuals, allowing the free enterprise system to stay in place for the rest of the population. In many ways their thinking mirrored the views of the American Medical Association. Conservative minded governments in Ontario, Alberta and British Columbia also favored a targeted subsidy system. Doctors expressed concern that a public system would violate their civil liberties, restrict professional independence and reduce the quality of health care (Crichton and Hsu, 1990: 161–2, 171–5; Naylor, 1986) Medical opposition resulted in a bitter, unsuccessful 23-day strike in July of 1962. Canada had become a battleground for two different visions of health care in developed countries. While the CCF government drew inspiration from Britain's National Health Service, strikers received support from the American Medical Association and other provincial associations.

The Canadian Medical Association appealed to the federal government to form a royal commission to look into the issue of medicare in the hope that their position would be strengthened. Much to their surprise, the Royal Commission on Health Services came down squarely on a universal, publicly funded national health care system. The Commission declared a healthy Canadian population to be in the national interest because it would raise productivity and strengthen national unity. Voicing skepticism that private insurance funds would cover the whole population and citing the greater cost of piecemeal subsidization the Commission concluded that:

> Canada requires the establishment of health insurance funds, provincially administered, contributed to by the Federal Government from general revenue, and by provincial governments as they may determine, structured along lines similar to the Hospital Insurance Programme. (Royal Commission, 1964: 743)

Within two years the minority federal Liberal government passed the Canadian Medical Care Insurance Act with the support of all but two Members of Parliament.

Echoes of the medical association battles of the 1960s were heard in Ontario during the summer of 1987. Doctors went on strike in response to the Liberal government's attempt to end extra billing. The provincial Liberals were responding to the 1984 Canada Health Act which was designed to firm up the universality of public medical care. Provinces that allowed doctors to bill their patients in addition to billing the government faced the prospect of reduced transfer payments from the federal government. Faced with the loss of revenue, provinces moved to end the practice. Backed by the public, the Ontario government easily rode out doctors' protests (Tuohy, 1988).

The Canadian domestic battle over public health care is perpetual. In the early 1990s, neoliberal-leaning governments once again mounted an attack on the universal health care system. In an attempt to reduce its budget deficit the Conservative federal government reduced transfer payments to the provinces. It particularly targeted the wealthier provinces of Ontario, Alberta and British Columbia. In August 1991, the Quebec government health minister passed a law requiring visitors to hospital emergency wards to pay a five dollar fee in order to discourage *unnecessary* visits. The government called it a referral fee, but many others saw it as a user fee.

United States

Whereas public funding accounts for the vast bulk of health care spending in Canada, only two-fifths of total American medical expenditure is from public resources (Wilson, 1987: 29). Despite numerous attempts to move toward a more public system, the American model demonstrates a belief that operation of the private marketplace should be the prime determinant of the provision of hospital and medical care. With the exception of programs and hospitals run by the Veterans Administration and the Armed Services, the American government leaves the private sector to provide hospitals and medical care. Americans pay for medical bills through the purchase of health insurance on an individual basis, through employer plans and government assistance. About 13 per cent, or 35 million people, are not covered by any form of medical insurance and face severe financial difficulty if in need of medical care (Karger and Stoesz, 1990: 192).

The US offers assistance to low income groups through two major programs. The Medicaid program allows patients to visit physicians who agree to treat them in return for payment from the federal government. Medicaid allows individual states considerable leeway to determine eligibility and scope of services. Although targeted towards the poor, Medicaid has numerous gaps. In 1986 it omitted about 32 per cent of the poor, covering only 22 million of the 32.5 million eligible people (Karger and Stoesz, 1990: 197–8). The Medicare system provides prepaid hospital insurance for the aged and offers the option of medical insurance for the same group. The elderly have benefited from this program as they pay about 40 per cent of their own medical costs, compared to 71 per cent paid by people between the ages of 19 and 64 (Morris, 1985: 116).

In the 1980s the spiraling cost of health care prompted a search for new models in the US. The Reagan administration's solution was to cap or reduce spending in Medicare and Medicaid programs. Senator Edward Kennedy has used the opportunity to press for a National Health Insurance Program. Under Kennedy's plan, all Americans would have compulsory health insurance, but it would still be run by private companies. It would be funded by employer, worker and government funds. The plan has not been accepted, nor has much support been gathered for a proposal for a National Health Service, similar to Britain's. Despite making health care reform a central plank of his 1992 Presidential campaign, President Clinton was unable to defeat insurance lobbies in 1994 (Rubin, 1994). Interestingly, Canada's health care system has featured prominently in US debates (National Planning Association, 1991; Andreopulos, 1975). The reduced administration costs of the Canadian system have been praised, but the American Medical Association remains fierce in its resistance.

The American medical system provides good care to middle and upper class individuals who have adequate insurance. Lower income groups are not as fortunate and even better off individuals can be bankrupted by the costs of extended or chronic illness. In addition to not providing universal and equal treatment, there is also some question about the efficiency of the American system.

SUBSIDIES AND THE PAST

This chapter has been a comparative review of Canadian and US public policy in a number of fields of importance to the subsidy dispute issue. The common thread binding these policies in each country is that they are a product of conflict between groups and classes. As such, they represent a domestic balance of power and interests between various social forces in each policy area. Yet, these balances are fragile as groups continuously try to shift the balance in their favor. Negotiating a bilateral subsidy code can intensify domestic conflict by reopening these issues and threatening to encase new balances in international agreements.

Although Canadian policies appear to be set, one is struck by their relative youth, some dating back only 30 years. It is also interesting to note the degree to which Canadian initiatives have been in reaction to US policies or examples. Canadian governments have been far more ready to use public enterprise and ownership to address social and economic needs. The theme of Canadian unity is often invoked as justification for action in a particular manner.

While the US system gives more leeway to the free enterprise system for policies in the area of culture, health care and regional development, government intervention in defense related spending and on the state level is quite pronounced. Rather than arguing that American governments intervene less in their economy, it would be more accurate to say that intervention comes in a substantially different form. It is these historical differences that make it difficult to resolve the subsidy issue. Yet, US policy is also capable of change and evolution. The reduction of defense spending following the end of the Cold War and serious consideration about universal health care are two areas where policy may begin to resemble those of other industrialized states.

Extrapolating from the shades of liberalism found in Canada and the United States one could venture a prediction about what policies each government would suggest should be bound by subsidy codes. A US administration would likely push for a code that conforms to its view of a hyperliberal economic structure. This would involve restricting attempts at conscious industrial strategy unless it is under the guise of national security, reducing the role of redistributive and regional development programs, and restricting Canadian government involvement in the economy unless it directly benefited the US. For example, Canadians might be 'allowed' to continue to subsidize energy projects whose primary function was to export energy south of the border. State capitalist approaches, which emanated more from Canadian society than the 1984–93 Conservative regime, would attempt to keep as many government policy levers available as possible. In particular, programs that target valued industries or assist in worker adjustment or in redistributing wealth would be favored. These are seen as essential for developing economic potential and maintaining an efficient, contributing work force. Similarly, broad based social programs such as universal health care are also seen as being vital for Canadian society as a whole. An extra area of Canadian concern is state activity that is designed to protect culture or reinforce national unity. Such a prediction would not be far off the mark.

4 Subsidies and the Free Trade Agreement

This chapter reviews the role of the countervail/subsidy dispute in the negotiation of the Canada–US Free Trade Agreement. The first section examines Canada's decision to petition the US for a free trade agreement and why the US agreed. It includes a review of some important CVD cases. This is followed by consideration of the crucial role the subsidy issue played in delaying, and almost destroying, the eventual deal. The subsidy issue proved difficult to resolve because of fundamental differences over what constituted a subsidy and which country needed to restrain its practices in this area. The clash of views and interests was a product of the different historical experiences examined in the previous chapter.[1] Canadian fears of moving towards a US style socioeconomic system prevented the concessions the Americans felt were needed to settle the issue. The final section reviews Canadian and US reactions to the deal. The boundaries to US sovereignty transfer are illustrated in Senate concern about the constitutionality of this modest agreement.

MARKET ACCESS

One of the major reasons that Canada petitioned the US for a free trade agreement in the 1980s was the desire to secure access to the US market.[2] A definition of market access is 'a foreign seller has market access if that firm can capture a reasonable market share relative to firm size and degree of competition in the market, provided the product is offered at favorable price–quality terms relative to the home-produced product' (Harris, 1989: 264). Canadians were concerned that their access was threatened by the rise of US protectionism. The business community, spooked by deteriorating Canadian–US relations and an aggressive Congress, brought the issue of market access to the attention of politicians, bureaucrats and academics. Canadian business, liberal economists and Conservative government officials, fearing the rise in US protectionism, sought a solution to the harassment of Canadian exports. They required a mechanism that would insulate the US trade system from protectionist pressures.

Improved access to the US market was declared vital to Canadian prosperity. Canada's Deputy Chief Negotiator for the FTA, Gordon Ritchie, summarized the view before negotiations this way: 'As the only industrialized country without free access to a major consumer market, Canada's prospects for diversifying from excessive dependence on volatile international resource-commodity markets hinged on enhanced and secure access to her giant neighbor to the south' (Crispo, 1988: 16). Such thoughts were echoed by economists Richard Lipsey and Robert York who stressed that 30 per cent of Canada's income was generated by exports and that 'Together with Australia and New Zealand, Canada is the only developed country whose industries do not have free access to a market of at least 100 million consumers' (1988: 4). Market access was also at the forefront of Prime Minister Brian Mulroney's explanation for pursuing an agreement, 'Our highest priority is to have an agreement that ends the threat to Canadian industry from US protectionists who harass and restrict our exports through the misuse of trade remedy laws' (Doern and Tomlin, 1991: 283). High on the list of obstacles to Canadian exports was the functioning of US trade law and the threat of countervailing duties in particular. In the mid-1980s approximately $7 billion in exports were directly threatened by US protectionism and 80 per cent of that was in three industries: softwood lumber, carbon steel and Atlantic fish (Percy and Yoder, 1987: 10).

The CVD Threat

Although the United States did not start to use its CVD laws against Canada in a meaningful way until the 1970s, they had previously been used in the early 1960s in order to force a change in Canadian automobile policy. In reaction to low productivity in the domestic automobile industry, the Canadian government instituted a plan that would remit duty on imported parts if the company in question exported a sufficient volume of parts or vehicles. This 1963 duty remission plan was seen by some in the United States as a subsidy for the Canadian automobile industry and in April of 1964 the Modine Manufacturing Company of Wisconsin launched a petition to this effect. Canadian desire to increase efficiency in a manner that would be acceptable to the United States led to the negotiation of the 1965 Canada–US Auto Pact (Beigie, 1970: 3–4, 38–9). Similar fears and desires would result in Canada pressing for a comprehensive trade agreement 20 years later.

In January 1973, the US Department of the Treasury announced that it would impose countervailing duties on X-radial steel belted tires imported from Canada. In May of the previous year, citing the use of federal, provincial and local subsidies, the US Rubber Manufacturers Association had launched a CVD petition against the operations of Michelin Tire Corporation operating in Nova Scotia. Canada did not dispute that incentives had contributed to the establishment of plants in Bridgewater and Granton, Nova Scotia. The federal government contributed a $16 million grant and tax breaks, the provincial government gave a $50 million loan and a grant of $7.6 million, while local governments reduced property tax and donated land for the Bridgewater plant (Guidi and Morrone, 1974: 238–9).

The Canadian government argued that these incentives were given in order to encourage economic development in an economically depressed area, rather than as a boost to exports. The implication of the CVD petition was that the grants were meant to encourage exports to the US by attracting France's Michelin to Canada. The Canadian government argued that its incentives were similar to programs available to tire makers in the US and pointed out that US firms had made use of similar programs when they had set up operations in Canada. In addition to procedural arguments, Michelin claimed that the intent of firms backing the CVD petition was to stop or delay the introduction of higher quality radial tires into the North American market, rather than address questions of unfair trade.[3] These points did not sway the Treasury.

Prior to the Michelin case, the US Treasury had exercised considerable discretion by levying CVDs on benefits that had been primarily designed to stimulate exports. Domestic programs that benefited exports by chance were ignored because legislation whose primary focus was domestic was not considered to be of concern to the US government (Guidi and Morrone, 1974: 241). The Michelin case set a precedent for countervailing regional development programs.

Many cases have been aimed at Canada's fishing industry. Between 1977 and 1986 eight actions were undertaken by the ITC to determine if US interests were being injured by Canadian fish or seafood products (Rugman and Anderson, 1987: 57). In August 1985, the North Atlantic Fisheries Task Force of Gloucester, Massachusetts and the Boston Fisheries Association filed a petition against the subsidized export of Canadian groundfish. The petitioners targeted over eighty-five different examples of subsidy activity from the federal and five provincial governments. The ITA ruled that 55 of the programs bestowed countervailable subsidies and established a subsidy level of 5.82 per cent (ITRD, 1984).

Federal regional development programs, such as the Industrial and

Regional Development Program were found to be countervailable because they were 'limited to companies within specific regions' (ITRD, 1984: 1854). Provincial programs, no matter how small, were also found to be offenders. For example, the Prince Edward Island Fish Box Pool Program was deemed to confer a subsidy of 0.002 per cent. The fish box program allowed members of the industry to purchase new, more sanitary, containers through loans at a 5 per cent interest rate.

A Canadian study listed a number of basic objections to the US subsidy ruling (Rugman and Anderson, 1987: 56–98). The first criticism was the failure to consider economic factors other than subsidization that might explain injury to US industry. Similar to other cases, subsidies may not be the cause of injury, but would receive the blame. The subsidy level reached by Commerce was about five per cent at a time when the US dollar had appreciated by *twenty* per cent. The process does not attempt to demonstrate any link between subsidized imports and injury. A second criticism focused on the practice of cumulatively adding various provincial and federal programs in order to determine subsidy levels even though no producer could take advantage of all of these programs. For example, a fisherman in Nova Scotia would not be able to benefit from the above mentioned PEI fish box program. The Commerce department did not see any difficulty with this methodology. A third point was the fact that petitioning firms most likely only represented a minority view within the US fish industry. The Commerce Department did not dispute this point, but required Canadian industry to prove that the US petitioners did not represent the majority of the industry. A related problem was that industry information came from questionnaires distributed to US industries which were returned in such low numbers as to make their use as evidence suspect.

The single positive aspect of the groundfish case from a Canadian perspective was that the ITA rejected the petitioners claim that Unemployment Insurance was a countervailable subsidy. The US firms had argued that the Canadian government gave special Unemployment Insurance benefits to Atlantic fishermen, but the ITA concluded that these were not substantially different from those generally available to all Canadian citizens.

Although the Canadian steel industry is not often subject to direct countervailing duty cases, CVDs are held in reserve with other trade actions to influence Canadian activity. Generally, it is the threat of a mixture of instruments such as CVDs, safeguards, antidumping or Section 301 investigations that is of concern to Canadian producers. Occasionally specific CVD action is launched against particularly successful

Canadian steel products. Thus, this example differs from the other cases in that the CVD law is not the prime threat.

The US and Canadian steel industry are similar in many ways – in their products, vulnerability to foreign competition and weak financial position (Hawes, 1986–7). The primary difference is that the US industry no longer relies on exports, while the Canadian steel industry exports about 25 to 30 per cent of its steel and most of that goes to the United States. Canadian share of the US market has fluctuated from 1 per cent in the early 1970s, to 3 per cent in 1985, to 6 per cent in 1987 and back down to 3 per cent in 1989 (Wrobel, 1990: 6). The Canadian increase in market share coupled with other foreign competition has led to bilateral trade disputes.

In addition to quotas the US steel industry uses the CVD and antidumping laws to coerce other countries to the bargaining table. It has been successful in this task, but constantly returns for more protection. In 1986 the Department of Commerce ruled that Canadian exports of some hollow steel products used in oil and gas drilling were subject to duties of 0.72 per cent. Saskatchewan's IPSCO was the company primarily hit with duties.[4] A 1989 case found subsidies on some new steel rails equivalent to 113 per cent (ITRD, 1988: 1412–29; 1753–64). Regional development measures were the primary culprit. Canadian industry objects to US practices to the degree that they affect Canadian exports. Since Canadian steel is also threatened by offshore producers, their optimal position would be to have an exemption from US law for Canadian products, but a continuation of quotas for other producers! (Hawes, 1986–7: 53–6).

Case Trends and Implications

A background paper prepared for the research branch of the Canadian Library of Parliament outlines a number of trends in the evolution of US countervail cases against Canadian products (Smith, 1989). The major finding is that regional development policies are a target for countervail as federal programs or tax expenditures aimed at specific regions are considered countervailable subsidies. While regional development subsidies are usually not large enough to meet the minimum level needed for a countervailing duty, when combined with other forms of subsidization the 0.5 per cent *de minimus* level is often reached. A second trend is that government equity infusions are also likely to be defined as subsidies. About one-third of the calculated subsidy in the Atlantic groundfish case was equity infusion into fish processing companies. A third trend is targeting programs where governments exercise some discretion over availability. The ITA cited the government's role in awarding access to Crown lands in Softwood Lumber and stabilization payments in Swine and Pork cases as contributing to making countervailable subsidies.

If Canadians are harmed by US trade laws, why don't they give the Americans some of their own medicine? Most observers argue that Canada would be at a severe disadvantage if it retaliated against US trade actions by vigorously enforcing its own antidumping and countervailing duty laws. Due to the asymmetry in size, an escalation of these cases would do Canada far more harm than the US. Canadian producers would be cut off from a market ten times their own size, while US producers would lose a market that is only one tenth of its domestic size (Rugman and Anderson, 1987: 49).[5] This great difference in market power has inhibited Canadian retaliatory practices.

US trade law has imposed a direct cost on the Canadian economy, threatens a potential cost and has resulted in specific political action to deal with that threat. During the 1970s and 1980s Canadian exporters assumed the high cost of fighting US legal actions. Even if the result was a legal victory companies were required to spend large sums of money protecting their interests. It is estimated that the Canadian steel industry spent over one million Canadian dollars in ITC cases in 1983–84 (Rugman, 1987: 373). In attempting to deal with seven allegations brought by just three US producers in the Atlantic groundfish case, the Canadian industry spent over one million dollars. (Rugman and Anderson, 1987: 80). The Canadian softwood lumber industry is estimated to have spent $11 million in legal and consulting fees in its unsuccessful fight in 1986–7 (Percy and Yoder, 1987: 138).

In addition to direct financial costs to specific industries, a second area of concern is that uncertainty about access to the US market might hinder foreign investment in Canada and adversely affect Canadian investment decisions (Ontario, 1988). Investment is vital for economic growth and Canada is heavily dependent on foreign capital for investment. Uncertainty about access to the US market may cause investors to go south of the border. This would apply to Japanese and European investment seeking a base in the North American market, as well as the decisions of Canadian companies expanding their operations.[6]

While US trade law posed a threat to some Canadian industries in the 1980s, it is useful to question its actual danger. Although there was a sense that US protectionism was on the rise, CVD cases against Canada did not threaten the health of the whole economy. Investigations numbered one in 1978, one in 1979, zero in 1980, three in 1981, two in 1982, four in 1983, zero in 1984, three in 1985, five in 1986, two in 1987, one in 1988, three in 1989, one in 1990 and probably one or two in 1991.[7] The US issued only five CVD orders against Canadian products between 1980 and 1987, touching on a small fraction of Canada's exports. If the total value of goods covered by the steel, fish and softwood lumber cases in the 1980s was applied to Canada's exports to the US in 1986, they would represent less than seven per cent of the total.[8]

While the total dollar value of the CVD actions may not have been extraordinary, the effects were felt sharply in Canada's outlying regions which were either economically depressed or heavily dependent on resources. More recent examples are US CVD investigations against the use of cheap Quebec electricity rates to lure magnesium or aluminum operations to that province (*Globe and Mail* 3 December 1991). Such actions threaten the Quebec government's choice of hydro power as a cornerstone of its economic development program. The US will tolerate Canadian subsidization of energy projects if the cheap energy is shipped south, but will not tolerate Canadians using subsidized energy to bolster other productive enterprises. Thus, although the CVD problem may not have been as severe as it was portrayed, powerful business and regional interests lobbied for action.

One of the contributing factors underlying CVD conflicts that can be gleaned from cases reviewed in this section is the presence of integrated regional economies divided by the boundaries of two states. US firms suffering economic difficulty and wanting to reverse their decline can use trade remedy laws to attack competitors across the international boundary. For example, the groundfish case was an East Coast dispute between the New England and Maritime fish industries, while the softwood lumber conflict involved lumber producers of the US Pacific North West and Canadians in British Columbia (Rugman and Anderson, 1987: 86). The tendency is to target firms operating under the rules of a different state.

Geographic and economic forces in North America often run north–south across state boundaries, rather than conform to political divisions. When considering this fact some have even suggested that 'Canada is a nation created in defiance of geography' (Mackintosh, 1988: 15). Geographic studies of the two northern countries in America can be undertaken so that regions are defined on a north–south axis with titles such as Pacific Coast, Interior Plains or Eastern Seaboard. Economic analysis can also examine regions that fall across state borders (Shipman,

1986). It is the presence of separate, sovereign, political structures straddling these economic and geographic regions that sets the stage for subsidy disputes.

In a 1987 book, the vocal Canadian critics of US trade law, Alan Rugman and Andrew Anderson, suggested that Canada seek complete exemption from US trade law procedures such as antidumping duties, escape clause actions, unfair trade practices and countervailing duties. They argued that as a fallback position Canada should secure an offset provision which would determine CVDs as the net difference between Canadian and US subsidies (in place of the practice of looking only at Canadian subsidies). Canada should be willing to give up trade related subsidies but keep internal subsidies such as the health care system, unemployment insurance, welfare and regional development programs. Canadian exemptions should apply only to 'those critical Canadian sectors necessary to retain the social, political and cultural fabric of the nation' (Rugman and Anderson, 1987: 4). The authors failed to address the question of what is or is not a critical Canadian subsidy and who makes such decisions.

Canadian business, liberal economists and conservative government officials, fearing the rise in US protectionism, sought a solution to the harassment of Canadian exports. The move towards dispute settlement and subsidy definition can be seen as an attempt to insulate trade policy from the pressures of those displaced or disadvantaged by a freer market. The solution was to take politics out of trade. The most obvious (but not necessarily desirable or practical) method was to eliminate the state boundary. Simple harmonization of economic organization would not resolve the problem because the ITA does not consider whether there are similar US programs or policies. Rather than dissolve the state boundary in a literal sense via political union, the Canadian government decided it would make it less salient through a free trade agreement.

The problem of securing market access reveals a political conundrum. When the world and domestic economies are running smoothly, protectionism tends to be less strident and the problem of access does not loom large. As a result, it slips down the political agenda. As the economy stagnates and protectionism increases, countries like Canada make market access a priority. However, the courtship of large markets occurs at a time when it is least likely that petitions will fall on friendly ears (Smith, 1987: 51). Bargaining concessions will most likely have to be larger in order to secure a result that could have been had at an earlier date.

Although most business organizations supported the idea of a free trade deal to increase and secure access, it was the Business Council on National Issues (BCNI) that was most influential in putting this option high on the government agenda (Langille, 1987). It began to publicly back a comprehensive trade deal (as opposed to sectoral initiatives) in 1983, following discussions with USTR William Brock. The BCNI represents the interests of Canada's largest companies (many of which are US transnationals) spanning the banking, manufacturing, resource and financial industries. Shortly after the September 1984 Conservative victory the new Trade Minister, James Kelleher, reacted positively to the BCNI's proposition to pursue a bilateral free trade deal.[9] Six months later, at the Canada–US meeting known as the Shamrock Summit, Primer Minister Brian Mulroney and President Ronald Reagan announced their willingness to begin investigating a free trade pact.

While not quite as influential as the BCNI, the conversion of the traditionally more protectionist Canadian Manufacturers Associations (CMA) was vital to advancing the free trade initiative. Throughout the 1970s the percentage of CMA members relying on exports had increased from 15 to 40 per cent (Doern and Tomlin, 1991: 49). This created a greater awareness of the importance of foreign markets and the sacrifices that might be required to secure them. Battered by the 1982 recession, and seeing freer trade as an opportunity to increase their own competitiveness, the CMA signed on to the quest for market access.

SUBSIDIES IN THE NEGOTIATIONS

Free trade negotiations began in May 1986 and were required to end by midnight, 3 October 1987 if they were to take advantage of Congressional fast track procedure.[10] Whereas the Canadian team arrived with detailed proposals and were eager to get down to business, the Americans seemed ill prepared and not anxious to get into specifics. Canada's Simon Reisman presented the Americans with a plan for a big deal that would eliminate virtually all barriers to trade. If the US would treat Canadian products similar to American products (national treatment), he was willing to extend the provisions to include investment and intellectual property. The principle of national treatment would solve the trade remedy law problem, as there would be no distinction between US products and Canadian imports. The Americans, led by Peter Murphy, were unwilling to agree to national treatment, as they felt unable to offer any restriction of their own trade law. The US position was that there was no problem with their legal system as the countervail measures were sanctioned by GATT. Canadians had it within their own hands to solve the irritant. They simply had to remove the offending government subsidies.

In a July 1986 meeting the Canadians tried another approach aimed at dealing with the subsidy conflict. Countervail laws could be limited if there was an agreement upon what subsidies were permissible and which ones were actionable. This would allow the Canadian government to operate in a few vital areas with the rest of the economy functioning unimpaired by the US trade actions. The Canadians compiled lists of US subsidy practices in areas from aviation to shipping as evidence that subsidization occurred in both countries. The Americans were not enthusiastic. Again, they argued that Canada could resolve the problem on its own by stopping its subsidy practices. The US had eliminated virtually all of their subsidies, claimed Murphy. If this was not so, why were there so few Canadian countervail cases against the United States?

While negotiations inside were going poorly, bilateral trade relations were being strained by other actions. In May 1986 the United States slapped a 35 per cent safeguard duty on Canadian cedar shakes and shingles. In the summer of 1986, the softwood lumber case was also brought to the fore, with US industry demanding a 27 per cent duty. Canadian opponents to closer economic ties with the United States portrayed these actions as negotiating tactics and attacked the government for not being tough enough in its own stance.

Negotiations proved to be exceedingly difficult, becoming acrimonious and bitter. The Canadians developed a sense of contempt for the American's inability to deal with the issues, while the Americans were unimpressed by Reisman's outbursts of temper and abusive nature. Peter Murphy's strategy was to delay as long as possible. Keeping the desires of Congress in mind, he refused to offer large concessions, feeling that any deal would have to be made at a higher political level. He was content to let the deadline approach to increase pressure and was willing to risk failure rather than show his cards. There was extremely little movement for fifteen months.

Finally, at an August 1987 meeting there was some movement. The Canadians had proposed that subsidies be divided into three categories, similar to GATT initiatives. This 'traffic light' approach stipulated that some subsidies would be prohibited (red) under any circumstances while others would be permissible (green). The remainder would be left in a grey area (yellow) and subject to binational arbitration. The Americans likened their approach to 'bright lines and safe harbors'.

US against Can subsidies - protectionism

The bright lines would be forbidden Canadian practices, and safe harbors would be provided for a small number of programs. All remaining subsidies would be dealt with by the US countervailing duty process. The US also wanted to distinguish between disciplining subsidies that had an export effect and allowing those that influenced the domestic market. The effects of such a proposal would be to target only Canadian subsidies, excluding US defense spending and state policies. While Reisman himself was unsympathetic to most Canadian subsidy practices, the federal government could not risk regional development programs so they prevented the acceptance of such a one sided proposal. Even supporters of the trade deal acknowledge that the limited progress made on a draft subsidies code was such that it would most likely have produced even stronger opposition to the Free Trade Agreement in Canada than was otherwise the case (Lipsey and York, 1988: 101). In a desperate effort to emphasize the seriousness of the situation, Reisman suspended negotiations.

Peter Murphy was correct to assume that the dispute had to be handed over to the politicians. A group of Canadian officials flew down to Washington on 2 October 1987 in a last ditch effort to bridge the subsidy problem. Mulroney's chief of staff, Derek Burney, was accompanied by Finance Minister Michael Wilson, International Trade Minister Pat Carney, Wilson's deputy Stanley Hartt and Burney's assistant Donald Campbell. They were joined by Canada's ambassador Allen Gotlieb. The US team was dominated by Treasury Secretary Jim Baker supported by his assistant Peter McPherson and Clayton Yeutter the USTR. As working groups tried to settle other issues, the subsidy-trade law road block resisted resolution. The pressure increased as discussions came closer to the midnight deadline on Saturday 3 October 1987. The Canadians were ready to terminate the negotiations when the final US position was delivered by Baker shortly after ten in the evening. Under tremendous pressure, tired and hungry, the negotiators finally agreed and sent the letter notifying Congress that a deal had been struck five minutes before midnight.

The solution was based on a proposal by democratic Congressman Sam Gibbons of Florida who suggested that each country maintain their laws, with disputes going to a binational panel that would examine whether or not the laws had been applied consistently with domestic legislation. The issue was dealt with through a threefold interim undertaking detailed in Chapter 19 of the Free Trade Agreement. The three most important articles are 1902, 1904, and 1907.

Article 1902 allows each country to retain their existing legal practices.

While both sides keep their trade remedy rules, they undertake to notify and consult about any future amendments. Any amendment must specify that it applies to goods from the other country, must be compatible with GATT and the 'object and purpose' of the FTA. In addition, any amendment may be sent to an FTA panel for a declaratory opinion of its consistency with the above terms. If the panel finds the amendment inconsistent with the FTA, the countries negotiate a solution or the aggrieved country may implement mirror legislation or withdraw from the agreement.

Article 1904 creates a binational panel to review the application of domestic law.[11] The panel reviews decisions of final determination, replacing domestic judicial review. Once a final determination of a countervailing or antidumping duty is made the other party has 30 days to appeal the decision to the binational dispute panel set out in Chapter 19. The panel's task is to consider whether or not 'such determination was in accordance with the antidumping or countervailing duty law of the importing Party'. The decision of the panel is binding on both parties unless it can be shown that a panel member was guilty of gross misconduct, the panel departed from a rule of procedure or exceeded its powers.

Article 1907 commits Canada and the US to negotiate new rules with regard to subsidies and dumping. A working group is to be established that will:

(a) seek to develop more effective rules and disciplines concerning the use of government subsidies;
(b) seek to develop a substitute system of rules for dealing with unfair pricing and government subsidization; and
(c) consider any problems that may arise with respect to the implementation of this Chapter and recommend solutions, where appropriate.

The provisions of Chapter 19 were to be in effect for five years from the signing of the Agreement, pending the development of new antidumping or countervailing rules. If no new system of rules could be agreed, a two-year extension would be given. After that date either party could withdraw from the agreement on a six-month notice.

Free trade negotiators found the subsidy/countervail issue so contentious that it almost scuttled the deal. It was not possible to reach a resolution to this problem because the negotiating teams did not agree on the basic issue of dispute. The Canadians argued that the problem was US abuse of its trade law and that any deal on subsidies should curb its use. The Americans viewed the problem as being Canadian subsidization of industry. Canadian negotiators wanted to link a precisely defined subsidy code with restricting US trade law, but American negotiators sought to eliminate Canadian subsidies and keep their law unchanged (Hart, 1989a: 27). While the American team was clear about the need for Canadians to reduce subsidies, little time had been spent by the US Congress to consider what subsidies they were willing to forego (Horlick and Steger, 1989: 14).

There are two reasons why the US would take such a firm position. The first is the notion that Americans do not subsidize. Subsidization is largely seen as a foreign practice. It was difficult to get US negotiators to admit that they actually subsidized in a meaningful manner. A second factor is the US view that subsidies which deter imports are not as large a problem as those that boost exports. US negotiators reasoned that Congress and the states should be given wide latitude to subsidize because 'Canada is rarely a major destination for subsidized US production, while the United States is frequently a major destination for subsidized Canadian production' (Schott and Smith, 1988: 189). Since a large percentage of Canadian products receiving subsidies find their way into the US market, while only a minor share of US production finds its way into Canadian markets, Canadian subsidization is a big problem for the United States, but the converse is not true.[12] This position suggests that subsidies assisting exports distort trade to a greater extent than domestic subsidies that preempt imports.

The difference in the size of each country's market and degree of export dependence was reflected in a different interpretation of the problem. For Canada, the dilemma was (and is) that export subsidies can be handled by unilateral action on the part of the importing country while subsidies that displace imports or distort trade to third countries must be settled by negotiation on a multilateral (or bilateral) basis (Hart, 1989a). Canada must address American concerns about subsidies that assist export into the US because they can use countervail, but the United States need not review its domestic subsidization policies that boost domestic production. Canada can be shut out of US markets by defense industry procurement or have their wheat sales to Russia undercut by US assistance to farmers, at the same time that Canadian resource management practices are found to be subsidies and therefore countervailable.

Canadian Reaction to the Subsidy Provisions

Similar to the FTA itself, Chapter 19's provisions concerning antidumping and countervailing duty laws are the subject of some dispute.[13] While a Canadian FTA negotiator (Hart, 1989a: 27) described the three part interim remedy to the subsidy and countervail problem as 'imaginative', others have given a less positive verdict. There are a number of points of dispute. The first argument revolves around the failure to agree on a subsidy code and the ensuing charge against Chapter 19 that it did not secure Canada's primary objective, leaving the most contentious bargaining to a later date. One Canadian nationalist asked: 'Having given away all of these bargaining tools and become more and more dependent on the American market, how are we ever going to bargain as to what constitutes a subsidy?' (House of Commons, 1986: 20–1)

Others counter this view by declaring that a great deal was achieved and one should not ask for the impossible. Economist Richard Lipsey (1988) makes a forceful argument that a high degree of access was achieved in the FTA. Going through the agreement, article by article, he cites 19 technical measures that increase access, nine steps that increase the security of access and two actions that will improve future access. Claiming that exemption from US trade law was never a realistic or sensible goal, Debra P. Steger proclaims the critics mistaken about Canada not achieving its primary objective:

> First of all, the dispute settlement mechanisms are the least important means of obtaining greater security of access to the U.S. market. Tariff reductions, rules of origin, and the reduction of non-tariff barriers, such as import and export restrictions, discriminatory technical standards and government procurement practices are the basic elements of any free trade area agreement and will do a great deal to enhance the flow of trade between Canada and the United States. (Steger, 1988: 185)

While it may be difficult to come to a conclusion about whose interpretation is most accurate, one can start with being clear about the difference between enhancing and securing market access. Lipsey and Steger are correct in citing the many ways in which market access has been enhanced, such as the elimination of tariffs or removal of technical irritants. Securing access, however, implies that a mechanism is established which would turn back protectionist pressures. A report written for the Ontario government following the FTA acknowledged that there would be increased access to the US market because of the elimination of US tariffs, but not a great deal of security. Despite the agreement 'American industries would continue to have complete access to the wide range of trade remedy laws which remain in place essentially as currently written. . . . Canada did not meaningfully achieve its key objective of secure access to the US market' (Ontario, 1988: 36–7).

Evaluation of the Chapter 19 dispute settlement mechanism is also a matter of controversy. Advocates claim that the notification requirement will inhibit Congress from making US laws more protectionist, the binational panels will increase the impartiality and objectivity of domestic final determinations, and the system will be made faster, simpler, and cheaper (Steger, 1988: 183–4). Critics charge that since the antidumping and CVD laws will continue as they were, not much has changed. US administrative discretion will not be curbed. While the panels will operate faster than the US Court of International Trade in reviewing final determinations (ten months versus two or three years), the bulk of harassment takes place at the beginning of the petitioning process and will remain intact (Quinn, 1988). The test of the dispute settlement mechanism is how it works in practice.

Views on whether Chapter 19 is a success or not are divided. Those who compare the provisions with the time period before it was signed claim substantial progress has been made. Those who compare it to the declared goals of the Canadian negotiators find it falls far short. Indeed, some would argue that while access has been increased through decreasing tariffs, trade laws have not been tamed (Cameron, Clarkson and Watkins, 1988). The result may be that the competitive pressures created by increased liberalism will only fan protectionist fires demanding increased and more innovative use of trade laws.

US Reaction

With regard to the issue of Canadian subsidization, the Congress made it clear that it wanted to see more results and regarded the FTA as a starting point for further discussion. While members of the Senate Finance Committee stressed areas that were of concern to their states (coal mining, oil and gas production, nonferrous metal mining and smelting [i.e. copper, lead and zinc], agricultural, forest and fisheries products), they indicated that the general issue of subsidies would continue to be important. The Committee called for:

(1) Achievement on an expedited basis of increased discipline on government production and export subsidies that have a significant impact, directly or indirectly, on bilateral trade; and,
(2) Attainment of increased and more effective discipline on those Canadian Government (including provincial) subsidies having the most significant adverse impact on U.S. producers that compete with subsidized Canadian products in the United States and Canada. (Congress, 1988a).

In the Congressional and US industry view, the practice of Canadian subsidization had not been sufficiently curbed and pressure would continue in the future. Senators from states involved in CVD cases against Canada expressed reservations that the bilateral panels were a significant US concession and left the impression that they would be closely monitored (Morton, 1989: 26).

From the beginning of the bilateral negotiating process the US representatives made it clear that they were not interested or able to offer the Canadians a deal which restricted the Congress' power or greatly interfered with the US judicial process. Simon Reisman's vision of a big deal which would eliminate the applicability of US trade law to Canadian products was a non-starter south of the border. Even the provision for binational review of US law aroused Congressional concern. Fears were raised that such a measure infringed upon US sovereignty and might even be unconstitutional (Congress, 1988b). Indeed although there has not been a successful challenge to the constitutionality of the binational mechanism doubts about the institution continue to be expressed (Chen, 1992; Ohana, 1989)

Several years after its implementation some US trade officials continued to question the soundness of a legal process which allowed foreigners to determine whether the United States was following its own laws.[14] The system is unique in this respect. It is not an international court applying international laws that both parties have created and agreed to respect. Chapter 19 sends the message that US administrative bodies are not trusted to do their job properly and that US appeal courts are similarly likely to be influenced by political rather than legal priorities. Some Americans might be displeased with a system that suggests they need foreigners to tell them how to operate their own trade law administration.

5 North American Subsidies in the 1990s

This chapter pursues the Canada–US subsidy/countervail dispute beyond the negotiation of the FTA. The first section examines the lack of progress in dealing with the subsidy issue following the Free Trade Agreement. This includes a review of the most serious obstacles, suggestions for solutions and explanations for delay. The three original reasons for delay were the difficulty in reaching an agreement, the ongoing GATT negotiations and the decision of Mexico to join the NAFTA. The second section outlines the terms of the subsidy provisions under the NAFTA and broadens the discussion to include other controversial aspects of rule-making in NAFTA. Because NAFTA subsidy provisions essentially reproduced the holding pattern of the FTA, little was accomplished. The conflictual aspect of rule-making in domestic domain was transferred into two other areas – labor and environmental legislation.

POST-FTA HURDLES

The working group to develop new subsidy, countervail and antidumping rules was set up in March 1989. The Canadian team saw its first priority as assembling a comprehensive list of Canadian and US subsidy practices. It was hoped that Canadian practices could be safeguarded by pointing out the existence of US activity. In the 1989 prenegotiation hearings before the Committee on External Affairs and International Trade, the Canadian head of the subsidy team made it clear that certain things would not be negotiated away: 'Canada intends to preserve its capacity to pursue regional development objectives. Furthermore, Canadian social programs and cultural identity will not in any way be at issue in these discussions' (House of Commons, 1989: 6–7).

Despite these reassurances, committee members, especially opposition Liberal and New Democrats expressed grave suspicion about US targeting of regional development, social and cultural programs. With regard to regional development, concern was expressed that specific programs such as the Western Diversification Office, Atlantic Canada

Opportunities Agency and Northern Ontario Development Office would come under threat. Drawing on themes from the 1988 election it was made clear that some members also saw broadly based activity such as health care or unemployment insurance, as well as specific programs protecting culture, to be at risk. Indeed, the negotiations were to be difficult as the Canadians and Americans remained divided over crucial issues. Key problems included the continuing legal confrontation, divergent objectives, subnational activity, calculation of subsidy levels and the problem of import-diverting subsidies.

Legal Issues

The first category of events that posed a problem for subsidy negotiations was the reemergence of trade disputes that many thought had been formerly resolved. Continued bilateral conflict over hogs and softwood lumber threatened increased tension, while the ubiquitous question of cultural industries lay in the background of bilateral negotiations.

Swine and Pork

The 1980s had seen a number of countervail cases launched against Canadian export of live swine or frozen pork into the US market. The cases were based on the argument that federal stabilization payments under the Agriculture Stabilization Act are a countervailable subsidy because the level of support varies between commodities and amongst the same commodity. Disputes over trade in pork products continued in the 1990s and were the basis for the first serious threat to the dispute settlement mechanisms agreed to under the FTA.

From a Canadian perspective, the reactivation of the swine and pork case raised questions about a central provision of the FTA. In late March of 1991, the USTR brought the usefulness of the dispute settlement mechanism into doubt by appealing one of the FTA dispute settlement panel's decisions. Following a review of the ITC's injury determination, the panel had declared that injury to the US pork industry by Canadian products had not been demonstrated. Over $20 million dollars in duties paid by Canadian pork producers would have to be refunded. From a Canadian perspective, the FTA panel had worked perfectly by ensuring the ITC used a correct statistical methodology. Its decision served as a signal that US administrative bodies would have to be a little more careful in their deliberations.

Springing into action, the US National Pork Producers Council enlisted the help of 38 Senators, including all of the members of the Senate Finance Committee and 51 members of the House of Representatives, to press the Bush administration to launch an extraordinary challenge of the panel's decision (*Toronto Star*, 31 March 1991). These groups felt that the binational panel had exceeded its powers. The USTR initiated an extraordinary challenge claiming that the FTA panel had 'seriously departed from a fundamental rule of procedure or manifestly exceeded its powers or jurisdiction in five instances' (Binational Secretariat, 1991).

The US administration listened to the pork producers' complaints because it was in the process of seeking fast track negotiating authority to complete the Uruguay Round and start free trade negotiations with Mexico. The parallels with the 1986 softwood lumber dispute are striking, as the Administration attempted to change the rules in specific cases in order to pursue broader trade agreements. As mentioned in the previous chapter, appeals of the FTA dispute settlement panels must be made on the basis of gross misconduct, a failure to follow correct procedure or exceeding powers. These seem to be relatively restrictive conditions, but if the pork appeal was successful, it could be invoked in many other cases as well, threatening the utility of Chapter 19 panels.

Canadian Prime Minister Mulroney indicated that he viewed the pork appeal as an abuse of FTA provisions and threatened not to participate in North American Free Trade talks (*Financial Post*, 1 April 1991). Although the threat may have rung hollow, it gained US attention. The special review panel hearing the challenge was able to delay the delivery of its decision until after the date that the President had secured fast track approval for finishing the GATT Round and starting negotiations with Mexico. This may have been arranged so that political fallout from a decision favoring Canada would not scuttle fast track authority.

The appeal was heard by three former federal court justices – one who had sat on the US Court of Appeals and two former Ontario Chief Justices. On 14 June 1991 the three declared that 'the allegations did not meet the threshold for an extraordinary challenge' (*Financial Post*, 17 June 1991; Binational Secretariat 1991). The decision made it clear that the Extraordinary Challenge Committee should only be used in 'exceptional circumstances'. Canadian pork producers were able to secure their $400 million a year export market and were to be given $33 million in refunded countervailing duties. Canadians claimed victory and hoped that the ruling would discourage American challenges.

The pork ruling increased Canadian confidence in the temporary dispute settlement mechanism as a means of preventing some US abuses. A different ruling would have given the Canadian government a fair bit of political trouble as opponents could have claimed that even the minor benefits of Chapter 19 were flawed.

US pork producers were not happy with the ruling and threatened to restart trade actions if Canadian exports grew much beyond their existing 3 per cent share. While some in Congress may have been displeased with the Committee's backing of the wide ranging panel decision, the issue was not pursued.

Softwood Lumber

If Canadians had been concerned by the possible breakdown of the dispute settlement mechanism, Americans were angered by Canada's decision to renegotiate the softwood lumber memorandum of understanding (MOU). Eventually the softwood lumber saga would lead to another extraordinary challenge and a Constitutional challenge of the panel system. As will be recalled from Chapter 2, Canada agreed to institute a 15 per cent export tax on its softwood lumber cases, responding to US pressure in 1986. Due to its competitive position the Canadian industry was initially able to weather this additional burden. Five years later, as Canada suffered through recession and macroeconomic conditions changed, the tax weighed heavily on the Canadian industry. In addition to the export tax and recession in both countries, softwood lumber producers saw their competitiveness undermined by the rise of the Canadian dollar from $0.72 US in 1986 to $0.86 US in early 1991 and $0.88 US in the autumn of the same year. The cost of the Canadian product had risen over 20 per cent due to currency fluctuations and 15 per cent because of the export tax. Canadian forestry officials claimed that the export tax was primarily responsible for the loss of 7000 jobs in 1990 (*Toronto Star*, 19 August 1991).

In response to this situation, the Canadian government began to lobby for a renegotiation of the deal in March 1991. It is possible that the Prime Minister believed he had earned some credit from the US President for Canada's firm support in the Gulf War. What was not clear, however, is why US producers or Senators would want to renegotiate the arrangement that had served them so well. Indeed, Canadian desire to renegotiate was interpreted as breaking a deal and risked renewed trade law cases. As the chairman of the US Coalition for Fair Lumber Imports saw it 'The Canadian Government should be held to its bargain' (*Financial Times of Canada* 22–28 April 1991).

On 3 September 1991 Canada gave the US thirty days' notice that it was withdrawing from the MOU. Canada argued that in light of the exchange rate fluctuation, decrease of market share from a third to a quarter, and the tripling of stumpage rates in British Columbia, the conditions of the MOU had changed. Canada's finance minister expressed confidence that any US attempt to prove Canadian subsidy practices would fail (*Financial Post*, 4 September 1991). US Senators led by Bob Packwood (R–Org) and Max Baucus (D–Mon) urged the President to institute a 15 per cent import tax on Canadian softwood lumber as soon as the MOU expired. They claimed that Canadian subsidies could be as high as 25 per cent (*Financial Post*, 20 September 1991). A day after the MOU expired, the USTR announced that they were relaunching the softwood lumber investigation. In addition, exports from provinces that had not raised their stumpage rates were subject to bonds (USTR, 1991a). British Columbia, Canada's largest exporter, was not liable to a bond, making the immediate US response tolerable. The real extent of the damage would have to await the new CVD ruling, which would probably make its way to an FTA panel hearing.

The CVD process was put into action by the Commerce Department and the results were not surprising. Commerce found that subsidies did exist and the ITC found that there had been injury. A complicated series of reviews of the administrative agencies' decisions by FTA panels followed. In May of 1992 the ITA found that Canadian stumpage programs conferred a subsidy of 6.51 per cent. The FTA panel disagreed with the ITA's methodology and sent the decision back to be reconsidered. In September, the ITA reported back that upon further investigation it had now found a subsidy of over 11.54 per cent (*International Trade Reporter*, 22 September 1993: 1573). The ITC's original decision that the Americans were being injured by Canadian subsidized softwood lumber was also remanded by an FTA panel. In its reply the ITC confirmed a finding of injury in October of 1993. The Canadian government expressed concern that US administrative institutions were not heeding panel guidelines, but officially expressed confidence that a satisfactory solution would eventually emerge through the dispute settlement mechanism (*International Trade Reporter*, 10 October 1993: 1757).

Continuation of the softwood lumber case posed a difficulty for both governments. As a high profile case it was symbolic to the Canadians as an example of US harassment. To the US lumber industry and some Congressmen, it represented all that was wrong with Canadian practices and the new dispute settlement process. An inability to reach a mutually agreed resolution could jeopardize trading relations and future agreements, by putting pressure on both governments to rewrite trading rules. In late 1993 it appeared that the US government was moving ahead with punitive CVDs and the Canadians geared up to make further use of the dispute settlement process. The ensuing twists and turns of the case will be recounted in the NAFTA section when consideration is given to the constitutionality of the binational process.

Culture

One of the groups most displeased with the FTA was the US entertainment business. The key political player in the industry is the Motion Picture Export Association of America (MPEAA). Their complaint lies with the FTA's cultural exemption clause (Section 2005). While the MPEAA is concerned about Canadian policy, the primary fear seemed to be the precedent this has set for other negotiations 'The US/Canada FTA has been repeatedly cited from Turkey to Indonesia by countries that claim US submission to a "cultural" exemption was a sign that trade restrictions are permissible if imposed to protect local "culture".' (MPEAA, 1990: 1). Particularly galling for the MPEAA has been the EU's broadcast directive stipulating that a majority of prime time programming should be reserved for European programs. When trilateral trade talks between Canada, the United States and Mexico were announced in 1990, the MPEAA declared that it would seek elimination of the cultural exemption clause.

The views of the MPEAA have some importance in trade issues because they are able to bend the ears of Congressional officials. The Association has impressive access and financial clout. Jack Vallenti, the association's president, sat on President Bush's advisory committee on trade policy and negotiations. The Association runs private Congressional screenings of first-run movies in order to keep in touch with Senators and Representatives. Contributions to Congressional campaigns by Walt Disney, Warner Brothers, Paramount and MCA/Universal studios have risen from $179 694 in 1981 to over $1 173 800 in 1990 (Stokes, 1991: 435). The industry also contributes to the Democratic and Republican coffers at the national level.

Although the movie and film business is large, it leads a precarious existence. Costs are high and domestic demand has stagnated. As a result, the industry relies on export revenues to bolster domestic profit. In 1989, exports accounted for 35 per cent of industry revenues. Whereas the movie *Rambo III* pulled in $55 million in the United States, it garnered $105 million abroad (Stokes, 1991: 434). As a matter of self-interest this has led to more concern about access to foreign markets.

The MPEAA can appeal to Congress playing upon notions of fair trade and redressing trade imbalances. With a $4.5 billion trade surplus, they lag behind only the aerospace grouping in contributing to US export strength (Stokes, 1991: 433). Claiming that the manufacture of films and TV programs is the one area where the Japanese and Germans are unable to compete, Jack Vallenti has suggested that 'the US film industry wants no special treatment. All we ask is fair treatment' (1990: 5). In order to ensure *fair* treatment, the MPEAA has threatened to work against the ratification of any trade deal that does not ensure open access for its audio-visual products.

From a Canadian perspective, the renewed call for action in the cultural sector was a worrying development. As outlined in Chapter 3 cultural industries are seen as vital for national survival. It is extremely unlikely that any Canadian government could give much ground on this issue. For their part, US industry officials are unlikely to cease pressing for change, as invoking culture is seen as an excuse to protect industries.[1]

Divergent Objectives

As in the FTA subsidy negotiations, Canada and the US had different objectives. Canada was trying to secure access to the US market by softening US trade law. The Americans were concerned with disciplining Canadian subsidies rather than making their trade laws more liberal. The tradeoff, similar to the GATT round, might have been for Canada to give on subsidies in exchange for US action in the trade law area. Yet, if there was not some restriction on US subsidization, Canadian producers would still be denied access to the US market as those subsidies displaced Canadian products. Canada's position was weak because it was making two demands on the United States while the US had a single goal. The Americans wanted to reduce Canadian subsidization. The Canadians wanted to curb US trade law and make sure that the Americans were not left free to subsidize in any manner they wished.

Canadians had to address US concerns about subsidies because of their fear of US countervail, but Canada had no similar stick (that it was willing to use) against the US (Winham, 1988: 208). The Conservative government (1984–93) demonstrated a reluctance to play trade hardball with its most important trading partner. The difficulty that the

Canadian government had in getting the FTA accepted during the 1988 general election indicated the Canadian perception that a large number of concessions had already been granted. The problem was whether anything remained for the Canadian negotiators to bargain away which would persuade the US to agree to a code that protected vital Canadian programs, offered refuge from US trade law and limited American import displacing subsidization.

Subnational Units

A further complicating factor has been the role of subnational governments. The influence of subnational governments poses two fundamental problems for subsidy negotiations. The first is whether subnational governments are bound by any bilateral deal and if they will abide by them. If New York or California recreate subsidy programs at the state level that have been bargained away at the national level, not much will have been gained from a Canadian perspective. As outlined in Chapter 3, subnational governments are potent economic actors and their activity has some impact on trade flows. For example, one study has concluded that Canadian provincial subsidies to business as a share of total subsidies has risen from 21 per cent in 1976 to 38 per cent in 1987 (Bence, 1990: 29).[2] It is estimated that a third of the subsidies go to agriculture, but it varies from province to province.

A methodological problem is posed by the extreme difficulty in quantifying and analyzing the policies of 50 states and 10 provinces. This is especially true in the US as a great deal of state activity takes the form of tax expenditure, of which there is often no record. State or provincial governments may give tax holidays or create tax free zones in order to encourage business to establish in a particular area. The amount of revenue forgone is as real as a grant, but it does not appear in public accounts. Whereas Canadian governments tend to favor visible grants, US states rely heavily on tax expenditures. Thus, when the available data are compiled it appears that there are more subsidies north of the border because Canadian methods of subsidization are more easily quantifiable.

Subsidy Calculation

The challenge of determining what is a subsidy and how to calculate it is a philosophical problem about what form of government assistance is acceptable and what is not. Calculation of subsidy levels and programs is central to perceptions concerning which states must undertake a restructuring process. Definitions are also important when governments prepare lists of subsidies they might want to trade off against other states' programs. As was suggested in the previous chapter, there is a perception that US industries are the innocent victims of vicious attacks by countries that subsidize their exports (Gill, 1990b). The impression of innocence is bolstered by studies using a methodology which ignores areas of heavy US subsidization such as state expenditures and defense research and development (Hufbauer, 1983). It is not surprising that this leads to a view that curbing subsidy practices is primarily a task for other countries. The aggregate subsidy level is a function of what is put into the calculation. For example, a study of federal subsidy levels in non-agricultural production in 1984 found overall subsidies to be equivalent to 1.0 per cent of the cost of production in Canada and 0.5 per cent in the United States. Yet, if defense procurement is added to this calculation, as Canadian negotiators might suggest, the American figure doubles to 2.0 per cent (Bence and Smith, 1989: 18). Using this method, Americans subsidize more than Canadians, which changes the dynamics of the negotiation.

Determining whether or not US defense spending constitutes a subsidy is an extremely controversial decision and will most likely be the subject of some debate. It is doubtful that the Americans would concede this point in negotiations. Similarly, Canadians have the view that regional development programs should be exempted from subsidy calculation. Again, the Americans are unlikely to agree. The difficulty in agreeing what is or is not permissible stems from the differing historical experiences outlined in Chapter 3.

Import Displacing Subsidies

As alluded to in the previous chapter, the US position tends to be that export subsidies are a problem, but import diverting subsidies are not a large concern. Since Canada exports a greater share of its production to the United States, the result of this approach is to target more Canadian subsidies. In preparing for post-FTA negotiations, the Canadians made it clear that they wanted discipline on export enhancing and import diverting subsidies. The head of the Canadian team declared that subsidy disciplines 'would apply to programs irrespective of whether the product was exported'.[3]

Extending discipline to import displacing subsidies is an ambitious and controversial task. The United States channels billions of dollars to industry through its military industrial complex and would be unlikely to change such practices for the sake of subsidy negotiations. For Canada the danger of taking this approach is even greater. Measures aimed at protecting Canadian culture or enhancing regional development may displace imports and influence investment decisions. Similarly, if the subsidy net is cast as wide as possible, programs completely unrelated to trade may be caught. Canadian concern has been expressed about the targeting of its health care system, for example.

The question of whether health care would be threatened by the FTA proved controversial during the 1988 election.[4] Similar concerns were raised about the subsidy negotiations. In the summer of 1989, two former US FTA negotiators, Peter Murphy and Bill Merkin, denied that Canada's health or social programs would be considered in the upcoming talks. They described the possibility as 'unthinkable and inconceivable' (*Financial Post*, 29 June 1989). However, the argument could be made that Canada's system acts as a subsidy to some industries. In the US automobile industry car makers and their employees pay health care bills, while in Canada the cost is spread out among all tax payers. The US automobile industry could claim that the health care system reduces the costs of Canadian operations. While doubting that the US government would raise the question of health insurance as a subsidy, the head of the US negotiating team, Ann Hughes, indicated that a case could be made: 'You could, if you were of a mind, see some subsidy element there, especially since health costs tend to be about $300 to $400 a car' (Marshall, 1989: 686).

It is possible that Canadian health care policies could be targeted by large US companies resentful about bearing the full cost of their employees' health insurance. Chrysler Corporation's vice-president in charge of Washington affairs indicated that health care costs may be a factor in deciding the location of production facilities. Citing health care costs as being $700 per car in the US and $223 in Canada he claimed that Chrysler is moving towards increased production in Canada, 'We're asking, why are we in the US?' (*Vancouver Sun*, 22 June 1990). Yet, health care is also an important domestic US issue. In November 1990, a relatively unknown Democrat, Harris Wofford, came back from a 44-point deficit in the polls to defeat the former Attorney General, Richard Thornburgh, for the Pennsylvania Senate race. Wofford launched a populist attack on Thornburgh, wooing the middle class with a vision of affordable health insurance. Wofford's most effective line declared 'If criminals have the right to a lawyer, I think working Americans should have the right to a doctor' *(Washington Post*, 7 November 1991).

US health care is very expensive for individuals and businesses. In 1990 the US spent approximately 12.2 per cent of its GNP on medical care, three per cent more than Canada, Germany or Sweden. US businesses have been unable to stem rising health costs, with some companies facing increased premiums of over 15 per cent, despite stringent reduction attempts (*Washington Post*, 17 November 1991). Under increased competitive pressure, businesses will be forced to get a handle on costs. US business in competition with foreign companies have three options. They could reduce the amount of coverage given to their workers, but this would encounter stiff resistance from unions and white collar employees. A second option, suggested earlier, would be the use of trade law to force other countries to abandon programs or pay penalties. This would encounter immense opposition in other countries and generate a great deal of conflict.

The third possibility would be some form of domestic reform which spreads the cost among the whole population through the tax system and reduces bureaucratic costs by eliminating or reducing the number of private insurers. This faces the opposition of the American Medical Association, private insurance companies and public resistance to higher taxes. President Clinton made health care a central plank in his election platform and put Hillary Clinton in charge of proposing a scheme which would provide coverage for all Americans. However, by the autumn of 1994 the President's plans had been defeated. Thus, the use of trade law is possible if a domestic solution is not found to rising medical costs.

The political sensitivity of targeting other countries' health care systems and the possibility of a domestic solution prevented this area from becoming a subject of serious subsidy negotiations. It does, however, serve as an example of the virtually unlimited reach of a subsidy definition that can be employed if one is interested in dealing with all subsidies or forcing other countries to bear increased costs of production.

Resolution Strategies

Two approaches to resolving the unfinished Canada–US subsidy issue were contemplated by those concerned with the negotiations. The first option was to come to an agreement about what are permissible or prohibited subsidies. As mentioned in Chapters 4 and 6, this is called the traffic light approach and was pursued at the GATT and in the FTA negotiations. Some subsidies would be prohibited (red) under any circumstances while others would be permissible (green). The remainder would be left in a middle category (amber or yellow) and subject to binational negotiation. Similar to problems with this approach at the GATT, this would probably leave most of the contentious issues in the yellow area with relatively short red and green lists.[5] This sheds doubt upon the utility of such an approach because conflict may not be reduced. Governments may simply convert their subsidies from red to yellow areas and spark more dispute and debate. The Canadians were unable to get the US to adopt such a strategy in the FTA negotiations due to disagreements concerning the size and breadth of the green category. Not a great deal has changed since those early discussions.

Regional development programs offer an example of the difficulties involved in the traffic light approach. As explained in Chapter 3, the Canadian government views regional development programs as an important tool for national unity and a commitment to poorer areas. They need regional development programs to be in the green category because of domestic imperatives. From a US perspective, Canadian regional development programs are usually seen as a cover to subsidize at will. They would probably not have agreed to a special green category designation for Canada.

The second strategy was to abandon the search for a solution to defining subsidies in favor of making technical changes in US trade law that would curb its effects. This solution was put forward by those who saw large obstacles in negotiating a subsidy agreement. (Bence and Smith, 1989). Some advocated a hybrid solution of trying to define a subsidy first and moving to technical adjustments if unable to get an agreed upon code (Horlick and Steger, 1989). Michael Hart (1989b), a former Canadian FTA negotiator, suggested that the participants prepare themselves for a *second best* regime of tinkering with the laws themselves. It may not be the most desirable solution, but seeing the benefits of the rest of the FTA over the seven year negotiating period may 'make it possible to live with what at first may seem like a failure'.

One of the proposed technical changes was the implementation of a net subsidy approach. The amount of subsidy would be determined by the difference between subsidies granted to imports and those given to domestic production (Rugman and Anderson, 1989). This would greatly reduce the subsidy level from present calculations which only measure the subsidies given to imports. Alternatively, the level at which subsidies are found to be countervailable (*de minimis*), 0.5 per cent, could be raised to 5 per cent. This would reduce the number of CVD cases that harass imports receiving a negligible amount of subsidies. There are a large variety of changes that could be implemented to reduce the CVD threat, but they stood little chance of being enacted.[6]

The major obstacle to the incremental approach was political. The US Congress must be given something in return for approving a restriction of their law. As outlined in Chapter 2, trade remedy laws are a valuable tool for dealing with disgruntled constituents and threatening foreign competitors. Something extremely enticing would have to be given in exchange for such a restriction. Canada did not have much more to give away that would satisfy the US Congress. By already agreeing to reduce tariffs and liberalize investment, Canada lost the single largest bargaining tool that would convince a large section of US multinationals to lobby Congress for changes to domestic law. Tariff reduction is crucial to gaining broad support because it acts like a tax cut to TNCs moving goods across the border. Canada might have been able to offer further concessions in intellectual property rights or cultural industries, but it is doubtful that those sectors alone could sway Congress.

As mentioned earlier, the US Congress would not be interested in limiting its trade laws only for Canada's sake. The US has even larger disputes with the EU and Japan. It would not make a great deal of sense to disarm themselves of the countervail threat for a country that amounts to only 20 per cent of US exports. From a Congressional point of view, the US would be fighting the subsidy wars with one hand tied behind its back solely for Canada's benefit. Such a situation was not acceptable to US legislators.[7]

NAFTA SUBSIDY PROVISIONS

At the same time that lack of progress at the multilateral level stalled bilateral negotiations, a new complicating factor arose. In the spring of 1990 the government of Mexico began to push for its own trade agreement with the United States. Having abandoned a nationalistic development strategy in the wake of the 1982 debt crisis, the Mexican government was eager to institutionalize its liberalization initiatives and willing to stake its development hopes on a free trade with its northern neighbor. Not wanting to be caught out, the Canadian government joined the United States and Mexico in a February 1991 announcement of trilateral talks to create a NAFTA.

The governments of Canada, the US and Mexico signed a NAFTA on 12 August 1992. The subsidy and countervail provisions of that agreement largely reproduced those of the Canada–US FTA. A review system similar to the FTA's in which panels would monitor the application of domestic laws was instituted. Article 1905 of NAFTA adds an additional dispute settlement mechanism to settle disagreements if a domestic law or court overturns or does not allow a panel ruling. This was implemented primarily because of US fears concerning the operation of the Mexican domestic legal system.[8]

NAFTA eliminated the Working Group on Subsidies established by the FTA and replaced it with a milder commitment to 'consult on the potential' of developing more effective rules.[9] The working group had made little progress in its four years of operation and there seemed little prospect of achieving any success in the future. Although allowed to lapse, the issue still remained of concern to the Canadian government. As the Canadian government advanced domestic implementing legislation it stressed the continued attempt to resolve subsidy issues through consultations. A Canadian government press release indicated that 'the successful conclusion of these processes will result in improved dispute settlement'. A USTR press release indicated that the discussions demonstrated US desire to consult with its partners, but that it in no way committed them to any particular outcome. The administration would continue to work closely with Congress and private sector interest groups and the best chances for resolving dumping, subsidy and trade law disputes would be a successful conclusion of the Uruguay Round (*International Trade Reporter*, 8 December 1994: 2051–2).

In a subsequent meeting in the first quarter of 1994 the Canadian government continued to express its interest in pushing the consultations forward. Acknowledging that the Uruguay Round agreement was a positive step Canada's International Trade Minister reaffirmed his desire to create better continental rules (*International Trade Reporter*, 19 January 1994: 84; 16 March 1994: 427). However, the Canadians did not have a particular plan to resolve the dispute or a clear objective to be achieved. In light of US disinterest it seemed a futile exercise. There are a number of explanations for such an approach. The first is that the Canadian government did not understand the degree to which the US was unwilling to move further. While this might be true of some Liberal politicians who had just come into government, it certainly was not true of Canadian diplomats and negotiators who had been working on this issue for years. A more plausible explanation is that the struggle was continued for the benefit of the domestic audience, to give the impression that the government was still working on the issue.

There was little incentive for any of the three governments to push for a fresh approach to the subsidy issue or a resolution of previous problems. The Mexican government had little interest in dealing with the subsidy issue. Following the debt crisis, the state resources for subsidies were relatively small. There was much more concern that the US would use antidumping measures against Mexican exports.[10] By this point the Canadians were well aware of the difficulties of reaching agreement. Both Canadian and US officials wanted to see the results of the GATT Round. The tradeoffs necessary to temper US practice were not possible on a bilateral level.[11] The Canadians had grown to appreciate the binational panel system which was enjoying some success in disciplining US practice. They were reluctant to change a system that seemed to be working.

Constitutional Concerns

As a result of the NAFTA arrangement, the three North American states are now committed to a subsidy system which was meant as a temporary measure and created at a moment of crisis in the Canada–US negotiations. It has provided Canadian industry with some protection, but trade disputes still flare between the two states. For example, in the spring of 1994 the US government attacked durum wheat as Canadian market share increased (*Globe and Mail*, 2 and 17 May 1994). While the US political system has digested the notion of a binational review of US law, concern remains about the operation and legality of the system. There is a fear that the panels are making new law rather than implementing existing law. If two identical subsidy cases make their way through the United States' administrative system but the accused subsidizers are Canada and another state, there is a possibility that the law will be applied differently. The Canadians can appeal their case to the binational panels and stand a better than average chance that the findings of the domestic US agencies will be overturned. The other country must take its appeal to the US Court of International Trade (CIT) where chances of winning an appeal are less. Whereas the CIT might overturn three of ten decisions the panels are more likely to overturn seven of ten.[12]

If the laws are applied in a different manner in Canadian cases, the law itself is being changed by the panel system. Whereas Canadian firms and trade officials had formerly complained that the US administrative process resulted in the perversion of US law, US officials might now claim that the FTA and NAFTA arrangements transform aspects of US trade law. This was indeed the intent of Canadian negotiators. The political difficulty arises because such a change was not the intent of the US Congress. Their desire, as outlined in the previous chapter, was not to bind US law, but to eliminate Canadian subsidy programs. Rather than accept the new role of panels and the application of US law, the reaction is more likely to be a search for other methods to address the same problem. The continuing bitter trade disputes between Canada and the US indicate that existing legal frameworks are inadequate to quell larger socioeconomic disturbances.

Although there have been murmurings about the possible unconstitutionality of the panel system, it has not yet been tested in Court. It appeared that such a test would finally occur as a result of the ongoing softwood lumber case, mentioned earlier in this chapter. It will be recalled that after Canada ended the MOU the US proceeded with CVD actions. On 17 December 1993, an FTA panel ruled for the second time against the Commerce Department's finding of a subsidy. The panel claimed that the Commerce Department did not demonstrate that the stumpage fees were specific nor that they distorted normal competitive practice. In particular, Commerce failed to show that they benefited a specific enterprise or industry. Unfortunately for the panel, the decision broke along national lines with three Canadians faulting the Commerce Department and two Americans supporting their decision. This was the first occasion that a decision had split in such a manner and it provided ammunition for those groups angered by the substance of the decision. For example, the attorney for the Coalition for Fair Lumber Imports indicated that they would push for an extraordinary challenge committee because the panel had acted beyond their scope and in a political manner (*International Trade Reporter*, 5 January 1994: 25). The Commerce Department dropped its finding of subsidy, but voiced its objection to the decision. US Senator Max Baucus from the state of Montana declared that the problem lay not with US process but with the FTA panel (*International Trade Reporter*, 12 January 1994: 61–2).

In February 1994, the USTR announced the launch of an extraordinary challenge to the FTA panel's ruling. In addition to dealing with the substantive issue, a question of conflict of interest would be raised. Two of the Canadian panelists were alleged to have interests which were in conflict with sitting on a panel to decide a bilateral lumber case. One panelist belonged to a firm that represented Canadian lumber companies while another had previously litigated a number of lumber cases (*International Trade Reporter*, 2 March 1994: 350).

Similar to the first extraordinary challenge, the Extraordinary Challenge Committee ruled that the FTA panels had behaved in a proper fashion. The allegations of conflict of interest and incorrect application of the law were not accepted. However, unlike the first extraordinary challenge, but similar to the panel decision under question, the panelists split along national lines. The single US judge, Malcolm Wilkey, wrote a vigorous dissent strongly challenging the views of his Canadian panelists, claiming that the decision 'may violate more principles of appellate review of agency action than any opinion by a reviewing body which I have ever read' (*International Trade Reporter*, 10 August 1994: 1245). The national split of panelists and forceful dissent of Judge Wilkey provided the opportunity for US lumber interests to mount a constitutional challenge to the FTA panel system. In September 1994, the Coalition for Fair Lumber Imports filed a challenge to the panel system in the Court of Appeals for the District of Columbia Circuit. They alleged that the operation of the panel system changed the balance between the legislative, executive, and judicial branches of the US government, that it violated the Fifth Amendment of the Constitution which provides for due process of the law, and that appointments to the panel violated US law (*International Trade Reporter*, 21 September 1994: 1456–7).[13]

Although the Constitutional challenge was initiated years after the FTA had come into force and even after a similar NAFTA mechanism had been established, it posed problems for the bilateral relationship. A decision that the panels were operating in a manner which violated the US Constitution would revive the market access issue in Canada by placing the subsidy and countervail agreements into doubt. A successful challenge was unlikely, but it highlighted continued resistance to binational arbitration, limits to future international tribunals and the potential fragility of North American institutional arrangements to domestic opposition. Some influential US producer interests remain steadfastly opposed to a legal mechanism that removes decision making from processes that they can influence. The activity of an external agency monitoring the application of US law also remains controversial and must await the ruling of the Court. A decision against the panels would set limits to future US commitments to be bound in a similar manner in other areas of international economic adjudication.

In the late Autumn of 1994, the Coalition for Fair Lumber Imports demonstrated that their true interests were in managing commercial relations rather than acting as protectors of the US Constitution. They dropped their Constitutional challenge in return for a new industry and government cross-border consultation mechanism. This arrangement seemed to satisfy all parties, but the termination of the case was unfortunate from a long-term institutional view. An important decision about the compatibility of this international mechanism with the US political and legal system has been postponed. It may well be that a future Court will decide against the arrangement and bring the issue of dispute settlement back to the top of the bilateral agenda. In June 1995, Judge Wilkey renewed his attack on the panel system at Congressional hearings concerning the extension of NAFTA to Chile (*Ottawa Citizen*, 22 June 1995). The dilution of US sovereignty in the area of subsidy disputes remains a potentially volatile issue.

Whose Rules?

Heated debate emerged in both the FTA and NAFTA initiatives around the subject of common rules and enforcement. Canadian and US negotiators did not even come close to agreeing new rules overseeing state intervention in the economy. The subsidy issue proved so intransigent that little effort was made to resolve it in the following NAFTA negotiations. The question of whose rules and how they would be enforced became an even larger issue in the NAFTA debate, but in the area of environmental and labor standards. Similar to the subsidy solution, the side agreements stipulated that there would be no set of common rules. The most that could be achieved was a monitoring institution to pressure each state to respect existing domestic regulations.

The inability to fashion common rules revealed political opposition to authority transfer. With regard to the subsidy issue, the US Congress was adamant that its sovereignty would not be limited. In NAFTA, it was business organizations and the state elites of Canada and Mexico that opposed a common standard. Varying standards were in transnational business interests as it would provide another factor of production to be exploited. Canadian based business and state elites worried that exports might be slowed by enforcement measures. Their original goal for entering into institutionalized liberalization on the American continent was for unimpeded access to the US market. For the Mexican elite one suspects that opposition was a combination of fears about sovereignty and a desire to maintain the 'advantages' that would continue to attract investment. Mexico had adequate legislation in these areas; the 'danger' was if enforcement became trilateralized and the government was forced to put substance behind the legal framework.

In NAFTA the answer to 'Whose Rules?' has been a resounding

'Our own!' While satisfying concerns about formal sovereignty, the lack of common rules maintains certain problems. Canadian exports remain vulnerable until such time as the Uruguay Round provisions demonstrate their worth. There is some reason to hope in this regard, but as is argued in the following chapter, much depends upon implementation. Labor and environmental groups will continue to press for revision in their areas both continentally and multilaterally. From the perspective of those advocating increased liberalization, separate rules may prove difficult to the extent that they are the cause of conflict and impede smooth cross-border flows. There are limits to economic integration if the three North American states continue to follow diverse rules in state intervention, labor and environmental standards. As Chapter 8 will show, the Europeans saw control over state aids as an integral part of their drive to an internal market. North American liberals are equally ambitious about liberalization and integration. It will not be long before further measures are proposed and the question of common rules is once again on the agenda.

6 Subsidies at the GATT

This chapter examines the subsidy issue at the multilateral level through the negotiations at the GATT. Attention will be focused on the role of the EU and North American states because they have been the primary actors in this field and they are also the subject of this study. The subsidy issue poses particularly difficult problems for the multilateral system because it challenges state sovereignty and core values represented by individual states. In North America, the Canada–US dispute has been tied to developments at GATT while the EU's Common Agricultural Policy's (CAP) subsidy program has been influenced by US–EU wrangling. This GATT history of dealing with subsidies in non-primary products will account for the bulk of this chapter. It sketches out the origins of the subsidy issue and the attempts to resolve it. The following chapter turns its attention to two narrower issues in the multilateral subsidy saga, agriculture and aerospace. The major lesson gleaned from a study of the multilateral subsidy issue is the difficulty of reconciling domestic imperatives with international pressure for change.

Before looking at GATT it is useful to recall that subsidy issues were an element in the agreement for the failed post-1945 International Trade Organization (ITO). The draft ITO charter, known as the Havana Charter, was drawn up in March 1948 (Stone, 1984: 50–6; Brown, 1950). In addition to addressing tariff policy it contained sections on employment and economic activity, economic development and reconstruction, restrictive business practices and intergovernmental commodity arrangements. US demands at the ITO negotiations for a free trade regime were weakened by an internal split between the State Department and the Department of Agriculture. The State Department was ideologically wedded to free trade following the ideas of Cordell Hull who saw an inextricable link between free trade and a peaceful international system. The Agriculture Department insisted upon protecting US agriculture by violating free trade principles. As a result, the Americans pushed for free trade as widely as possible, but were committed to securing the use of quantitative restrictions for agricultural products and the allowance of export subsidies in this area. Agriculture will be more closely examined in the following chapter, but its importance here is that the US desire for protection in agriculture forced it to sanction protectionist policies of importance to other countries.

The ITO's provisions for subsidies strongly discouraged export subsidies, but permitted domestic subsidies. Export subsidies were those that directly or indirectly affected the exports of the subsidized product while domestic subsidies did not result in an increase of exports or decrease of imports (Kock, 1969: 48–9.) Areas where subsidies were permitted included the promotion of economic development, diversification of industry and protection of national security. Two years after the Charter had come into force countries were not to subsidize exports with the possible exception of agriculture (Wilcox, 1949: 126–30). Although the Canadian government suggested even stricter discipline on export subsidies by demanding that they be given prior approval from the ITO, this was eliminated from the text.

Countries agreeing to the Havana Charter made their ratification conditional upon US ratification. US liberalization would be required before weaker countries felt they would be able to gain sufficient benefits to themselves liberalize. When the US was unable to ratify, the ITO failed to come into existence. With echoes of the Senate's refusal to endorse Woodrow Wilson's effort to have the United States join the League of Nations following the First World War, the US Congress refused to give its agreement to the ITO. More influential than isolationists in rejecting the agreement were liberal forces who heartily condemned the concessions the US negotiators made to other countries. The US branch of the International Chamber of Commerce opposed the ITO because it was based on economic nationalism and jeopardized the free enterprise system (Kock, 1969: 59). Congressional opinion was so set against the ITO that in December 1950 the US administration dropped the initiative and asked Congress to continue giving its support to GATT.

THE GENERAL AGREEMENT ON TARIFFS AND TRADE

In December 1945 the United States invited fourteen countries to begin negotiations on liberalizing international trade.[1] The negotiations followed two paths. The first was the above mentioned attempt at creating the ITO and the second was an initiative to quickly implement an agreement to reduce tariff levels. The tariff cutting exercise resulted in the General Agreement on Tariffs and Trade which was signed on 30 October 1947. Once the ITO was complete the GATT would be subsumed in the larger organization. Because the ITO was never ratified, the 'temporary' GATT instrument became permanent and was left as the primary legal framework governing international trade.

GATT's role was to assist in liberalizing world trade by providing the following services: a framework for ongoing international consultations, a common set of international trade rules, facilities and procedures for resolution of trade disputes and the collection and distribution of trade information (Stone 1984: 23–4). Its primary method of accomplishing this task was through a series of negotiating rounds aimed at reducing tariff levels. During these negotiations tariff levels were reduced and then 'bound' so that they could not be increased.

GATT strove for the lofty goal of free trade, but implemented what was most feasible. Although the Agreement aims for liberalization on a nondiscriminatory and multilateral basis, major exceptions to these principles have been allowed to accommodate diverse concerns.[2] There are exceptions from GATT rules for textiles, agriculture, regional trading groups, developing countries and safeguards to prevent serious injury to domestic producers. GATT does not demand the politically impossible – that all nations liberalize immediately and unconditionally. GATT members, or Contracting Parties, are not coerced into accepting complete liberalization. States must balance domestic interests and make whatever concessions they deem feasible. One observer has described it as a 'disarmament treaty for mercantilists' (Wolf, 1990: 44). Small steps are gradually taken over a long time period to reduce trade barriers and liberalize trade flows among countries. Indeed the liberal commitment to free trade was embedded in domestic commitments to stabilization and full employment (Ruggie, 1982).

When Contracting Parties have a disagreement, they can utilize GATT's dispute settlement procedure which is covered by Articles XXII and XXIII.[3] Article XXII provides for consultation if Parties believe that they are not receiving GATT benefits, while Article XXIII allows the matter to be brought before the GATT Council. Since 1962 it has become GATT practice that disputes which cannot be resolved through consultation (Article XXII) are handed over to a Panel which examines the issue. Once the panel has considered the issue a report is presented to the Parties. If they cannot work out an agreement based on this report within two weeks, it is transmitted to the GATT Council. At the GATT Council (an assembly of all GATT Contracting Parties) a decision can be taken to accept a report, but only if it is unanimous. The party which has 'lost' the case must agree to the report. Reports usually demand that a country terminates an offending practice or authorizes the aggrieved party to undertake countermeasures or retaliation.

Although the GATT dispute settlement process has had some success it has also had two major weaknesses. The first is the ability of a contracting party (prior to completion of the Uruguay Round) to veto the process at numerous stages. A dissatisfied party could block the creation of a panel, block adoption of the report by the Council or fail to undertake the obligations outlined in the report. Contracting Parties had to agree that their activities violated the rules and should be changed. A strong domestic interest often militated against such a position. The second problem has been that even if a panel report is accepted by the country in question, it may choose to keep the offending policy, leaving the injured party to suspend benefits in kind. The dispute then falls back on to unilateral action by the aggrieved party. The party which has had its complaint supported by a panel must undertake retaliation through its own domestic legislation. This could take the form of tariffs or suspension of trade benefits to the offender. Offenders are not sanctioned, they just have benefits of equal value withdrawn by the complainant.

The unilateral nature of the process raises serious problems for the whole system. The countries able to take unilateral measures will tend to be the economically powerful such as the US, Japan and the EU. Smaller states are less likely to take action against the giants because they fear a trade war which would cost them dearly. One of the purposes of having an international legal framework for trade is to facilitate relations based on rules rather than power. Law should restrain powerful states from abusing their economic power to the cost of smaller states. Since the GATT process relied so heavily on unanimity, this goal was difficult to achieve.

Subsidies in GATT Law

The issue of subsidization and countries' response to subsidization (countervailing duties) are handled under two separate GATT Articles. Article XVI deals with subsidy practices while Article VI concentrates on the domestic legal remedy to those practices – countervailing duty law. The original subsidy measures in *Article XVI* were much more modest than the Havana Charter proposals. No reference was made to export subsides as a distinct category. Countries granting subsidies (agricultural or industrial) that would have an effect on exports and imports were required to notify GATT concerning their nature, extent and effect. If the subsidies had a negative effect on other countries there would be an obligation to consult with those countries. This is the present section A of Article XVI. This stipulation had little effect on government behavior so in 1950 Contracting Parties agreed that a time limit for notification of existing subsidies should be instituted and members should be reminded of the obligation to notify new subsidies. A 1952 GATT report concluded that the primary problem caused by subsidies was to reduce the opportunities for other countries in third markets. The example cited was that US subsidies to sultana production did not harm the domestic sultana industry of Greece or Turkey, but did hurt their exports to other countries. Greek or Turkish exports to Europe would have to compete with US subsidized sultanas (GATT, 1953).

Momentum gathered for a change to the rules which resulted in the 1955 revision. Stricter action on subsidy practices would require greater differentiation of the forms of acceptable and non-acceptable subsidies. Prohibition of all subsidies would not be accepted nor would prohibition on export subsidies in the field of agriculture. Agreement would require a reversion to aspects of the Havana Charter where agricultural, industrial, export and domestic or production subsidies were treated differently. It is at this point that the present Article XVI becomes more visible. Subsidies were divided into a number of subcategories and differential treatment was given to the various entities – domestic, export, primary and nonprimary. Article XVI states that a subsidy includes 'any form of income or price support, which operates directly or indirectly to increase exports of any product from, or to reduce imports of any product, into its territory' (Stone, 1984: 35).[4] Discipline is greatest upon export subsidies for manufactured goods, and far weaker for domestic subsidies or agricultural/primary product subsidization. Subsidies whose sole or primary purpose is to assist the export of manufactured goods or industrial products are prohibited. This was the result of a declaration in 1960. Agricultural and primary product export subsidies are permitted as long as they do not give a country 'more than an equitable share of the world export market in that product' (GATT, Article XV13). Subsidies whose primary purpose relates to the domestic economy are tolerated, but countries must give notification of such policies and agree to discuss them if they injure the interests of other countries.

What accounts for this differential treatment? The division between export and domestic subsidy was based on the belief that export subsidies were illegitimate because of their mercantilist nature in attacking other countries' home markets. They recalled the interwar beggar-thy-neighbor policies which the postwar arrangements were designed to avoid. The second split between primary (agriculture) and non-primary (manufactured goods) was based on the special position of agriculture in the dominant political economies. As will be seen in the next chapter, both the Europeans and the Americans heavily protected their agriculture and treated it as a product unlike manufactured goods.

A weakness of the system was that the GATT relied upon its members' discretion to notify it of offending subsidy practices. Individual states were free to determine whether their own industrial subsidy policies had any direct or indirect effect on exports or imports. Many countries would not admit that their subsidy policies had a trade-distorting effect so few policies were notified. A 1961 Panel of Experts concluded that there were few or limited subsidy practices that affected exports or imports in industrial goods despite the clear evidence that in areas such as shipbuilding massive subsidy programs existed (Kock, 1969: 159).

If countries violate Article XVI, Contracting Parties may make use of *Article VI*, which authorizes members to levy a countervailing duty. It must be demonstrated that the effect of the subsidy is to 'cause or threaten material injury to an established domestic industry, or is such as to retard materially the establishment of a domestic industry' (GATT, Article VI:1). The existence of a subsidy is not enough to trigger CVDs – it must injure industries in the market in question. Such a requirement reduces, but does not eliminate, the possibility that the laws will be applied at will to any product as a protectionist tool. After some discussion prior to drawing up the Agreement it was decided that an injury clause would be required (Brown, 1950: 110–11) However, the only country that actively used the CVD measure – the US – was exempted from using such a test. They successfully argued that since their law predated the GATT and did not contain an injury measure, the GATT provisions were not applicable. Rather than being satisfied with this legal explanation it would be more accurate to say that the US did not want to be bound by such a restriction.

The failure to bind the US through an injury tested reduced the effectiveness of Article VI to ward off the threat of US protectionism in this manner. Yet, this was not a serious drawback to the Agreement as countervail was not a very salient issue at the time. Contracting Parties were far more disturbed by the use of antidumping duties to protect domestic markets from competition. During the Kennedy Round of negotiations, antidumping legislation was seen as such a problem that a Code governing its activity was introduced, but no such measure in the countervail field was produced (Dam, 1970: 166–79). Although included in the original GATT, the issue of countervail did not take on any great importance until the 1970s and the start of the Tokyo Round negotiations. It was at that time that a subsidy code was added to the GATT and CVD rules were tightened.

Before proceeding to a review of the subsidy issue since the Tokyo Round, it is helpful to make a couple of points about the political sensitivity of addressing subsidies. The first is that the most intense conflict centers around domestic (sometimes labeled 'production') subsidies that are not undertaken primarily for export benefits. These subsidies are primarily focused on activity within the state and address domestic priorities. The issue was less visible before the Tokyo Round because it was not until the 1970s that the US did not target production subsidies. A key event was the 1973 Michelin tire case against Canada in which the targeting of domestic subsidies became concrete.[5]

The second point is that unlike the other major international legal recourse for unfair trading practices (antidumping measures) the remedy for dealing with subsidy disputes (the countervailing duty) targets government policy. Antidumping measures are targeted at unfair pricing by rival firms. Rather than questioning the commercial policies of particular firms, CVDs challenge the sovereignty of other states. While it is true that the conflict in CVD cases is between rival firms, the threat is also leveled at government policy. For example, the steel company in country A may be attacking its rival steel makers in country B, but the case challenges the authority of the government in country B to pursue chosen objectives in a particular manner (for example, regional development). The dispute thus escalates from being between firms to being between states.

The clash of interests is between one state's desire to promote domestic social and economic objectives and another state's fear that its producers are being injured. John Jackson (1989: 263) has suggested that by permitting subsidies that do not cause material injury, the CVD law provides a method to mediate between these states' interests. As long as a domestic subsidy only causes an insignificant amount of damage to another country's producers it is free to pursue its domestic goals. In this view, the CVD law strengthens the multilateral system by allowing countries the autonomy to pursue policies deemed essential for domestic social and economic welfare. The CVD law can serve as a buffer between states. While plausible in theory, such an explanation breaks down in practice as political power, rather than an absolute standard, tends to dictate the degree of injury that triggers CVD cases.

Tokyo Round

US preparation for the Tokyo Round is important for the subsidy dispute because the United States' use of CVDs forced the issue of subsidies to the top of the bargaining agenda. As with other GATT negotiations, the initiation and progress of the Tokyo Round revolved around US desires and needs. US concern about its deteriorating trade position spurred interest in the areas of foreign barriers to trade and subsidies. Initiating another GATT round was part of a general US plan to modify the international economic system so that it would deliver greater benefits to the United States and force allies to absorb increased costs.

US determination to rewrite international rules was underscored by the Nixon shock of August 1971, which took the US dollar off gold and featured a 10 per cent import tax. President Nixon and his advisors determined that the United States was disadvantaged by the monetary and trade rules of the international economic system and took dramatic action to press home their concerns to the Europeans and Japanese. By breaking the link between gold and the dollar, other currencies rose in value, increasing the competitiveness of US exports. The 10 per cent import tax was a stern message to other countries reminding them of their dependence on the US market for economic growth and indicating a desire to restructure trade relations. As part of this general move to change international monetary and trade arrangements, a 1973 presidential commission on international trade identified nontariff barriers (NTBs) and subsidies as areas of major concern (Twiggs, 1987: 9–21).

In preparing for a new round of multilateral trade negotiations, the US Administration modified the manner in which it dealt with Congress and the private sector. These changes influenced the outcome of the Tokyo Round. The first change dealt with the role of Congress in approving the results of the negotiations. Since the Tokyo Round involved discussions about nontariff barriers, as well as tariffs, the previous forms of enabling legislation allowing the President to negotiate a particular percentage of cuts were no longer deemed sufficient. Congress had previously signaled its desire to influence detailed NTB measures when it rejected two commitments that had been the product of the previous Kennedy Round.[6] The effect of such a move was to undermine the credibility of the US negotiators abroad. How were other states to know if a deal would make its way past the particular interests of Congress?

In an effort to make the passage of any multilateral deal more likely, the Nixon administration persuaded Congress to agree to a 'fast track' negotiating procedure. The fast track procedure meant that, subject to a strict timetable, Congress was committed to vote up or down on the whole package presented by the executive. It was hoped that such a vote would avoid the possibility of delaying the deal or potentially troubling additions to or deletions of small sections of the agreement.

For its part the administration tried to build Congressional support for the eventual agreement by bringing members into the multilateral negotiating realm. Members of the House of Representatives and Senate went to Geneva as official advisors, keeping their fellow members informed of the direction of the talks and offering views about the feasibility of particular proposals. Congressional input was also expanded by allowing Congress to draft a version of the implementing legislation that it would find acceptable.

A second major change was bringing private industry more closely into the negotiations to provide information to US negotiators and create political support for the final deal (Twiggs, 1987: 35–44). Forty-five private sector committees, encompassing over one thousand participants, were divided into three fields – industry, agriculture and labor. Committee members gave advice on technical matters as well as broad policy issues. The government used this opportunity to explain their problems in negotiating specific deals to industry as well as get their input.

Gilbert Winham (1990: 811–13) likened the Tokyo Round's negotiating dynamics to a pyramid. Deals were usually arranged at the top of the pyramid between the United States and the European Community (EC) and then presented to middle and smaller powers further down the structure in an effort to establish a consensus. The negotiations dealing with subsidy and countervail followed a similar pattern with the EC and the US being the primary participants. Once a tentative agreement was reached other states such as Canada, Japan and the Nordic countries were included. Later negotiations brought in the developing countries.

The US position at the beginning of the Tokyo Round was that the issue of subsidies was of greater concern than their own CVD practices.[7] If countries eliminated offensive subsidy practices, there would be no need for countervailing duties at all. This view was to reappear in the Canada–US FTA and GATT Uruguay Round negotiations a decade later, so it is worth considering an official statement on the matter.

> The United States has underscored the point that emphasis on CVD's [i.e., countervailing duties] is misdirected, since subsidies, not CVD's are the basic problem. Subsidies are serious trade distortions that must precede countervail action. Therefore, why should the onus be on the countervailer rather than the subsidizer? Logic suggests that a satisfactory solution on subsidies should largely resolve the countervail issue. (Winham, 1986: 119, n.41)[8]

A number of points flow from this early US position at GATT which also reappear in the Canada–US negotiations. The first is that the problem lies in subsidy practice, not the legal remedy (CVDs) to those practices. Stop subsidizing and CVDs will disappear. Second, the operation of US CVD practice is not an issue as it is deemed to be impartial and simply reacts to others' unfair practices. Third, it is implicitly suggested that foreigners subsidize, but Americans do not. The US had been the major enforcer of fair trading relations through the vigorous and proper use of its CVD process.

The US argument was that subsidies simultaneously distorted trade in three markets. Take the example of US trade with country X which subsidized its car exports. Subsidization would prevent country X's home market from feeling the force of US exports in cars because X's cars would be cheaper. This would have the effect of an import substitution policy. Secondly, the US market would be distorted by the presence of Country X's subsidized exports. American car makers would lose domestic market share. Thirdly, US market share to third countries would be undermined by country X's subsidies. For example, the Japanese would buy more of X's cars and fewer American cars than otherwise would be the case.

Concerns about subsidies and countervailing duties built up in numerous countries during the 1970s. In the United States, consternation about the growth of subsidies in other countries led to the desire to impose CVDs or to eliminate other governments' practices in these areas. The US Senate Finance Committee Report on the 1974 Trade Act declared that: 'Central to the forthcoming multilateral negotiations should be the establishment of acceptable international rules governing the use of subsidies.'[9] The American desire was to curb foreign subsidization in all its aspects – export, agricultural and domestic. Much of the rest of the world, however, was unconcerned about subsidization, feeling that US use of countervailing duties was the major threat to trading relations because it restricted access to the world's most wealthy market.

EC–US trade conflict and subsidy disputes in particular came to be a regular feature of GATT hearings. In a statistical analysis of GATT lawsuits between 1960 (the year the EC became a full GATT participant) and 1985 Robert Hudec (1988: 18, 24, 25) found that one-third (26 of 80) of the cases were between the US and the EC while only 9 of 80 involved neither party. Thirty-nine per cent (13 of 33) of complaints filed against the EC dealt with subsidy issues and 47 per cent (8 of 17) of US complaints against the EC were subsidy related. Thirty-eight per cent (6 of 16) of the cases directed against the United States were against its antisubsidy measures. Four cases were against US countervailing duty law and two against exports subsidies in retaliation for other countries' subsidy practices.

It soon became clear that the issues of subsidies and countervailing duties were two sides of the same coin. The Europeans and developing countries were concerned that US law was not consistent with GATT because it did not require a demonstration of injury to domestic industry before CVDs were imposed. In contrast, the Americans were apprehensive about other countries using export and domestic subsidies to gain unfair trade advantages.

The US suggested a traffic light approach to dealing with subsidies. This approach divides subsidies into three different categories and variations of it have been central to GATT and Canada–US negotiations. In its original form the US proposed a threefold division. The first category would be prohibited subsidies (red) which other nations could countervail at will without having to demonstrate injury. This was the US practice at the time. The second category (yellow) would include subsidies that were permissible, but still subject to countervailing duties if material injury could be demonstrated. This would have been a concession in that the US would have to incorporate an injury test into its legislation. The third group of subsidies (green) would be allowed and immune from CVDs.

Such a proposal had a number of difficulties. The first was determining which subsidies would fit in which category. Agreement would be elusive as the United States tried to limit the subsidies in the green area and the Europeans tried to expand it. Similarly, the red area proposal did nothing to limit unilateral US CVD law being applied against foreign programs that did not necessarily injure US producers. In this category US law would still not conform to GATT principles. The traffic light approach was not taken up in the Tokyo Round, but it would reappear in the Uruguay Round.

By December 1977 the EC and the US were able to draft an outline agreement which acknowledged the essential trade-off. In return for European recognition that subsidies had serious trade effects, and an illustrative list of prohibited practices, the US would adopt an injury test into its domestic legislation. By the Bonn economic summit of the Group of Seven in July 1978, an outline agreement had been reached. On 19 December 1978 the major participants agreed to a subsidy/countervail code to temporarily settle the debate. The 1979 Tokyo Round Subsidies Code dealing with this issue required the US adopt an injury test to discipline its use of CVD laws in return for other countries restricting their subsidy practices (Rivers and Greenwald, 1979: 1477–95). This is sometimes referred to as a two-track solution (Barcelo, 1982; Jackson, 1989: 258–61). Track I deals exclusively with limiting the reach of CVD laws and Track II with curbing subsidy practices.

Although Contracting Parties agree to a similar final document, GATT law is implemented by slightly different means in each country, resulting in varying patterns of enforcement and administration (Jackson, Louis and Matsushita, 1984: 203–5). In the US case, the inclusion of an injury test in domestic law had an effect opposite to the intention of restricting the use of CVDs. Pressure from the steel industry and Congress resulted in the definition of material injury being watered down to such an extent that it did nothing to discourage the use of CVDs. Similar to attempts at limiting antidumping laws, the relevant statutes needed to set up such limits actually created stronger rights and provided a more legitimate mechanism for domestic petitioners (Finger, 1990: 161–2). Contrary to the hopes of the United States' trading partners, the use of CVD laws increased dramatically in the early 1980s following the Tokyo Round. The question of limiting the use of US CVDs was not satisfactorily resolved.

The solution to controlling the use of subsidies proved to be equally disappointing to the US. Contracting Parties were not able to agree on a definition of what actually constituted a subsidy. Drawing on a 1960 GATT Working Paper, they compiled an illustrative list of subsidies on the export of nonprimary products that would be prohibited.[10] For example, the 'full or partial exemption, remission or deferral specifically related to exports, of direct taxes' (Section c, Balassa, 1989: 159). The common element amongst the measures on the list was that the availability of the subsidy had to turn on export performance. As such, it did not directly target domestic subsidies.

Some impact was made in dealing with domestic subsidies, because they were actually addressed in the agreement. This led some observers (Jackson, 1989: 259; also see Winham 1986: 220) to comment favorably that subArticle 11 of the Subsidy Code (Subsidies Other than Export Subsidies) is the 'first general multilateral treaty discipline on government use of domestic subsidies which have an impact on international trade.' However, the language is deliberately ambiguous and reflects Contracting Parties' varying perceptions of the problem. Subsection 1 acknowledges that domestic subsidies are 'important instruments for the promotion of social and economic policy objectives' (Article 11:1, Balassa, 1989: 148). These policy objectives include regional development, economic restructuring, retraining, research and development, and environmental measures. The next paragraph focuses on the potential trade-distorting aspects of domestic subsidies by declaring that they may 'cause or threaten to cause injury to a domestic industry of another signatory or serious prejudice to the interest of another signatory or may nullify or impair benefits . . .' In the end, countries are asked simply to 'seek to avoid causing such effects' (Article 11:2, Balassa, 1989: 149). As with other aspects of the Code, this provided a temporary, but ultimately unsatisfactory solution to the subsidy issue.

There was also an inconsistency between the two elements of the code dealing with countervailing duties and subsidies (Tracks I and II). The CVD section or Track I allows importers to impose CVDs on domestic or export subsidies as long as they cause material injury. It pays no attention to the justification or intention of foreign domestic subsidies. In contrast the section on subsidies (Track II) did set out provision where social or economic justifications would allow such practice. It is another example of a compromise which creates confusion and wide latitude for multiple interpretation.

In addition to the domestic subsidy quandary, the Code left two other gaps. The first was that any practice not specifically cited on the illustrative list would become a matter of dispute. Governments could repackage subsidy programs, leading to increased controversy at the initiation of countervail actions. The second problem area was in agriculture. US farmers pushed for a prohibition on primary product export subsidies similar to the one on export subsidies for industrial products. EC opposition restricted the United States to firming up the language on ambiguous phrases such as 'more than an equitable share of world export trade'.[11]

In retrospect, the Tokyo subsidy code made extremely limited progress in addressing the basic issues of disagreement. Agriculture was left out, but would return with a vengeance in the following round. The US continued to target foreign subsidy practices and this habit accelerated in the early 1980s. The Congress in particular continued to operate under the assumption that subsidy programs were the domain of others and were not applicable to US domestic policy. For their part, the Europeans continued to operate programs that because of their economic power at home or abroad would attract US attention.

THE URUGUAY ROUND

The latest round of GATT negotiations was launched in Punta del Este, Uruguay, in September 1986. Fifteen negotiating groups were set up to cover topics such as market access, reform of GATT rules and new issues such as services and trade-related intellectual property questions (Winham, 1990: 796–822). With regard to the subsidy/countervail problem, impressions at the beginning of the Uruguay Round were that previous measures had not lived up to expectations (Hufbauer, 1989: 13; Twiggs, 1987: 77). The US felt that trade rivals were making increasing use of subsidies, while other states witnessed a dramatic increase in the use of US CVD law. Compared to the Tokyo Round, pressure to do something about subsidies was even more intense. The US trade deficit had soared and some Americans were focusing on 'fair trade' and creating a 'level playing field' as a method of redressing the deficit. Agreement on subsidies became the make or break issue of the negotiations, with the sharpest conflict in the field of agricultural subsidies.

The US position during the Uruguay Round with regard to limiting its trade laws was straightforward and echoed sentiment from previous negotiations – the practices that stimulate them must be eliminated. Countries seeking refuge from unilateral US actions must trade *fairly*. A staff member of the House of Representatives Ways and Means Committee indicated that some minor changes might be possible, but 'only if, and not before, there are assurances of stronger rules and disciplines on the underlying unfair trade practices themselves, that is the dumping and subsidy behavior' (Smith, 1990: 166).

By 1990 a draft subsidy agreement for discussion purposes, based on the traffic light approach, had been hammered out.[12] Prohibited (red) subsidies would be subsidy actions that are clearly unacceptable and remedy would be sought through the GATT dispute mechanism and multilateral sanctions. Actionable (yellow) subsidies would be objectionable practices that were not on the prohibited list. They would be dealt with through the countervail procedure in national courts. The third category of non-actionable subsidies (green) would be particular government spending instruments not subject to trade law activity. Disagreement centered around which subsidies should be on the green list and what level of domestic subsidization would be deemed to result in serious prejudice.

More than other countries, the US wanted to limit the green category and was reluctant to agree to exceptions for regional development programs.[13] Similar to the bilateral trade negotiations, the Canadians were trying to protect their room for subsidization and were eager to protect generally available programs such as 'social assistance, public welfare, education, environmental management and conservation, national identity, and natural disaster relief'.[14] The Europeans were also eager to protect key areas of subsidization.

The dispute concerning agricultural subsidies delayed negotiations repeatedly as is outlined in the following chapter. In an attempt to get the negotiations back on track, the Director General of GATT, Arthur Dunkel, circulated a draft package of Uruguay Round agreements in December 1991 which were to serve as the basis for final agreement scheduled for April 1992. That deadline also passed, but his version ('Dunkel Draft') served as the basis for further negotiation. Its subsidy provisions were largely incorporated into the final text, but the changes are important in that they highlight the conflicting interests of the major actors. It is helpful to outline the major features of the draft and the changes made.

Dunkel Draft

The Dunkel text subsidy provisions adopted the traffic light approach of prohibited, actionable and non-actionable.[15] Section 1 of the subsidy code provides the first GATT definition of a subsidy as a financial contribution from government which confers a benefit. Prohibited subsidies (Article 3) include export subsidies and those that depend upon a minimum amount of local content. Prohibited subsidies do not require an injury test, their very existence is enough to allow the Committee on Subsidies and Countervailing Measures to authorize countermeasures.

Non-actionable subsidies (Article 8) are those that are generally available rather than specific to particular industries. These subsidies are usually not susceptible to another country's countervailing duties or to GATT Code discipline. Provision was also made for government assistance to educational institutes or firms providing it covers no more than 50 per cent of the costs of basic industrial research or 25 per cent of the costs of applied research. In addition, it must be limited to costs that arise directly as a result of research activity. Such an exception is of great use to wealthier states actively involved in supporting research and development.

The other non-actionable category was assistance to disadvantaged regions, permitting regional development programs. Such programs must target an identifiable region and be generally applicable to firms operating there. The region must be shown to be disadvantaged according to economic indicators and a ceiling of aid to each project must be stipulated. Qualifying regions must have either a GDP per capita not over 85 per cent of the country as a whole or an unemployment rate of at least 110 per cent of the granting state. Both figures must be measured over a three-year period.

To be eligible, any such program must be notified to the Subsidies Committee before implementation. Notifications must contain information on the form of the subsidy, the amount of subsidy per unit, the policy objective, duration of the subsidy, and data on its trade effects of the subsidy. Annual updates indicating expenditures and program notifications are required. Other Contracting Parties may seek information about these programs, seek consultation or request that the Committee review notifications. Even if the programs comply, parties that feel their domestic industry may be threatened can request consultations and seek a Committee review in the hope that they will recommend the program be modified.[16]

Subsidies that are not in the prohibited or non-actionable category are in the actionable category. Here, the important qualification is specificity which is used to identify illegitimate subsidies. Subsidies which are specific are 'actionable' which means they may be subject to CVDs by other states. Specific subsidies are those that in law *or in practice* are available only to a single enterprise or industry or select group of industries. All export subsidies are deemed to be specific. The controversy over specificity lay at the heart of the Canadian Softwood Lumber case outlined in Chapter 2. GATT has now recreated the US use of the term. In an even bolder move programs available to all enterprises within a designated area were deemed to be specific. Thus, state or provincial level policies could be branded as specific unless they qualified for some other form of exemption such as assistance to research activities or assistance to disadvantaged regions. As a result, the draft provided sharp new disciplines on subnational governments by defining many of their programs as specific subsidies. This is particularly problematic for federal states where separate political jurisdictions are desirable features of the system because they allow diversity in political and economic organization. The Dunkel Draft threatened to undermine diversity in favor of national and international harmonization.[17]

Another import element of the agreement was the move to add weight to the notion of 'serious prejudice'. Subsidies which adversely affect another country's trade interests are classified as causing serious prejudice and must be withdrawn or redesigned to remove the harmful influences. Serious prejudice is presumed to exist where the cost to government of a subsidy program exceeds 5 per cent of the value of the product or when subsidies are for debt forgiveness or to cover operating losses. The serious prejudice section of actionable subsidies allows countries to seek redress for subsidized products entering third markets or disrupting imports. Earlier Canadian proposals had made the point that 'present rules do not adequately address trade distortions that may occur as a result of subsidies that displace imports in the home market of the subsidizing country or in third country markets.'[18] Trying to curb domestic subsidies to deter imports may have been formulated with the US in mind, while subsidies influencing third markets could apply to either the EU or US helping its grain farmers to take away traditional Canadian markets. Once serious prejudice is found, the offending country has the opportunity to rebut the presumption if it can be shown that there was no trade effect, it was the result of special circumstances such as strikes or natural disasters or that there is already an explicit trade arrangement in the product such as a voluntary export restraint.

A third crucial provision of the Dunkel Draft was the measures for dispute settlement mechanisms which reversed the unanimity straightjacket on panel reports. Panel reports would be automatically adopted 60 days after being issued unless there was a consensus that it be *rejected.* Since the side benefiting from the report would be unlikely to agree to reject, it seems most probable that a consensus to reject would very rarely be achieved. Such a procedure would result in almost every panel report being adopted, even if it went against the interests of the larger states. Thus, a major step was taken to turn a system from one which encouraged delay by favoring unanimity of acceptance, to a speedier process which could override the wishes of particular states. This is a move away from a system of negotiation which was traditionally the preferred option of the Europeans to one of adjudication, the aim of the US.

A number of measures to tighten the application of CVD were undertaken to meet the interests of countries concerned about US practice. Petitions to invoke CVDs must demonstrate that they are supported by the domestic industry rather than just a few troubled firms. A *de minimis* level of 1 per cent is established which means that subsidies less than 1 per cent of the value of the goods will be considered too small to be countervailable. This is a very low level and the practice of adding up various subsidies should ensure that most controversial programs will easily vault the 1 per cent level. The code also stipulated that injury findings must demonstrate that injury was caused by the subsidies rather than other factors. A sunset provision was also included to encourage the elimination of CVDs once the injurious effects of the subsidy are no longer pertinent.

The Final Agreement

The Uruguay Round Agreement was eventually concluded on 15 December 1993. The subsidy issues were settled two days earlier on the 13th. They varied from the Dunkel Draft in three major areas: Research and Development, Regional Development and Environmental protection.[19] Agreement was greatly facilitated by a change in administration in the US. Under President Bush, the US position had been that all subsidies were harmful and had to be eliminated. President Clinton's team took a more activist approach to government and believed that industry and the economy could be assisted by selective government intervention. This was particularly true with regard to the high technology industry.

A prominent figure brought into the Clinton administration was Laura D'Andrea Tyson who took up a position as the chair of his Council of Economic Advisors. As an academic economist she had made the case that the US high technology industry required government support if it was to compete on an equal footing with other countries (Tyson, 1992: 280–6). Taking the label of a 'cautious activist' Tyson argued that trade laws such as CVDs were not satisfactory solutions to high technology problems. Americans needed a clear industrial policy and measures to match foreign subsidization. Rather than levying CVDs the United States should consider countervailing subsidies. In her analysis a broad based funding program to support American research and development was also required.

In addition to a more favorable intellectual climate for intervention there was also increased need for assistance by some branches of the high tech industry following the end of the Cold War. US military spending was being cut back, as were some of the lucrative high tech contracts. This was especially true for basic research such as SDI. Numerous defense firms were forced into severe restructuring and defense labs scrambled for support. Defense expenditure was being cut in numerous areas, drawing money out of the economy. In 1994 it was estimated that in real terms weapons purchases had declined from a 1985 high of $132 billion to $48 billion. US defense industry employment had fallen from 1.35 million in 1990 to an estimated 800 000, and the purchase of only 28 fixed-wing combat aircraft was a far cry from the 293 bought in a relatively quiet post-Vietnam 1975 (*Financial Times*, 11 August 1994). The cuts forced contractors to reduce their research and development in response to a deteriorating economic outlook.

In November 1993 Senator Jeff Bingaman wrote to President Clinton urging reconsideration of the US negotiating position with regard to subsidies for commercial research. Bingaman, Senator for New Mexico, was especially concerned as his constituency contained a number of key government defense research laboratories. His view was that the Dunkel Draft was detrimental to US interests because it discouraged technology partnerships between private industry and the federal government. Writing on behalf of a number of colleagues he stated that 'We believe that inadequate consideration has been given to this position. If adopted it would be extremely detrimental to US interests' (*International Trade Reporter*, 24 November 1993: 1957). Bingaman then went on to argue that the transfer of technology from federal labs to US industry was a legitimate effort to capture economic benefits of federal research.

While some Democrats and high tech industrialists urged increased flexibility in the subsidy negotiations, others tried to hold the line on the Bush approach of complete opposition to subsidy practices. Senators Baucus and Danforth sent a letter to the President dated 8 December reaffirming their support for a more traditional US position which would not allow regional development and R&D subsidies to be exempted from countervailing duties (*International Trade Reporter*, 19 January 1994: 103).

The White House took a sympathetic position to the more interventionist strategy and reversed its GATT negotiating position with regard to R&D subsidies. Under the Dunkel Draft subsidy limits of up to 50 per cent of the cost of basic research and not more than 25 per cent of applied research were proposed. Prior to the Dunkel Draft the US had been arguing that even rates of 15 and 20 per cent were too high. Following the change in Administration, and lobbying on behalf of high technology industries and states, the US position changed to expanding the limits to 75 per cent of costs for basic research and 50 per cent for applied. The EU which had formerly been arguing for rates of 15 and 20 per cent against the American desire to lower them, now was in the position of finding the US proposal too generous! Should such a proposal be accepted they may find themselves put under pressure to raise their own Community limits! The higher limits of 75 and 50 per cent were indeed the levels that the US Trade Representative Mickey Kantor and EC trade negotiator Sir Leon Brittan agreed to on 8 and 9 December.[20]

A change in the US position indicated that the Dunkel Draft was not cast in stone, creating an opportunity for the United States' North American neighbors to secure modifications. An important side deal was made with Canada over the desire to keep subnational subsidies. Section 2.2 of the Dunkel Draft's subsidy section had stipulated that a subsidy would be deemed specific, and thus countervailable, if confined to any geographic area irrespective of the level of government supplying it. The implication was that an identical generally available program, instituted by a subnational government, would come under scrutiny and possibly countervail action, but a national program would not. California's policies would be actionable, but not Germany's. This particular arrangement suited the EU countries as they would be allowed to continue subsidy policy at the Union and national levels while large US states would be disciplined more strictly. Although this issue was of some concern to the US federal government and some state governments, it was crucial for the Canadians. Such a measure would weaken the Canadian confederation by providing Quebec separatists with an excellent example of how autonomy would be increased by separating from the Canadian state. As a separate country Quebec government policies would not be under the same restrictions. Ultimately, the Canadians and Americans were able to prevail over the Europeans in an eight-hour negotiating session and the section was amended so that generally available subnational policies would not be automatically deemed specific.

As with the Canada–US negotiations there is some suggestion that the US was far more interested in monitoring and reducing other states' subsidy policies than their own. The amendment of the R&D proposals indicates a new found awareness of their subsidy practices, but there is little indication that much thought was given to what specific disciplines on subnational level might entail. Part of the Canadian case against the US government in bilateral subsidy negotiations was that US states used large amounts of subsidies to support industry. Under the stricter definition of specificity (drawn from US law) which insists that subsidies must not just be generally available, but must be used by a number of groups, billions of dollars of state expenditures may be questionable. In the future, aggressive US trade action could be met by equally aggressive opponents targeting a wide range of important state level economic development initiatives.

On the next to last day of the subsidy negotiations the Mexicans declared they wanted a green light in the area of measures that assist companies adapting to environmental standards. The GATT Director General and former EU Commissioner Peter Sutherland backed the initiative as it was essentially an old EU proposal. The Mexicans put the environmental proposal forward as part of a developing country initiative highlighting the fact that the subsidy package was primarily created to satisfy the interests of OECD states with no particular input from developing countries. Environmental issues were a concern in Mexico's case due to fears that environmental rules and regulations might increasingly be used by developed countries to block imports from developing countries. The Mexican government had previously used GATT to resist US restrictions on Mexican tuna imports that had been harvested in a manner harmful to dolphins (Skilton, 1993). This final agreement permitted one time subsidy measures for companies adapting existing facilities to new environmental standards limited to 20 per cent of the costs. This amendment was brought up very late in the negotiations and was agreed on the day the subsidy deal was sealed, 13 December.

The environmental exception may cause friction in the future as it goes against general US policy which tends to make the polluter pay for cleaning up their own industry. If US industries are unable to secure government support for environmental upgrades but other governments support their competing firms, American industries may be disadvantaged. They will not be able to take trade action because the foreign companies and governments will be protected by the subsidy code. The US government may have inadvertently agreed to a measure that will increase environmental spending to support domestic firms competing with companies based in countries with greener supporting governments.

In addition to tackling general subsidy provisions, three other areas were the subject of discussion. Agriculture which posed a special difficulty and aerospace which was not brought into GATT are examined in the following chapter. The third subsidy related area was the US favorite of entertainment or cultural industries. Stymied by the Canadian cultural exemption in the FTA and NAFTA, the MPEAA was determined that European policies would not receive GATT sanction. The two main areas of dispute were European quotas which limited the time of US airplay on television and subsidy policies such as the French tax on movies (including US) which was directed to French film makers. Arguments similar to those laid out in the Canada–US conflict were prominent, with the US claiming that the Europeans were protectionist and the French declaring that they would safeguard their right to create and distribute images of their own society.

President Clinton, who had received considerable financial support from Hollywood and was aware of the importance of California in any future reelection bid, met with the MPEAA and assured them of his support. In all-night negotiations on 13 December the USTR, Mickey Kantor, pushed the Europeans to budge on the cultural exemption, but to no avail. The French government was adamant that it would not make concessions in this area. As the deadline for agreement rapidly approached the US administration was forced to choose between scuttling the GATT deal on behalf of Hollywood movie interests, or reaching a GATT agreement which did not further the MPEAA's agenda. While the movie makers urged the US to sacrifice the agreement, the benefits in other areas could not be ignored. The United States capitulated to the European position.[21]

Having reached the GATT agreement the next challenge became ratification and implementation. In the message that President Clinton sent to Congress accompanying documents dealing with the Uruguay Round, he argued that the subsidy code was a balanced compromise providing clearer rules and stronger disciplines while making certain subsidies non-actionable (*International Trade Reporter*, 22 December 1993: 2158). He argued that clearer rules would benefit the United States and that the US had extended discipline to areas previously not covered, such as resource input subsidies. At the same time the Americans were able to maintain the effectiveness of their CVD rules and increase the level of obligations on developing countries.

The President's critics were unimpressed. A group of Republican Senators condemned the President for reversing US free market policies by agreeing to an arrangement which permitted subsidies. In a letter to the President dated 31 January 1994 they declared 'We believe the subsidies agreement raises a fundamental question about the proper relationship between government and the private sector . . . the new agreement promotes industrial policy' (*International Trade Reporter*, 12 February 1994: 178). Specific complaint was raised against the sections which permitted subsidization in the areas of R&D, regional development and environmental compliance. Senator Danforth, in particular, railed against the complete reversal of US antisubsidy policy, expressing fears that the US would have to find billions of dollars to compete with other governments. Senator Danforth is often on the front line of subsidy disputes as his constituency is home to some Boeing operations. The administration stressed both that the deal would allow them the flexibility to work with industry to create technologies of the future, and that they would continue to deal severely with others' unfair subsidization. The Deputy USTR stated that 'We intend to ensure that where there is discretion, we will [implement the Agreement] in a way that makes our laws truly effective and enforceable' (*International Trade Reporter*, 16 February 1994: 245–6).

As it came closer to the time for implementation of the GATT enabling legislation, the administration moved to bring the critics round. At a Senate Finance Committee meeting Senator Danforth indicated that there might be a way in which he could agree to back the agreement. (*International Trade Reporter*, 16 March 1994: 417). Article 9 of the code calls for consultations when subsidies are harming domestic interests of another state. A rigorous use of this clause might go some way to mitigating the GATT agreement. The difficulty for the administration in negotiating with Congress on such issues is that to gain domestic support they may need to bend the implementing legislation in such a way that it then becomes inconsistent with the multilateral agreement itself.

The fate of the subsidy provisions and the GATT agreement in general rested with the US Congress. Negotiations between the Senate and House over Uruguay Round legislation made it clear that the subsidy provisions would be applied as tightly as possible. Similar to previous trade legislation the Congress tried to reinterpret and mold the agreement to suit their domestic protective interests. The Senate stated that it would use the required GATT notification process to 'aggressively monitor the operation of the green light categories'.[22] For any program not properly notified the burden of proof would fall heavily upon the other country. It was also proposed that the USTR act as a watchdog over GATT developments, reserving the use of Section 301 in cases where a country hinders or does not comply with the GATT Subsidy Committee. A mechanism for channeling domestic complaints concerning the serious adverse effects of other countries' green light subsidy practices was also viewed as important. Ample opportunity should remain for what others will view as protectionist initiatives or harassment of imports into the US.

In the Balance

The issue of subsidies and their shadow CVDs pose a number of problems for the multilateral trading system. Increased focus on NTBs to trade highlights a contradiction the GATT system papered over at its creation in 1948. GATT tried to balance the drive for liberalization with the desire of governments to have autonomy in their domestic economies. As long as liberalization was primarily concerned with reducing tariffs in a time of economic expansion, governments were relatively free to pursue domestic priorities such as full employment. The elimination of tariffs, along with a shift in comparative advantage and a slowdown in growth and productivity has moved attention to the issue of subsidies and NTBs. The drive to eliminate or harmonize NTBs, and domestic subsidies in particular, attacks 'the policy tolerance which had been a central, if largely implicit element of the international consensus that had created and maintained GATT' (Destler, 1986: 34). Subsidy negotiations are difficult because they increase the possibility of exposing domestic policy to severe international constraints. The globalized financial system has placed limits upon how much governments can spend, while trade law is attempting to dictate how the money can be spent.

On the surface it appears that the Uruguay Round agreement on subsidies and countervailing measures has made considerable progress. The definition of subsidy has finally been agreed, the category of prohibited subsidies expanded, the specificity test enshrined, an area of non-actionable subsidies crucial to state autonomy has been delineated, demands for notification strengthened, a faster and more effective dispute settlement process created, and some restraint on countervailing duties implemented. Yet, one should not expect this to be the end of the story. Provisions in the area of restricting subnational subsidies will most likely be the subject of considerable dispute, as will the question of specificity and environmental assistance. Legal improvements have been made, but will they be enough to contain the underlying tensions?

The gap between the US and its trading allies concerning the appropriate role for subsidies remains and may be exploited in times of tension or recession. Republicans who took over majority control of the Congress in November 1994 remain ideologically opposed to the notion of green light subsidy practices. Their desire to modify the Code by making extensive use of Article 9 consultations indicates that subsidy disputes may continue even if a particular practice does not violate the code. Similar to the fate of the Tokyo Round subsidy agreements, a great deal depends upon implementation and the political mood in the US. Should the subsidy provisions of GATT live up to best expectations it is likely that they will dampen some subsidy conflicts, but they will also channel the underlying conflict into new issues and other trade actions.

7 Agriculture and Aerospace

Two sectors of the economy that have been of particular concern in subsidy disputes, but have been handled outside of the general provisions of industrial subsidies are agriculture and aerospace. Agriculture was an exception to postwar liberalization initiatives as most governments believed in the necessity of supporting the sector against the chaos of the international market. Agricultural disputes took center stage in the Uruguay Round and caused considerable delay in reaching a final agreement. Aerospace has also been a subject of intense conflict in the past 20 years as competition between the European Community's Airbus has threatened United States producers such as McDonnell Douglas, Lockheed and Boeing. Similar to agriculture, the primary protagonists have been the United States and the European Community with the latter declaring that its subsidy practices are justified. In both cases bilateral deals have been agreed which restrict but do not eliminate subsidy practices.

DOWN ON THE FARM

This section examines the European–US agricultural subsidy dispute as an example of the difficulties in trying to restructure the domestic policies of one country or region to satisfy powerful interests in another. Agricultural subsidies are particularly important because failure to reach an agreement threatened completion of the Uruguay Round. The primary axis of conflict has been between the United States and the European Union, but other major players include Japan and the Cairns Group. The Cairns Group is a coalition of middle powers whose treasuries are unable to compete with the United States or the EC in subsidizing agricultural exports. Its members are Argentina, Australia, Brazil, Canada, Chile, Columbia, Hungary, Indonesia, Malaysia, New Zealand, Philippines, Thailand and Uruguay. As a group they represent 500 million people and account for a quarter of world agricultural exports (Johnston, 1988: 3). From 1979 to 1985 the average annual US dollar value for agricultural support was \$53 billion for the EC, \$34 billion for Japan and \$32 billion for the US (Vitte and Langer, 1990: 5).

Efforts to liberalize agricultural trade conflict with domestic policies that have something other than efficient resource allocation as their primary objective. Countries may intervene in agriculture in order to ensure self-sufficiency, sustain a community and way of life, or to support or stabilize food prices. The theoretical case for free trade is often traced back to David Ricardo's theory of comparative advantage. Ricardo used the example of Britain exchanging its manufactured goods (textiles) for Portugal's wine to demonstrate that countries would gain from trade if they specialized in the products in which they had a comparative advantage (Hollander, 1979: 462–70, Ricardo, 1992: 77–93). There is a crucial difference between these products and food, however. If production is reduced in either Britain or Portugal, the product will be missed in the other country, but the hardship will be tolerable. A country that has its food imports reduced or halted due to war, pestilence or natural disaster faces the prospect of starvation. Thus, because of fears of dependence or the commitment to support a particular way of life states are generally reluctant to be totally dependent on others for food, even if it is economically more efficient.

Although protectionism in agricultural products violates liberal theory and has drawn considerable criticism in the last 20 years it is not an exceptional occurrence. Free trade in agricultural products, with the exception of Great Britain during its hegemonic era, has not taken place in the modern age. Starting from an unrivaled industrial lead, British governments opened their markets to cheap food imports in the 1840s. Not only did this conform to liberal theories of comparative advantage, it assisted industrial production by allowing employers to limit or decrease wages to workers who bought the cheaper imported foodstuffs. After flirting with free trade Germany and France both pursued protectionist agricultural policies. At the founding of the United States, small independent landholders were seen as the key to a strong and vigorous democracy and steps were taken to ensure that foreign products did not disturb this state of affairs. Managed trade was the rule as European colonial powers established exclusive bilateral arrangements which funneled agricultural trade (often tropical) from the colonies in exchange for manufactured goods. Prior to the First World War Europe occupied the central position in world agriculture as it was both the leading importer of temperate zone and tropical products and the largest producer of agricultural products. It accounted for over half the world's wheat, barley and oats production, 90 per cent of beet sugar, 30 per cent of cattle and half the pigs. North America held the edge over Europe in cotton, tobacco and maize (Nagle, 1976: 4).

The First World War disrupted European agricultural production, especially in Russia, but by the 1920s prewar patterns were reestablished. With the onset of the Great Depression, agricultural protectionism increased as prices collapsed in many countries. For example, in major agricultural exporters such as Argentina, Canada and the US prices in 1932 were approximately half of their 1929 level (Nagle, 1976: 7). In Britain a number of steps such as subsidies for oats, barley and wheat production, a levy on imported and domestic flour to subsidize domestic producers and internal marketing boards were introduced. At the Ottawa Conference of 1932 Britain and the Commonwealth countries solidified a preference system which gave favored access to British manufactured goods in return for privileged access of Commonwealth agricultural products.

The US response to the Depression and agricultural crisis was to introduce a set of support measures which later had a decisive impact on postwar trade arrangements. The 1933 Agricultural Adjustment Act (AAA), the 1936 Soil Conservation and Allotment Act, Agricultural Marketing Agreement Act of 1937 and Agricultural Adjustment Act of 1938 were designed to raise farmers' incomes by a combination of production restraints, cash payments and import controls. An executive order of October 1933 created the Commodity Credit Corporation (CCC) which was authorized to buy or deal in any agricultural productions targeted by the President. Two aspects of these acts are of particular importance. The first is the concept of parity. Parity was the goal of giving farmers a purchasing power for their agricultural products equivalent to what it was between the base period of August 1909 to July 1914. The second aspect was that in order to do this the President was given the power to impose import quotas or fees in addition to tariffs to protect the domestic market.

Because of the strength of domestic interests, interwar US farm arrangements had to be accommodated in the postwar structure (Kelly, 1963: 174–226). Initially the gap between trade and agricultural policy was not great, as both were protectionist in the early 1930s. Yet, as US trade policy moved in a more liberal direction and agricultural policy moved to offer increased support for domestic farmers, the tension became more pronounced. For example, a year after the Trade Agreements Act of 1934 backed away from the protectionist Smoot-Hawley tariff of 1930 by granting the President authority to reduce tariffs in international negotiations, Congress amended the AAA of 1933 to provide protection in support of agricultural domestic policies. Section 22 was added establishing the principle that imports ought not frustrate AAA programs. This allowed the President to institute import quotas to protect the AAA. Section 32 was added supporting the principle of export subsidies and mandating the setting aside of 30 per cent of customs revenues for this and other purposes by the Secretary of Agriculture. Such measures were required to support the AAA because high domestic prices would be undermined by a flood of cheaper imports. Export subsidies would be required to sell domestic produce abroad if the US price was above the world price. In a time of considerable domestic economic instability and crisis in the agricultural sector, Sections 22 and 32 were politically untouchable and trade agreements would have to accommodate their provisions. In the struggle over principles and policy Secretary of State and free trader Cordell Hull was not able to outmaneuver the Agricultural Secretary. Sections 22 and 32 were not actually used until the late 1930s as droughts in 1934 and 1936 forced the importation of large amounts of agricultural products.[1]

Rather than return to pre-Depression policies following the Second World War, support for US agriculture expanded in the 1940s. The principle of parity as well as the number and scope of products qualifying for support expanded. The Congress was determined to protect US agricultural interests from a downturn in agricultural demand expected following the end of hostilities. In addition to supporting domestic programs directly, the United States made provisions to assist in the sale of its exports. Under the 1954 Public Law 480 supplies of agricultural products were made available on easy terms of credit. In 1955 as much as 35 per cent of US agricultural exports benefited from export assistance (Nagle, 1976: 20). This continued protection required the molding of international agreements to support domestic programs. In postwar negotiations the US suggested that the prohibition of import quotas should not apply to agricultural import quotas. They were also opposed to restrictions on agricultural export subsidies which might restrict their domestic programs.

The provisions of the failed ITO tried to discourage export agricultural subsidies, but did not prohibit them. States paying exports subsidies were committed to negotiating international commodity agreements to share markets and deal with low prices. During negotiations states were prohibited from initiating or increasing subsidies. However, if negotiations did not succeed or members considered that their interests were prejudiced they would be free to subsidize agricultural exports (Wilcox, 1949: 128–9).

From its very inception, GATT was not up to the task of liberalizing agricultural trade and it has struggled since that time to plug holes and reform the system. Agriculture was made an exception to a number of GATT rules because the US resisted efforts at liberalization in this area and this suited most other countries as well (with the exception of major agricultural exporters like Canada) (Stone, 1984: 155–65). In drafting the GATT, the US ensured that its own domestic protectionist agricultural policies would be protected by inserting Article XI:2(c) which allowed quotas to protect domestic price support programs.

It was not long after the GATT agreement had been reached that pressure for the US to break away from the weak discipline in place began to build. In the early 1950s US exports began to fall and protectionist pressure increased. Congress changed Section 22 from declaring that it must be consistent with international obligations to declaring that international obligations must be consistent with Section 22. The Congress ordered the President to violate GATT if it conflicted with the domestic agricultural system. Inventive Congressional agricultural interests managed to amend the 1951 Defense Production Act to include cheese as a strategic material and worthy of protection! Insistence at maintaining dairy restrictions pitted the US against the Netherlands, Australia, Canada, Czechoslovakia, Denmark, France, Finland, Italy, New Zealand, Norway, the United Kingdom, and Sweden (Hudec, 1990: 181–206). GATT's threat of sanctions failed to sway the US. Following a positive verdict from the GATT the Netherlands exercised its right of retaliation and reduced it imports of US wheat as compensation. The action had little effect on US policy as by 1953 complete embargoes on foreign dried whole milk, dried buttermilk and dried cream were instituted.

Increased use of Section 22 by the United States in violation of GATT principles after 1952 meant that unless either Section 22 or GATT was amended, GATT rules would be discredited by constant violation. The solution was that in the annual review of 1955 GATT granted a waiver to the United States for Section 22 actions that '. . . effectively removed US agriculture from international constraints' (Gavin, 1987: 279). It excepted Section 22 from GATT disciplines for an indefinite period of time. In turn the United States agreed to consult with other countries and recognize their right to retaliate. This waiver was later held in reserve by the European Economic Community in case the provisions of the Common Agricultural Policy (CAP) were challenged at GATT. Although minute progress was made during the Kennedy and Tokyo Rounds to deal with some specific issues, countries were generally able to do as they pleased in agricultural policy (Tangermann, 1989).

Until the 1970s, US agricultural policy neglected export markets in favor of controlling domestic overproduction, maintaining income levels and preserving the family farm. By controlling supply the US price for agricultural products was maintained above that of the world market. Domestic prices were kept up by restricting supply through payments to farmers for reducing the amount of crops they planted. Low-priced imports were kept out of the market by quantitative restrictions.

Similarly to the US, European governments organized their agricultural industries so that they focused on domestic markets following the Great Depression and the Second World War (Cafruny, 1989: 111–37). Having experienced food shortages and in some cases starvation during the war, Europeans concentrated on stimulating production through subsidies and price support systems. As in the US, Europe kept out low-priced competition through the use of import controls. Any surplus from its agricultural policies was exported or given away as aid in order to prop up domestic prices. A 1967 EC study estimated that the percentage of support measures in agricultural income was 44 per cent in the US and 50 per cent in the EC (Nagle, 1976: 21).

When the six founding members of the European Coal and Steel Community (West Germany, France, Italy, Belgium, Netherlands and Luxembourg) decided to deepen integration by creating the European Economic Community in the late 1950s agriculture was a key element. In 1958 24 per cent of the French, 16 per cent of Germans and 33 per cent of Italians were engaged in agriculture (Nagle, 1976: 22). Across the new Community 20 per cent, or approximately 15 million people, were engaged in farming (Swann, 1992: 222). The central political deal was trading German desire for free access for its manufactured goods against the French desire for access for its agricultural goods. The CAP was created to regulate the EC's agricultural policies.

The five primary objectives of the CAP as set out in articles 39 of the Treaty of Rome are: (1) to increase agricultural productivity; (2) to ensure a fair standard of living for agricultural communities; (3) to stabilize markets; (4) to provide certainty of supplies; and (5) to ensure supplies to the consumer at reasonable prices. Although some of these objectives would prove to be in conflict, such as ensuring a fair standard of living for farmers and reasonable prices for consumers, these were the goals to guide policy. The objectives were pursued by manipulating the internal market prices for products. The Community would buy products at official rates to support prices, while steps would be taken to ensure cheap imports did not undercut the Community price.

A threshold price for commodities would ensure that cheaper imports would pay a tax to make up the difference. The Community instituted a variable levy rather than a regular tariff. The variable levy would rise as the world market price fell, and fall as the world market price rose, to keep inputs at a fixed level with internal prices. Any surpluses would be disposed of on the international markets.

By 1968, the Community eliminated agricultural protection between member states and replaced national systems of support with a Community system. Agricultural surpluses were bought up through the European Agricultural Guidance and Guarantee Fund (EAGGF). National governments also gave grants and aid. The policy was a success from a political vantage point as it was the most integrated form of collective policy making on a Community basis. However, as will become clear below, it violated another provision of the Treaty of Rome – Article 110 which states that Community policy should contribute to the harmonious development of world trade.

By the early 1970s the United States' and European Community's policies were increasingly in conflict and became a source of considerable irritation in the 1980s. On the European side, the CAP had stimulated production to such an extent that surpluses spilled on to the world market undercutting other countries' exports. At the same time, the US was starting to exploit a comparative advantage in agricultural product exports in order to redress their balance of payments deficits. The new US policy of placing more emphasis on export markets, combined with competition from other agricultural exporters, clashed with the established European policy of the CAP. The CAP has been the object of slightly over 30 per cent (25 of 80) of GATT lawsuits between 1960 and 1985. Fifty-eight per cent (25 of 43) of GATT lawsuits in agriculture were directed at the EC while more than 70 per cent of litigation against the EC involved agricultural issues (Hudec, 1988: 22–3). Conflict was heightened by the US 1985 Farm Bill, which decisively liberalized domestic US agriculture by rejecting supply management. This put more pressure on American farmers to rely on export markets for income.

In addition to attracting criticism from foreign governments and producers, the CAP has internal shortcomings which have been the subject of much comment. The primary criticisms have been that it costs a great deal of money and raises food costs to the general public. For example, at the beginning of the 1980s wheat prices were 30 per cent above world levels and beef was 90 per cent above world levels (Swann, 1992: 234). Some studies estimated that removal of the CAP would reduce agricultural product prices by an average of 30 per cent (Swann, 1992: 234). In addition to paying higher food prices, consumers paid to store and dispose of growing surpluses. By using a large slice of the Union's budget for the CAP less money was available for regional development and social funds. Another problem lay in the disparity of income levels among farmers in different regions and of different sizes. The system operates to the benefit of larger farming operations. It has been difficult to slow increases in production, which means that some of the surpluses get dumped on world markets, creating trade tensions. Numerous attempts have been made to reform it, but it is a slow process and critics are usually unimpressed (Fennel, 1987).

Vocal opposition to the CAP on the part of the US and the Cairns Group sometimes obscures the fact that there has been substantial reform in Europe's agricultural policies. During the 1980s it shifted from a policy that protected small family farms to one that encouraged its most competitive farmers to export (Phillips, 1990). CAP reform was initiated following the prospect of a budgetary crisis and the refusal of Britain to renegotiate budget contributions without increased discipline on agricultural spending. By 1984 the Council of Ministers had agreed to price reductions and production constraints, but these were insufficient to redress the budgetary problems or reduce surpluses. In 1984 reform began in the milk sector where quotas were imposed. The guaranteed price was on a stipulated quantity, subject to annual cuts. Member states also introduced outgoers schemes to encourage farmers to exit milk production. A coresponsibility levy was put on cereals. Further reform occurred in 1988 under the Delors package. Agricultural spending growth was capped at 74 per cent of EC GNP growth, an expenditure ceiling was agreed, disincentives to curb overproduction were introduced and set-aside schemes as well as early retirement schemes for farmers were created. Due to domestic changes in production, education and technology, many European wheat farmers are now competitive with their US counterparts. As a result the EC became willing to further reform its domestic agricultural policies on the condition that it could maintain its world market share of exports (Bulter, 1993: 164). While European willingness to reduce its subsidy practices may reduce other countries' complaints, its new taste for international markets is likely to increase conflict with other agricultural exporters.

The US Uruguay Round proposal for dealing with agriculture was extremely ambitious, if not impractical. Drawing upon nuclear weapons disarmament terminology the US proposed the 'Zero Option.' It called for a ten-year complete phase-out of all agricultural subsidies which 'directly or indirectly affect trade', an immediate freeze and phase-out of export subsidies, phase-out of all import barriers and harmonization of health and sanitary regulations (Petersmann and Hilf, 1987: 585–8). The Cairns Group proposal shared these goals, but did not foresee their achievement in a ten-year period. They were willing to take a decade to establish the means of achieving fully liberalized agricultural trade (Hoekman, 1989: 89). Former US Undersecretary of Agriculture Dale Hathaway characterized these groups as being in the reform camp. Their goal was to eliminate agricultural exceptions from GATT Articles XI and XVI, eliminate exceptions and waivers and eventually prohibit domestic subsidies that produce trade distortions (Schott, 1990: 52). He contrasts this with a group of countries urging restraint through a gradual lessening of protection and retaining of support. This group was led by the EC, but found support in Japan and some Nordic countries. For Japan the greatest difficulty lay in the liberalization of its rice market (Rapkin and George, 1993).

US proposals encountered stiff resistance from the EC. The Europeans were interested in stabilizing the market and gradually reducing subsidies, rather than a dash to liberalization. They proposed emergency action be taken on some commodities such as cereals, sugar and dairy products to stabilize the market. This would be followed by some liberalization and negotiations along certain product lines. European hesitation to move quickly was backed up by studies that suggested Europe and Japan would bear the brunt of adjustment from liberalization (McDonald, 1990).

Progress on the agricultural front was slow, with the US demanding complete liberalization within a decade and the EC demanding a much slower pace. The deadlock threatened the talks at numerous stages in the six-year Uruguay Round negotiations including the 1988 Montreal midterm review when the Cairns group refused to approve reports from other sectors in the absence of an agriculture deal. In an April 1990 GATT ministerial meeting it was agreed to that subgroups be formed in the agriculture group to look at issues of market access, domestic supports, export competition, and sanitary and phytosanitary regulations. The final week of negotiations were to occur in December 1990 because the US needed to get the proposals through Congress before its fast track negotiating authority ran out in June 1991. The US demanded a 90 per cent cut in export subsidies and a 75 per cent cut in domestic programs, but the EC offered only a 30 per cent cut to internal programs retroactive to 1986 (*Financial Post*, 14 December 1990). Europeans wanted the cut to be retroactive so that they would get credit for internal initiatives undertaken since their internal reform project began four years earlier. There was also failure to agree on a common methodology for measuring agricultural trade distortions. Attempts at compromise failed and on 7 December 1990, negotiations were suspended. It appears that the Americans expected the EC to collapse under immense pressure while the EC was unwilling to take action that would threaten the CAP.

Suspension of the GATT talks had diverse effects. The US House of Representatives leader, Richard Gephardt, threatened to introduce legislation that would force other countries to open their markets. Canada's Minister for International Trade, given to colorful rhetoric by nature, warned that continued failure would 'plunge us into trade disaster, a trading war, with more unilateralism and more protectionism' (*Financial Post*, 10 December 1990). Those with cooler heads began to patch a new deal together. Informal discussions began in early 1991 between the US and the EC in the hope that the agricultural issue could be resolved. US President George Bush was able to secure extension of fast track authority in June and work on the agricultural issue resumed. Another deadline had passed without serious repercussions as attempts to reach a compromise continued.

In turning down US terms in 1990, EC leaders decided that the domestic social balance struck with rural areas through the CAP was more important than immediately conforming to policies advocated by the United States and the Cairns Group. A leading decision-maker in this area is the largest economic entity in the European Community, Germany, whose agricultural policies exhibit a continuity of over a hundred years. Since the 1970s Germany has become more resistant to changes that might hurt its farmers (Hendriks, 1988/9). Any room that the German government had to move on the subsidy issue may have been taken away with German unification. The collapse of the East German economy, high unemployment and social strife following the fall of the Berlin Wall made stability in the agricultural sector even more important.

Institutionally and politically, the EC was in a much less flexible bargaining position than the US. The CAP was a central aspect of European integration and large scale changes would threaten that process. The CAP was of great importance to the more agricultural economies of the EC and of central importance to France. In addition, EC policy was institutionalized in such a manner as to give agricultural interests a strong position in the bureaucracy and in the decision-making body of the Council of Ministers. Agricultural trade policies were the domain of agricultural ministers of the member states and not subject to the same compromises as other industries. While the Director General for External Affairs is responsible for negotiating international treaties, the Directorate General for Agriculture exercises responsibilities in the agricultural field.[2] Despite the desires of some national governments such as Britain to go further in making concessions, agricultural interests maintained support through a Franco-German alliance. The French supported the German government's desire to oppose domestic price cuts which would hurt its small farmers while the Germans supported the French desire to ward off cuts to export subsidies. The rigid structure and conflicting interests resulted in a delay in agreeing a new EC position in the autumn of 1992. This arrived several weeks after the 15 October deadline for final GATT proposals and was one factor in complicating the 1992 negotiations.

Indeed, EC willingness to compromise in international negotiations is heavily conditioned by internal developments. Changes to the CAP are usually a result of a Community budgetary crisis as in the cases of 1984, 1988, and 1991. For example, the EC's 1991 proposals were in response to a looming EC budget problem where agricultural spending threatened to go over budget. These proposals, named after the Agricultural Minister Ray MacSharry, stressed internal problems of the CAP such as the productivity increasing by 2 per cent per annum while consumption rose by only 0.5 per cent, environmental damage caused by the support of intensive farming, and concentration of support on a small number of large farms. The MacSharry reforms were adopted in May 1992 and provided for a reduction in price support in the cereals sector to bring the levels down closer to world market prices, compensatory direct payments to farmers for lost revenue, and an expanded set-aside scheme where payments would be linked to taking land out of production. It was these reforms driven primarily by internal Community difficulties, but with an eye to the multilateral environment that allowed for later compromise at the GATT (Swinbank, 1993).

Agriculture became the make or break sector of the negotiations even though it was only one of 15 negotiating groups and represented a small percentage of world trade.[3] Robert Paalberg has suggested that an explanation for the deadlock was the United States' attempt to use the Uruguay Round as a lever forcing domestic agricultural reform (Paalberg, 1993). USTR Clayton Yeutter and his Undersecretary for Agriculture Daniel Amstutz hoped they could find liberal minded allies in the EC and Japan who would join them in creating an agreement which would reduce everyone's domestic farm support burden.

Unlike the Canadian FTA negotiators, the US GATT team were unable to find powerful like-minded counterparts in the EC and Japan. Support did come from the Cairns Group, but it was not sufficient. At home the domestic farm lobby was successful in holding the administration to its ambitious zero option proposals which made international agreement difficult, thereby ensuring the maintenance of US support programs.

Canada's position on agricultural trade mirrored some of the problems in the US–EC dispute. While trying to persuade other countries to eliminate export subsidies, Canada blocked access to its own domestic market. As a member of the Cairns Group, Canada has pushed for the elimination of subsidies on exports, especially grains. Yet, it strictly protected its domestic market via supply management policies for dairy products, eggs, and certain meat and poultry products. The Canadian message seemed to be that it was acceptable for countries to protect their domestic markets, but not subsidize their exports. The partial endorsement of agricultural liberalization reflects a deep regional split. Western Canadian grain farmers desperately need an open international market for their competitive harvest, while dairy and poultry farmers in Quebec and Ontario require a protected domestic market for their products. The result is an inconsistent liberalization policy because addressing the issue directly runs the risk of severe domestic regional conflict (Skogstad, 1992).

As GATT negotiations picked up in the fall of 1991, it became increasingly clear that Canada was losing ground in its efforts to keep marketing boards off the table while reaping the gains that might result from the elimination of export subsidies (*Financial Post*, 18 November 1991). The Europeans and even the Japanese were beginning to agree to a process whereby all forms of domestic protection would be changed to tariffs. This tariffication process would grant the same degree of protection, but would have the advantage of being subject to tariff cuts as had happened in previous GATT rounds with manufacturing products. Canadian dairy and poultry farmers feared that this signaled the beginning of the end of the marketing board environment. Some producers tried to use the threat of increased support flowing to the Quebec independence movement to bolster their hand with the government (*Toronto Star*, 23 December 1991).

One of the substantive issues blocking a GATT deal in agriculture was the ongoing EC–US dispute over subsidies to oilseed production (Brand, 1993). It reflected both the difficulty of dealing with the agricultural subsidy issue and differing interpretations of the role of GATT dispute settlement. Whereas the EC has traditionally viewed dispute settlement as a method to further negotiation, the US has viewed GATT as a litigation arena to force other countries to act properly. In January 1988 the USTR launched a 301 investigation of the EC's subsidy practices in the oilseeds field. This was followed by an April 1988 initiation of a GATT case on the same issue. The US argued that EC policy served to undermine the benefits that the United States should have received as a result of the lowering of tariffs in 1962 and that the EC subsidies to community producers and users discriminated against American exports. Prodded on by the threat of unilateral US 301 action, the EC consented to have GATT deal with the issue. Although a GATT panel ruled against a revamped EC subsidy policy, the US and EC were not able to agree upon adequate compensation. The final GATT ruling found that the European action nullified US expectation of gains, but was not in violation of GATT. The US was entitled to compensation, but the EC did not make an offer the Americans found acceptable. As a result, the US government announced in November 1992 that by December it would impose duties of 200 per cent on wine, cheese and other EC imports. On 20 November the US and EC reached agreement in which the Community would reduce the acreage entitled to subsidies, making a GATT agricultural deal more likely.

The agreement on oilseeds was part of a wider EC–US bilateral agricultural deal called the Blair House Agreement. It amended the agricultural sections of Secretary General Dunkel's draft text published in December 1991 (Ingersent, Rayner and Hine, 1993). The French government in particular had objected to portions of the Dunkel Draft and demanded changes. In the area of market access the EC agreed to the Dunkel Draft's tariffication of all NTBs, reduction of 36 per cent in specific tariffs subject to a minimum of 15 per cent in every category and minimum market access of 3 per cent of an importer's base period. This acceptance was traded in return for a provision that the EC could maintain a minimum 10 per cent import tariff. The EC agreed to the Dunkel Draft's provisions for a uniform cut of 20 per cent in domestic support, but was able to increase the types of programs exempted from this requirement. In the realm of export subsidies the EC agreed to the Dunkel provisions to cut budgetary expenditures on export subsidies by 36 per cent, but was able to reduce the restriction on reducing the volume of subsidized exports by 24 per cent to 21 per cent.

The French government extended its opposition from the Dunkel Draft to the Blair House Agreement. They sought clarification of restraints on export subsidies and pushed the EC both for further restraints on imports and increased funds to compensate farmers. French intransigence and the threat of a possible vetoing of the GATT deal led to minor revisions of the Blair House Accord which included an increase in the starting volume of subsidized exports that would be subject to reduction in the early period of the agreement. The reference years for production cuts shifted from 1986–90 to 1991–2 which would allow the Europeans to export an estimated extra 8 million tonnes of cereals (*Financial Times*, 16 December 1993). Other compromises included an extension of the Peace Clause shielding agricultural policy measures that did not violate the Uruguay agreement from six to nine years. The final text of the Uruguay Round Agreement sections covering agricultural issues closely followed the Blair House Agreement, but omitted some of the numerical details of particular commitments.[4] Numerical requirements agreed at Blair House with regard to export subsidies are included in the final text. A notable aspect of the agreement is the proportionately greater cuts in market access (36 per cent) and export subsidies (36 per cent budget, 21 per cent volume) than in cuts to domestic support (20 per cent with exceptions) (Ingersent, Rayner and Hine, 1993: 3). This reflects both the desire to reduce trade-distorting subsidies and an acknowledgment that support to farmers is a political prerequisite for such cuts.

French opposition to the Dunkel text and the Blair House Accord centered around its alleged incompatibility with the 1992 CAP reforms. Commission officials claimed that they were compatible, but their underlying assumptions that productivity growth would be below historical levels and that the Europeans would be able to reconquer internal grains markets from the United States were challenged (*Financial Times*, 2 April 1993 and 30 September 1993). In France there were objections to two aspects of the reforms. The first was that direct compensation to farmers reduced their sense of independence and highlighted their dependence on the state. The second was that plans for set-aside of agricultural production could leave vast areas of land unattended and contribute to desertification of the French countryside. French farm unions estimated that 1.5 million hectares of French production could be set aside – equivalent to the total land under cereal cultivation in Denmark or 10 times that in the Netherlands (*Financial Times* 24 June 1993).

Another factor weighing on the mind of any French government is the tradition of French agricultural interests taking direct action in commercial disputes. Blocking roads, burning tires, dumping agricultural goods in inconvenient settings, intercepting rival commodities and bloody clashes with riot police are standard weapons in what public choice analysts might dispassionately label interest group politics or rent seeking. In addition to the technical discussion about the influence of particular reforms and fears about electoral prospects, some consideration to social order bears on the minds of decision makers.

Prior to finalizing the GATT agreement the EC members most hesitant about a GATT deal were able to wring concessions from other Member States at a last minute summit. France was able to secure agreement that even if the CAP reforms resulted in a level of agricultural surplus above the allowed GATT levels, no more land would need to be taken out of production. Rather than cutting production, internal prices would be lowered to world levels and French farmers would receive increased direct compensation. This would allow wheat to be exported without export subsidies. The Germans were able to receive guarantees that their farmers would not be hurt by continuing strengthening of the German currency, and penalties on East German farmers, who had exceeded their planting quotas, were reduced. The British government was pleased that there would be no increase in the resources going towards agricultural spending. These agreements smoothed GATT acceptance, but could prove a source of confrontation if all the bills came due, upsetting British expectations of limiting spending (*Financial Times*, 13 December 1993). As the dust settled on the GATT deal, Commission officials warned that the promises made to Germany concerning currency and agricultural price guarantees might prove particularly troublesome (*Financial Times*, 19 February 1994).

The Uruguay Round agreements managed to extend GATT discipline to the agricultural sector. The tariffication of import barriers should result in reduction of obstacles to trade as these tariffs are gradually reduced over time. Agricultural export subsidies also face the prospect of quantitative targets which should be more effective than previous provisions limiting states to a fair share of the world market. However, agriculture remains an exceptional area in world trade as export subsidies are still permitted.

CONFLICT IN THE SKY

Subsidies have been of considerable concern in the aerospace industry since the 1970s. All large airplane manufacturers have benefited from government assistance although the method, amount and timing has varied considerably. It has not been possible to have a thriving aerospace industry since the Second World War without the support of national governments and taxpayers. Similarly to agriculture, state elites have been unwilling to let market forces determine outcomes. The primary conflict has been between the US and the EC and agreement has been to reduce, but continue subsidization in the field. An interesting point of the aerospace dispute is the role that the industry has played in pushing for reform, but counseling against trade action that might disrupt their own interests in the other continent.

Unlike agriculture, government support for aerospace receives some intellectual backing from mainstream economics as an example of a high technology strategic industry. In the 1980s some economists and policy analysts advanced the case for rethinking traditional free trade theory in the form of strategic trade theory (Richardson, 1990). Their argument was that in some sectors of the economy firms were operating in an imperfect market where a small number of participants could influence prices and harm rival firms' activities (Krugman, 1986). This is in contrast to the notion of a perfectly competitive market where a large number of small firms engage in competition. In strategic conditions, firms may be able to appropriate large 'rents'. Profits may be higher in the strategic industry than in other industries. An added impetus for government intervention is the notion of external economies or externalities. Having a particular industry located in one's country may lead to benefits that are greater than those reflected in the balance sheet of the industry in question. This is thought to be particularly true in high technology fields. Nurturing a high technology industry may assist in the provision of a highly skilled workforce which can be employed in other ventures. It may attract similar high value added service industries.

The aerospace sector fits the bill for strategic trade policy. The industry moves towards a natural monopoly due to immense technological risk and huge upfront development costs. Aerospace may be viewed as strategic in the economic sense of providing high wage, high skill research and development employment. Barriers to entry by new firms are great. Without government support it is unlikely that a country will develop a major airline producer. It is also a strategic industry in the military sense in that commercial airframe producers are major military contractors. The failure of a country's aerospace sector could have severe consequences for the purchase of military hardware and state security. There are a number of factors in addition to the economics of a particular venture that may persuade decision-makers to assist industry.

Following the Second World War the US quickly came to dominate the global aerospace industry. Although the Europeans had been the prewar leaders in aerospace technology and continued to introduce innovations, US companies were able to achieve a dominant position benefiting from the largest single market for airplanes, lucrative defense contracts, and a regulated market which encouraged airlines to compete through the purchase of new products. US companies benefited from an unintended but effective industrial policy through military spending. For example, Boeing's dominance of the wide body passenger jet market can be traced back to engine and design technologies it undertook for the B-47 and B-52 military bombers. Not profitable on the commercial side of its operations, Boeing was able to count on military contracts to keep it profitable during the first 20 years of its existence (Tyson, 1992: 169).

The US government assisted producers in other ways. Funds from the National Aeronautics and Space Administration (NASA) were used by US companies for R&D. In 1967 federal loan guarantees and a favorable anti-trust ruling by the government allowed for the merger of McDonnell and Douglas aircraft companies. In 1971 Lockheed was given a $250 loan guarantee to keep it out of bankruptcy. In the early 1980s when McDonnell Douglas was on the verge of closing its DC-10 production line the US Air Force bought 60 military versions of the aircraft allowing the company to weather the difficult period.

Following the collapse of a number of national airline production companies and under increased threat of US dominance in the aerospace industry, European governments worked to establish a consortium for aircraft production in the 1960s. The result was Airbus which is a consortium of French (Aerospatiale), British (British Aerospace), German (Deutsche Airbus) and Spanish (CASA) companies. By 1991 it had captured one third of the world market for large commercial jets, replaced McDonnell Douglas as the second largest producer and achieved technological parity with Boeing. Unlike US government intervention, European support has been blatant and intended primarily for commercial gains. It would have been impossible to jump the high entry barriers to the commercial aircraft market without massive development, production and marketing support. Although Airbus members are also military producers they have received a large amount of their support directly from governments in the form of loans, loan guarantees, guarantees against exchange rate losses, equity infusion and tax breaks.

The opportunity for Airbus to squeeze into the market came in the

1970s when McDonnell Douglas and Lockheed, backed by military contracts, decided to contest the wide body aircraft. As the DC-10 and Lockheed L-1011 engaged in disastrous competition, Airbus was able to launch and compete with a smaller airplane (A330) for shorter distance flights. The Airbus was well suited to the shorter haul European market and made inroads in the East Asian and Middle Eastern markets in the late 1970s. In a daring move Airbus was able to break into the US market by offering Eastern Airlines a deal which included a six-month free trial period, export credit and a guarantee for manageable operating costs. While there was some suggestion that the US should place a CVD on Airbus, an appeal by Eastern's CEO Frank Borman to the Treasury Secretary prevented such a step (Tyson, 1992: 197–9). Airlines in the US benefited from the Boeing–Airbus competition and faced the prospect of higher costs from a Boeing monopoly. For their part Boeing and the other aircraft producers pressed for more subsidies from the US government to fight off the European challenge.

Increasing US concern about Airbus activity led to the negotiation of the 1979 GATT agreement on Trade in Civil Aircraft. Its primary achievement was to create an environment of freer trade by eliminating trade barriers such as tariffs and quotas. Although this increased the flow of aircraft parts and components, it did not remove the tension in US–EC aerospace issues. The agreement recognized the need to curb subsidy practices and the desire of governments to support the aerospace industry. Governments were committed to seek to avoid adverse effects of such policies.

The aerospace industry subsidy dispute between the EC and the US intensified as Airbus enjoyed increasing commercial success in the 1980s. Between 1981 and 1985 Airbus A300 sales exceeded that of DC-10s and L-1011s while US exports of civil aircraft fell 50 per cent in 1982–4 from 1979–80 (Tyson, 1992: 202). The competitive pressure on US companies was increased as Airbus made a sale to Boeing's traditional customer Pan Am in 1984 and announced the introduction of a new aircraft (the A320) based on technology superior to existing US designs. By September 1985 Airbus was able to convince Air India to abandon a letter of intent to purchase Boeing 737s in favor of the A320. Airbus offered generous financial credits and offered to lease planes for Air India until the A320 was ready for delivery.

Boeing urged a prompt investigation of Airbus subsidy practices, but did not request that a Section 301 case be pursued as some other industries might have done in similar circumstances. This may have been because Boeing was well established in Europe and stood to lose a great deal in the closing of the European market. For example, in 1988 Boeing had 1000 aircraft operating in Europe while only 56 Airbus were in operation in the US. Although Boeing is clearly a US company and Airbus is European based, each depends upon access to the other's market and supplies. Boeing uses Rolls Royce (British) to produce some of its engines and Aeritalia (Italian) for some airframes, while Airbus uses General Electric engines (US) and over 50 per cent of Airbus A300s components were procured from US manufacturers. US airlines opposed trade action as they wanted a competitor for Boeing and the American administration remained divided.[5]

The US and EC entered into bilateral negotiations over the subsidy issue in 1986 and finally produced an agreement in 1992. Aerospace continued to be of vital importance to US trade interests as it maintained its place as the most valuable export sector with a surplus of $17.8 billion in 1991 (Tyson, 1992: 155). Generally, the European response has been to accept that it subsidizes Airbus and to claim both that such activity is legitimate and that US manufactures have benefited from their share of government assistance. Since assistance to US firms has usually been unplanned and undertaken through military sources and market structure, an American sense of grievance against a targeted European project has developed (Hayward, 1986: 157–92). Bilateral negotiations were difficult with Europeans pointing to past American subsidy practices and the US highlighting more recent European subsidies. In order to increase pressure on the Europeans the US initiated a 1989 case at GATT against a German exchange rate guarantee. When talks broke down in 1991 the United States launched a second complaint against Airbus subsidies. The exchange rate case went against the Germans in early 1992.

The 1992 bilateral agreement covered government involvement in the development of commercial aircraft of a hundred seats or more. It provided for a maximum allowable direct subsidy rate of 22 per cent for the development cost of a new aircraft and identifiable benefits from indirect subsidies were restricted to 4 per cent of the value of each firm's annual sales. Following the European position, the interest rate applicable to the repayment of aid used in the launch of aircraft is based on the cost of government borrowing rather than the commercial interest rate. As a compromise the Americans were able to accelerate the time for repayment of such aid. Transparency was also increased by requiring detailed reporting information. Annual meetings were mandated and a desire was expressed to multilateralize their deal through the GATT. The agreement contains an emergency escape clause which allows temporary derogation from its terms if the survival of a manufacturer is threatened. Trade laws in areas other than government support such as intellectual property or dumping are still applicable.

The 1992 EC–US agreement did not eliminate subsidies in the aerospace industry, but it is unlikely that such an agreement had been possible in light of heavy government involvement in the sector. Having achieved its goal of producing competitive commercial airliners by the mid-1980s, Airbus' need for heavy subsidies in its later years was less pressing. By the 1990s it was able to agree to an arrangement that set limits on government aid and European governments were also more willing to restrict their practices. For its part Boeing was anxious to put its competition with Airbus into a common framework. Its agreement to the limiting of indirect (military) subsidies and permissibility of more commercial subsidies may also reflect a trend in the United States where the volume of money from the defense establishment is declining and the technical spinoffs are now more likely to move from the civilian sector to the military than the former pattern of military to civilian path.

The 1992 bilateral agreement was extended by both parties, but tensions continued to come to the surface. The EC accused the United States of violating the subsidy agreement by giving indirect support through a special tax financing scheme exceeding the levels specified for indirect support, while the US continued to object to European subsidy practices (*Financial Times*, 31 March 1993). Attempts at GATT to multilateralize the bilateral large airliner subsidy EC–US agreement sharpened the conflict. The United States hinted that it would try to lower the limit allowed for direct subsidization from 33 per cent to 20 per cent. European producers felt this was an attempt to stall or derail Airbus' plan to develop a challenger to Boeing's 747 Jumbo. (*Financial Times*, 10 June 1993). The Community pressed for tighter control of US policies, fearing a more activist US government. Examples included President Clinton playing a key role in persuading Saudi Arabia to buy US airliners in February 1994 and increased spending by NASA to fund research into supersonic and advanced subsonic airliner technology. The GATT efforts failed as the United States rejected a draft agreement. The US would not agree to tighter controls on indirect government support, extension of subsidy discipline to aero-engines (main US objection) and the grandfathering of existing support for Airbus programs. The Europeans pressed for such changes because they felt that while the general GATT code on subsidies would restrict direct forms of aid used in Europe, it would have little impact on indirect US support (*Financial Times*, 19 and 20 May 1993).

Subsidy issues may yet become more heated if Airbus continues its commercial success, but the present framework may dampen down charges of unfair trade. In addition, US policy may shift toward a more commercial industrial policy as called for by former academic and now Clinton official Laura D'Andrea Tyson. Another interesting aspect of the EC–US agreement is its implications for newcomers to the aerospace industry, especially Asian aspirants. Having relied heavily on government support to carry them on the 20-year loss-making learning and production curve necessary to enter the market, the American and European giants may try to multilateralize their agreement in an attempt to diminish the likelihood of new competitors.

Hard Cases

These two cases tell us a number of things about the efforts to deal with subsidies on a multilateral basis. The first is that there are some sectors such as agriculture and aerospace where liberalization policies are more difficult to implement because they challenge other key policy goals and interests. In the high technology area there is even an attempt by some economists to provide intellectual support for such policies. A second point is that the changing nature of competitive advantage serves to fan the flames of subsidy disputes. The United States has been a prime exponent of curbing subsidy practices in agriculture as its competitive advantage increased and in aerospace as it started to come under challenge. A third point is that the difference in subsidy practices between political entities attracts attention from competitors. US condemnation of direct subsidies to Airbus and acceptance of its own indirect programs is an excellent example. A fourth point is that although the negotiations may be multilateral in that numerous countries are involved, the primary negotiations tend towards bilateralism between the major players, in these cases the US and EC. Finally, although liberalization has come slowly and with a great deal of verbal conflict and saber rattling, it has made inroads in these sensitive policy areas. Government subsidy activity has not threatened to destabilize the multilateral trading system and has been subjected to greater discipline. At most, subsidy practices and intergovernmental disputes have slowed the liberal juggernaut.

8 The Unique European Union Arrangement

Previous chapters of this book have exposed the difficulty of solving the subsidy/countervail issue on a bilateral and multilateral level. Struggles at GATT have been long and intense. Canada and the US have not been able to reach agreement despite their relatively similar economic and political systems. This section reflects upon the framework which has had the most success in addressing the issue – the European Union.[1] Consideration will first be given to how the EU deals with the subsidization issue and then an effort will be made to explain why they have succeeded where others have failed.

Government subsidization within the member states of the EU is referred to as *state aids* and its effects are dealt with under the rubric of competition policy. In most countries, competition policy is designed to protect consumers from unfair business practices of monopolies and oligopolies. Large firms may try to fix prices, carve up market shares among a cartel, prevent the entry of other firms, or engage in mergers and takeovers to cement domination of a particular market. Monitoring firm activity and screening mergers induces governments to take steps to ensure that the market remains competitive and functions in a more efficient manner. Unlike competition policy in the United States which is confined to anti-trust considerations (Comanor, 1990), the EU's interests also extend to government support for firms.

The European Economic Community (EEC) integrated provisions on subsidy measures into its founding treaty in a manner similar to its neofunctionalist predecessor the European Coal and Steel Community (ECSC). The ECSC was the first major integrative institution in Western Europe with supranational elements and was part of Jean Monnet's plan for an incremental path to European union (Monnet, 1978: 288–335; Schmitt, 1962). In an attempt to create a common market for coal and steel the ECSC forbade state assistance in any form whatsoever. Despite this bold declaration special arrangements allowing for subsidies were made for Belgium and Italy because of the weak state of their coal industries (Diebold, 1959: 194–222). Belgium, suffering from high unemployment, heavily dependent on coal production and riven by ethnic and religious rivalry between its less and more efficient coal producing regions, insisted upon support measures if it was to join the common market.

The ECSC went beyond approving domestic subsidies to taxing efficient producers in West Germany and the Netherlands to distribute its own subsidies to Belgian and Italian coal pits. From 1953 to 1957 the High Authority (similar to the EU's Commission) transferred $48.4 million to Belgium and $6.5 million to Italy (Diebold: 1959: 204). In Belgium these funds were matched by the national government. The ECSC had some success in eliminating export subsidies for coal and by 1958 the High Authority subsidies ceased. This left the Belgian and Italian governments to take up the shortfall. The High Authority was forced to retreat from its original stance of not permitting any subsidies to an acknowledgement that some national subsidies would be required in the weaker coal producing regions.[2]

The rules governing the EU procedures for state aids were set out in articles 92, 93 and 94 of the Treaty of Rome. The Treaty of Rome, signed in 1957, founded the European Community and serves as its constitution. Article 92:1 stipulates that any aid given by a 'Member State or through State resources in any from whatsoever' is incompatible with the common market when it favours some undertaking or goods production in such a manner as to distort trade between member states. Emphasis is placed on ensuring fair competition *within* the Community. This echoes passages in Articles 2 and 3 of the Treaty of Rome which state that competition in the common market should not be distorted so that European growth and standard of living can be increased.

Similar to the earlier discussion of GATT's operation, the Treaty of Rome outlines a number of exceptions to its prohibitions. Yet, these exceptions have been interpreted fairly strictly. Determining exceptions is a delicate balancing act where the goal of economic efficiency may be outweighed by other Community objectives such as regional development or social harmony (Mathijsen, 1975: 187). The first clause of Article 92:1 stipulates that competition policy applies 'Save as otherwise provided in this Treaty.' In operational terms this means the fields of security, agriculture and some transportation matters.[3] Article 92:2 sets out a number of state aids that are compatible with the common market. These include broadly based aid of a social character, assistance in the wake of natural disasters or exceptional circumstances and aid given to compensate some parts of West Germany disadvantaged by division following the Second World War.

Article 92:3 sets out state aids that *may* be considered compatible with the common market. The two most important are the cases of regional development and 'common European interest'. Article 92:3a reads as follows:

> (a) aid to promote the economic development of areas where the standard of living is abnormally low or where there is serious underemployment.

The EU's position is that by being strict with aid to wealthier regions, more money can be funnelled to depressed areas. This is meant to strengthen the cohesion of the Union by contributing to the development of poorer areas. For example, in 1991 the EC Competition Commissioner suggested that German aid to areas in former West Germany and Italian aid to northern Italian regions should be phased out in favour of aid to areas such as southern Italy or Portugal (EC, 1991a). The Commission allows up to 75 per cent of capital expenditure in the EC's poorest regions to come from state aid.

The following subsection gives conditional approval to:

> (b) aid to promote the execution of an important project of common European interest or to remedy a serious disturbance in the economy of a Member State.

Programs targeted at assisting research and development, assistance for small and medium size industries, environmental assistance, infrastructure projects and energy saving schemes may be exempted. A project may be confined to a single state and still serve the common European interest. To determine this interest the Commission examines expressed policy, resolutions from the European Parliament and pronouncements of the European Council (Schina, 1987: 57).

Before moving on to consider the evolution of state aid policy it is crucial to examine the key role of the supranational European Commission. It is the Commission which plays the central role in the enforcement of state aids policy. The Commission is the European Union's civil service and has a staff of almost 12 000 of whom about 2000 are interpreters. It is divided into departments overseeing issue areas such as competition policy or regional development. The department with oversight for state aids is Directorate General IV or simply DGIV. Commissioners are nominated by national governments and entrusted with overseeing a number of departments.

The Commission has a number of diverse tasks – it initiates proposals, administers and polices decisions and mediates conflicts between other EU institutions and between Member States. Its most prominent role is that of initiative. The Commission drafts proposals for initiatives to be considered by the Council of Ministers. The Council of Ministers is composed of the appropriate minister from Member States' national governments and has the final voice in EU decisions. If the Council accepts the Commission's proposals, either by qualified majority voting or unanimity, they are promulgated in the Official Journal and become law. If the Council does not accept a Commission initiative, it can only be amended by a unanimous vote. Alternatively, the proposal can be sent back to the Commission to be reworked. Successful Commission proposals can emerge in one of four forms – directives, decisions, regulations or recommendations. A directive carries the force of law and is aimed at member states, requiring them to change laws. They do not apply to companies or individuals. A measure backed by the force of law and aimed at a specific person, company or state is called a decision. A regulation may also be aimed at a specific entity, but has a general application. Finally a Commission recommendation is a measure that lacks the force of law.

The European Commission, subject to review by the European Court of Justice, determines which cases will be investigated and if exceptions are to be made in allowing the granting of state aids. Following Article 93 all state aids are monitored to determine if they remain compatible with the evolving common market and whether or not they should be abolished or altered.[4] If the Commission finds fault with an existing aid it must advise the state to abolish the aid or modify the programme to eliminate its faults. If a state ignores the Commission, compliance may be forced through the European or national courts. If the Commission does not take action and other states or corporations in competition with the alleged offender believe that the Commission has erred, they may appeal to the European Court of Justice.

The Commission must be informed of any new aid initiatives or plans to alter aid programs before they come into effect. If the Commission suspects that the aid is not compatible with the common market it can prohibit the state from implementing the aid until a final decision is reached. If state aid is granted without prior notification to the Commission, states are given a maximum of 30 days to provide the relevant information to the Commission. If the information is not forthcoming or deemed to be insufficient a provisional decision is issued requiring the suspension of the aid within 15 days and more detailed information is requested. If there is still a failure to comply, a final decision of incompatibility may be reached requiring the repayment of unlawful aid. Failing this, the matter is turned over to the European Court.

If aid is notified beforehand, the Commission then has two months to inform the state whether the program is or is not compatible with the common market. It may also launch investigations of any program that was not brought to the Commission's attention. If the aid is found to be incompatible with the common market, it will fix a date for the aid to be discontinued. The Commission also has the power to order the repayment of state aids that have been previously distributed. National courts are unable to declare a state aid compatible or incompatible with the common market. They must respect and enforce the decisions of the Commission and the European Court.

The European Court is available to parties who believe the Commission has not fulfilled its responsibilities adequately. This may be especially useful if a party believes that the Commission should have investigated an aid that it ignored or has not acted quickly enough to prevent unlawful implementation of an aid. However, the Court is restricted in its review powers to finding errors in facts or law or an inadequate Commission justification for a particular action. Backed by the European Court, the Commission has not been pressured into declaring a level under which subsidies would be considered harmless (*de minimis* rule). The Court may demand that the Commission provide further justification for particular decisions, but rarely challenges the content of the decisions. The Court has recognized that an essential element of Commission decisions in determining compatibility is the weighing of complex social and economic factors (Lasok, 1986: 81). Although the Court does not put it in the following terms, this is a blatantly political task and is therefore not one the Court participates in. These decisions are left to the Commission and occasionally the Council of Ministers.

The Commission enjoys considerable discretion both in determining whether a particular measure qualifies as a state aid and, more importantly, whether a state aid qualifies for an exemption from the general prohibition. For example, when assessing state aid to public companies the Commission has decided that aid need not lead to short-run profit, but can be used for longer term objectives which do not show an immediate commercial return (Hancher, 1994: 135). The Commission also has the key role of deciding if a project is in the common European interest. Is it in the common European interest that France emerge as a leading player in the high speed train market? If it is, subsidies may be approved for research into fast train technology as outlined above. The crucial point in this arrangement is that it is a bureaucracy engaged in bargaining with member states and commercial interests that makes the final decision. One might argue that questions such as what is in the common interest are political decisions which should be taken by political leadership responsible to the people as a whole.

There are two instances where the more explicitly political leadership, the Council of Ministers, may grant exemptions from the state aid prohibitions. Acting upon a proposal from the Commission, the Council may specify an exception if it is approved by qualified majority voting. This has been used to provide special exemption for the shipbuilding industry. The other option is where a Member State brings an example of state aid and seeks Council permission to implement it. In this case the state must demonstrate exceptional circumstances and the Council must be unanimous in its approval.

POLICY EVOLUTION

Although state aids measures were a part of the Treaty of Rome they played a minor role in the Community until the 1970s. The early years of the EC saw some measures taken against Member States' subsidy practices in those areas which tended to promote the purchase of domestic goods such as tax relief or that favoured exports to other Community countries (McLachlan and Swann, 1967: 42–55). One example was the French government's *carte d'exportateur* which gave tax benefits to firms with a high percentage of exports. Yet, the Commission was forced to accept that in some industries such as shipbuilding governments were reluctant to end subsidy practices. In these cases the most that could be hoped for was a harmonization of subsidy policies across the Community.

By the early 1970s competition policy took on a slightly higher profile. The European Parliament asked the Commission to submit annual reports on the evolution of competition policy for public scrutiny. The Commission's first report issued in 1972 reaffirmed the commitment to disciplining state aid, but stressed that a pragmatic approach was needed to facilitate the cooperation of Member States (EC, 1972: 16–19, 111–45). It stated that aids must be selective, degressive (decreasing over time), transparent and have the least possible effect on intra-Community Competition. The Commission's role of balancing restriction of state aid against Community goals was apparent from the beginning: 'The Commission will, therefore, intervene whenever national aid is likely to be harmful to the interests of nationals of other Member States without providing in return a generally improved operational balance or a more active growth for the Community as a whole' (EC, 1972: 113). Reviewing regional, sectoral, and export aid the Commission highlighted its desire to modify national policies so that aid programs would be undertaken in the context of Community rather than national interests. Acknowledging that there would be times when social and human factors would override 'strictly economic reasoning' the Commission outlined its view that measures should be taken which have the minimum distortive effect on the market and other Member States.

By 1978 new guidelines in response to economic stagnation and Japanese competition were introduced which recognized the valuable role state aids could play in speeding up the response of private enterprise to new investment and technological opportunities and the adaptation of industries which needed to redeploy resources. Following this, the Commission became more sympathetic to aids for R&D. Responding to fears about US and Japanese technological might, a Community framework for R&D was created in 1985. It stipulated that R&D aids must be notified like all others, the level of aid for basic research should not exceed 50 per cent of the research program and that the nearer the research is to the market place, the lower the level of allowable aid. Regional aid was also seen as a problem because states were engaged in expensive bidding wars against each other to lure production into their territories. Proposals were elaborated on the scale of permitted aid and these were revised in 1975, 1979 and 1988.

Elevation of state aid measures to a major role in Community affairs was an integral element of the 1980s attempts at increased integration and market liberalization. A number of factors including the reversal of French Socialist policy permitted elite consensus on the need to liberalize the Community market in order to boost economic growth. In 1985 the European Commission released the Cockfield Report or White Paper *Completing the Internal Market*. It outlined 300 measures that would have to be introduced if Europe was to complete the liberalized internal market. In the areas of state aids the Cockfield Report did not call for new legislative measures, but for more vigorous enforcement of existing treaty measures: 'As the Community moves to complete the Internal Market, it will be necessary to ensure that anti-competitive practices do not engender new forms of local protectionism which would only lead to a re-partitioning of the market. 158. In this context, it will be particularly important that the Community discipline on state aids be rigorously enforced.' (EC, 1985a: Paras 157–8) The Report also required the Commission to produce an inventory of state aids and to report on their policy implications.

In the December 1985 Luxembourg Summit the Single European Act (SEA) was negotiated. It was ratified in 1986 and came into force on 1 July 1987. The SEA of 1986 amended the Treaty of Rome to require the progressive establishment of the internal market by the end of 1992. The Single European Act had three important facets. It implemented a set of institutional reforms, directed measures meant to liberalize and solidify a competitive internal market, and outlined steps to mitigate the effects of increased liberalization through social, regional and industrial policy. The greatest weight was given to the economic elements of the initiative which was to work towards an internal barrier-free market by 31 December 1992. This was the primary thrust of the 1992 project, a single market without internal frontiers. The internal market project targeted what the Treaty of Rome was unable to adequately attack – non-tariff barriers. It was an attempt to eliminate as many obstacles as possible interfering with the free flow of capital, labour, goods and services. In this respect it was an extremely ambitious liberalization project, trumpeting the virtues of laissez-faire competition.

Creating a barrier-free market was a complicated task as a number of difficult issues would need to be handled. Disparate value added tax (VAT) rates would hinder the removal of border controls because governments would want to stem the tide of cross-border shopping and the immediate export and reimport of goods to take advantage of differing rates. Some progress would need to be made on the issue of harmonization or mutual recognition of product standards or else they would act as non-tariff barriers.[5] State aid policy was also targeted as an area that needed increased attention.

A primary assumption behind the creation of a European common market and the 1992 single market project was that Europeans would gain the economic benefits from a more competitive market. The Commission's 16-volume 1988 Cecchini Report undertook micro and macro analysis of the possible effects of an internal barrier-free Europe and stressed the gains to be achieved. Micro analysis focused on the benefits of reducing barriers on a sector by sector basis. It estimated benefits of 4.3–6.4 per cent of Community GDP. These would be once and for all gains. On the macro front, a number of scenarios were produced with the most supported being a medium term increase in Community GDP of 7 per cent and the creation of five million jobs (Cecchini, Catinat and Jacquemin, 1988).

Competition policy and regulation of state aids was given an important role in ensuring that these predicted economic benefits would be achieved. Sir Leon Brittan, the Commissioner for competition policy voiced fears that 'Member States will use state aids to protect certain industries from the full force of competition that will follow from the completion of the internal market' (EC, 1989a). Tariff barriers might be replaced by increased domestic aid to industries as uncompetitive firms sought government assistance in the wake of increased liberalization. Efficient firms would then have to compete with less efficient companies backed by their state treasuries. Liberalization would be frustrated by increased state aids. In order to benefit from a common market some action would have to be taken to prevent government subsidies from distorting the market.

The renewed emphasis on and expansion of state aids policy to assist the operation of the internal market is reminiscent of the spillover dynamic identified by neofunctionalist scholars 20 years earlier. Neofunctionalist theory, as put forward by Ernst Hass and Leon Lindberg, highlighted the role of spillover and stressed the importance of political elites in driving the integration process (Haas, 1958; Lindberg, 1963). Integration in one area could spill over into others as technicians and elites witnessed the increase in efficiency and welfare. Integration was seen to rely on the interaction of political forces such as interest groups, parties, governments, and international organizations in pursuit of their own interests. As one sector of the economy became integrated pressure groups in that sector would prevent backsliding and insist on further integration in connected sectors to reap greater economic benefits. Seeing the success of the original sector, other interest groups would push for integration in their field. Not only was action in the state aid section seen to be necessary for the 1992 project, but as the EC Competition Commissioner indicated (Brittan, 1992: 89), increased activity created a larger constituency demanding further action: 'More and more complaints are being made to the competition directorate and myself about aid in sectors never before investigated ranging from weather forecasting to football. Broadcasting, banking and insurance have become regular areas of our work.'

When Sir Leon Brittan became Competition Commissioner he launched a review of state aids policy. His goals in this area were threefold. Firstly, to create greater transparency about the levels of state aids being granted. Secondly, to take action against the most wasteful and anti-competitive policies and thirdly to roll back the general level of aid (Brittan, 1992: 16). In an attempt to get a better understanding of subsidy practices in the European Community, a task force was set up in June 1985 to carry out a state aids study. In December 1988 the

Commission published its first survey on state aids covering the 1981–86 time period. It examined state aid given in the manufacturing, agriculture, fisheries, railways, waterways and coalmining sectors and found that approximately 3 per cent of the GDP of EC states or 100 billion ECU was spent on state aid to industry (EC, 1988). In July of 1990 the Commission released the second report which updated the figures to 1988 and found that total aid had decreased to 2.2 per cent of GDP (EC, 1990a). The Netherlands, UK and Denmark were under the EC average, France, Portugal, Spain, Germany, were close to average, while Ireland, Greece, Italy, Belgium and Luxembourg were over the average. The report was firm in its conclusion that state aids remained a barrier to the benefits of the common market.

The result of enhanced vigilance has been an increased tendency of governments to consult the Commission about the suitability of particular aid programs (Ross, 1989: 192). Analysis of Commission activity in this region reveals that although the number of cases where an illegal state aid has been declared has remained stable, the number the Commission reviews has increased dramatically. Table 8.1 shows the number of cases in which the Commission has taken a negative final decision under Article 93 (2) has fluctuated from a low of seven to a high of 21 during the years 1981–92, but there has not been a rise in the number of cases over time. This might challenge the notion that state aid policy was invigorated following the SEA. Yet, if one looks at the number of cases that the Community has subjected to scrutiny the picture is quite different. From 1981 to 1986 the Commission usually approved between 80 and 90 programmes. This figure jumps to 160 in 1987 and continues rising each year until in 1992 there are 474 cases, 5 times the 1985 number. This rise is not explained by increased government subsidies on the part of the Community's largest member, Germany, following reunification in 1989. The German percentage share in notified programme numbers remains between 27 and 31 per cent between 1987 and 1992. Since the overall level of state aids in the Community was declining from 2.2 per cent of GDP to 2.0 per cent of GDP between 1986 and 1990 it is unlikely that the increase in cases is due to increased government activity (EC, 1992: 39). The UK, a country near the bottom of the tables in terms of government subsidization of industry, increased the number of programs vetted from 10 in 1987 to 88 in 1992.[6] The trend is for government to greatly increase the number of programs submitted to the Commission for clearance.

From the previous information it appears that the Commission has expanded its surveillance role while maintaining (in number of cases)

Table 8.1 EC State Aid Activity 1981–92

	Final "–" decisions	*No objection*	*Germany*	*UK*
1981	14	79	–	–
1982	12	79	–	–
1983	12	80	–	–
1984	21	111	–	–
1985	7	82	–	–
1986	10	98	6	2
1987	8	160	49	10
1988	10	189	52	16
1989	10	221	67	21
1990	10	364	116	60
1991	10	371	103	69
1992	11	474	131	88

Source: *Report on Competition Policy* No. 11–22, 1981–1992. Differences in the method of reporting prevent the inclusion of German and UK notifications before 1986.

its prohibitive role. Although some subsidy cases have been high profile, national governments have incorporated the Commission formula of allowable subsidy practices into their policy formation. Larger numbers of programmes are being scrutinized, but the failure rate has not increased. There is some evidence to suggest that the nature of national subsidy policy is changing. Between 1986 and 1990 there has been a shift of aid policy away from particular sectors to either horizontal or regional aid. Horizontal aids are those 'dispersed horizontally to different sectors which are not part of national sectoral or regional schemes and which are not specific to individual enterprises' (Schina, 1987, 94). Programmes falling in this category include aid to assist in environmental protection, support of small and medium enterprises, economization of energy and broadly based, non-sectoral and non-regional research and development initiatives. Comparisons of the periods 1986–88 and 1988–90 reveal that the percentage of manufacturing sector aid aimed at particular sectors has decreased from 26 to 20 per cent while the percentage for horizontal aid has risen from 40 to 42 per cent and the percentage of regional aid has risen from 34 to 38 per cent (EC, 1992, 27).

Restrictions on the granting of state aids have been particularly prominent in the automobile industry. Automobile production is a highly valued economic activity as it involves numerous well paying industrial jobs. As a result, competition for plants can be intense and governments often get involved to lure plants to their location. Unfortunately, the resulting bidding war undermines the tax base as governments compete to give large transnationals the best deal. Money is expended to influence plant location within a geographic area, but new production may not be stimulated. Alternatively, the support of numerous companies may result in over capacity, making the industry unprofitable for efficient firms.

To address this problem, the EC developed a state aid framework for the motor vehicle industry in January 1989 which was renewed for two more years in December 1990 (EC, 1990b). All aid packages to the industry must be cleared with the EC before implementation. The purpose of the agreement was to increase the transparency of state aid going to the industry and apply stricter disciplines. The Commission has greatly increased its activity in this area. In June 1989 Peugeot repaid FF500 million in loans from the French government following a Commission ruling of illegal state aid (EC, 1989b). The government of France was engaged in a lengthy dispute with the Commission concerning subsidies it had given its state owned car maker Renault. Under a centre right government France secured permission to give Renault subsidies to restructure and downsize its operations. The new Socialist government refused to cut production and the EC voided its subsidy approval (*Wall Street Journal*, 16 November 1989). Following difficult negotiations, the French government agreed to repay FF3.5 billion immediately and another FF2.5 billion over a longer time period (EC, 1990c). In July 1991 the Commission reached down into the affairs of the Derbyshire County Council (UK) and examined its sale of development land to Toyota. It concluded that the Council sold the land to Toyota for £4.2 million less than its market value and asked the car company to repay the council (EC, 1991b).

One of the most prominent examples of the EC's state aids policy occurred in 1988 when the British government of Margaret Thatcher enticed British Aerospace (BAe) to buy the car maker Rover by offering to write off £800 million of Rover's debt. The government negotiated exclusively with BAe, did not solicit competitive bids, nor did it explore the possibility that it could be sold for a greater price or with more debt. As a result of this cosy arrangement, the Commission announced that it would only approve a £469 million write-off. A day later BAe agreed to buy Rover on those terms, making the government appear foolish to have offered such a generous deal. The Commission had saved British tax payers £331 million. Reviewing the Rover case in 1990 the Commission discovered that the British government failed to give a complete accounting of its subsidy assistance. The Commission found additional subsidies in British payment to BAe to cover part of the cost of buying Rover shares from minority shareholders, the costs of allowing BAe to defer payment for six months and a number of smaller side deals. It requested repayment of £44.4 million in illegal subsidies.[7]

The fascinating point about the EU's activity in controlling aid in the automobile industry is that it is more comprehensive than any structure within the US or Canada. As mentioned in Chapter 3, US states continue to engage in destructive bidding wars to lure automobile assembly plants to their territory and the federal government is unwilling to do anything to stop this process.[8] The EU has also been active in the areas of regional development, R&D, environment and public enterprises.

Regional Policy

The EU's policy on regional development is a prime example of the commitment to mitigation of free market forces and attempts to distribute the benefits of increased liberalization. Central to the founding principles of the EEC, as indicated in Article 2 of the Treaty of Rome, was a commitment to strengthen the unity of the members' economies and to ensure harmonious development by reducing the differences between backward regions. Disparities between countries and regions have been stark and the political pressure to address them has also been evident. For example, at the founding of the EEC in 1958 the per capita income of the most favored region (Hamburg) was seven times that of the least (Calabria). When Britain and Ireland joined their GDP per capita was 70–80 per cent of the Community average while new members Greece, Spain and Portugal were at less than 72 per cent (Swann, 1992: 282).

The Treaty provided for the creation of a European Investment Bank with the task of providing loans and guarantees on a non-profit basis for developing backward regions, modernizing or converting undertakings, and projects of common interest. British demands upon joining in 1972 resulted in the creation of the main instrument used to assist regions – the European Regional Development Fund (ERDF). It participates in the development of lagging regions to correct imbalances. Other elements of Union policy that have a role to play include the European Social Fund and the CAP, which has tried to improve the incomes of farmers in depressed regions. Poorer members of the Community demanded that the move to further liberalization under the SEA be offset with additional aid for cohesion. This took the form of a new Treaty Title, Economic and Social Cohesion, and a commitment to concentrate aid in the poorer regions.

State aid policy accommodates regional objectives by allowing aid for regional development purposes. When assessing regional aid, the region in question must have a degree of structural unemployment and low level of per capita gross domestic product by Union, rather than national, standards. Thus a program aimed at Sicily would stand a better chance of approval than one aimed at the less developed areas of the Netherlands. The Commission is particularly supportive where aid is for infrastructure investment to allow a region to exploit natural resources.

The ambit of competition policy work with regard to state aids continues to expand. The Commission has approved regional assistance measures to the new states or Lander of former Eastern Germany.[9] The aggregate permissible assistance for projects in the area was set at 35 per cent (EC 1991c). The Competition Commissioner also took steps to ensure that the privatization of former East German industries is undertaken without resulting in state aid creating unfair competition or the violation of state aids provisions. The German Economic Minister Jurgen Molleman agreed that the privatization organization Treuhandanstalt would keep the Commission informed of its activities and submit regular reports (EC 1991d).

In addition to permitting state aids for poorer areas, the Commission policy has attempted to limit spending on the part of the wealthier states. By definition, poorer states cannot provide as much aid as wealthier states. Commission studies indicate that the percentage of state aid from the four largest countries (Germany, France, Italy and the UK) has increased from 75 per cent in 1986–8 to almost 80 per cent in 1988–90 (EC, 1992: 13). In addition, the four weakest countries (Greece, Ireland, Portugal and Spain) 'spend less on aid per person employed than the Community average, and significantly less than the wealthier and more central Member States' (Wishlade, 1992: 142–50). The results of such spending may well be to attract or keep industry that would otherwise migrate to the lower cost and less developed areas of the Community. In investment wars, weaker states are less able to compete with wealthier members of the Community. Thus, the Commission claims that a strict enforcement of state aids policy will assist in the Community goal of cohesion because the less developed states will be better able to compete for investment (EC 1993: 57–8).

Research and Development

Another area where state aids policy accommodates illiberal Union objectives is in the R&D field. In response to a sense of diminishing competitiveness on world markets in the 1980s, the Commission proposed a more dynamic technological response to the US and Japan. It proposed a plan involving the identification of areas of technological risk, collaboration to meet those challenges, an increase in the proportion of the Community's budget to R&D, framing of activities in a multi-annual framework, a concentration of R&D collaboration at the research end to prevent US trade law attack, the inclusion of non-EC countries such as EFTA and Turkey, and a suggestion that the Rome Treaty should more explicitly address itself to the research and technological challenge. Indeed, the SEA amended the Treaty of Rome to contain a new Title (VI) headed Research and Technological Development. Community initiatives included its own Joint Research Centre, Joint European Torus (JET) looking towards the possibility of fusion, ESPRIT in information technology and RACE assisting in telecommunications network.

Support in the R&D field is usually targeted at projects in which European companies are challenging powerful foreign competitors. Citing the need for Europe to regain its technological edge and increase its competitiveness, the Commission announced guidelines for Community policy towards research and development in December 1985 (EC, 1985b; Schina, 1987: 213–18). Fundamental research resulting in 'an enlargement of general scientific and technical knowledge not linked to industrial or commercial objectives' was declared compatible with the common market.[10] Basic industrial research, work furthering the advancement of the laws of science or engineering in areas that 'might apply to an industrial sector or the activities of a particular sector' is permitted up to 50 per cent of the cost of the project. This may be increased to 60 per cent if it is directed to small and medium size enterprises. Similarly higher levels may be permitted in exceptional circumstances or if the project is complementing other Community objectives such as regional development. As state aid moves into applied research and development, activities more closely related to the creation, establishment or improvement of new products, production processes or services, allowable percentages of aid are to be reduced.

Commission decisions in the early 1990s reinforced the perception that the EC was serious about funding high technology research with government funds. In July 1990 the European Commission approved the French government's plan to give FF445 million in grants to assist in the development of the next generation of the TGV (high speed train). The money was targeted for research into lighter building materials, a power unit that could adapt to various European power voltages, a braking system and improvements to take corners at higher speed. In addition to being of common European interest, the project was also approved because it would strengthen Europe's technological base and assist in environmental protection (EC, 1990e). The Commission also approved ECU 85 million of Italian and French state aid to electronic firms engaged in developing high definition television (HDTV) (*Financial Times*, 23 May 1991). It may be recalled from Chapter 3 that HDTV is an area where the US government has poured R&D funds through its defense establishment. The expenditure was justified by the Commission on the grounds that it was a project of common European interest.

Environment

Policy with regard to state aid and the environment has changed to become more permissive in the past twenty years (Evans and Martin, 1991: 103–4). The first guidelines in this area were published in 1974 (EC, 1977: 127–31). The intention was to have companies pay the cost of adapting to environmental regulations rather than the state. A transitional period for state aids in this area was established until 1980. This period was extended until 1986 by which time the Community's view on environmental protection had changed considerably. Aid policy was revised to permit state aids in the environmental field if it met the following conditions: it must facilitate the implementation of new environmental standards; the grant may not exceed 15 per cent of the value of the aided investment; the firms reviewing the aid must have been in operation for two years before the standards enter into force; and the eligible firm must bear the entire cost of normal replacement and operating costs.

Public Enterprises

An area of increasing Commission activity and conflict between member states has been the attempt to curb government subsidies to public companies. The Commission has estimated illegal state aid in the public sector at 10 times the flow of non-notified public subsidy to private companies (*Financial Times*, 17 June 1993). In 1980 the Commission issued a directive requiring Member States to make financial relations with public sector enterprises more transparent.[11] The Commission sought transparency of Member States' activities so that it would be able to determine public funds made directly available to public enterprises, public funds made available through intermediaries such as other public undertakings or financial institutions, and the use to which these funds are put.

In July 1991 the Commission expanded its reporting requirements by demanding states provide annual reports of assistance given to public manufacturing industries with a turnover of more than Ecu250m. New rules were proposed to make it easier to judge whether publicly owned companies were receiving subsidies from state financial flows. State capital injections, loans and return on investment for money going to public companies would be put under greater scrutiny (EC, 1991e). This step was taken to redress what was seen as the possible unfair advantage of state owned companies relying on governments to provide capital. The French government, which presides over an active state sector, successfully challenged the Commission's demands on procedural grounds, but this is most likely only a minor setback (*Financial Times*, 22 June 1993).

A good example of the clash between governments as well as between public and private enterprise can be found in the steel industry. Steel has been a troubling sector for the administration of state aid policy for two reasons. The first is because of chronic problems of overcapacity and the second is because of the presence of competing public and private steel producers. In 1989, the EC adopted a strict code dealing with state aids to the steel industry.[12] Permissible aid was limited to basic R&D, measures meant to increase environmental protection and closure aid. Temporary exceptions were also provided for Greece and former East Germany because they were seen to have particularly pressing restructuring needs. Closure aid is meant to help reduce steel production by assisting in the termination of unviable companies. Such aid can contribute to the cost of payments to laid off workers and early retirement incentives. Other closure costs may also be mitigated under the condition that the plants permanently cease production. Any plans to alter aid flowing to the steel industry must be approved by the Commission and Member States are required to submit aid reports every six months. The EC code was thought to be of such quality that it served as the basis for bilateral discussions with the US and multilateral discussion at the GATT.

Under pressure from overcapacity, recession and cheaper Eastern European imports, state owned steel makers were reluctant to implement surplus capacity cuts in 1993. Private steel makers from Germany, Britain, France, the Netherlands, Belgium and Luxembourg condemned the Commission for its laxity in forcing public steel makers into cuts and eliminating subsidies (*Financial Times*, 7 December 1993). Following a great deal of debate and intense bargaining the Commission was eventually able to reach agreement with governments in weaker areas of the Community to allow some state aid in return for capacity cuts and some closure. The most difficult problems were in Italy, but plants in Spain, Portugal and former Eastern Germany were also included (*Financial Times*, 20 December 1993). A bitter British Steel official, who had been pressing for stricter cuts and discipline, commented 'This is a compromise, driven by political expedience' (*Financial Times*, 18 December 1993). The interpretation was quite correct, state aid was being used as one of the thousands of constant bargains needed to keep Community integration moving forward by ensuring weaker members secured some benefits.

Although the EU approach to subsidies has been relatively successful, the increased focus on curbing public enterprises highlights tensions.[13] The most serious difficulty is that its decisions impose larger costs upon those countries that have a tradition of greater subsidization and direct government involvement in the economy. Italy and France face larger adjustment problems than Britain. Recently even Germany has tried to use subsidies to prop up its devastated eastern economy in the wake of unification. An additional difference is that southern EU countries France, Italy, Greece, Portugal and Spain tend to favour explicit industrial strategies and the nurturing of EC champions while Britain, Germany and the Netherlands take a more free market approach (*Washington Post*, 21 April 1991). These differences can spill into political conflict when a state is determined to aid a sensitive domestic industry and other states object. Such is the case with French assistance to its computer maker Bull (*Financial Times*, 11 July 1991). Other examples are French and German assistance to their national airlines which harms the interests of the larger and more efficient private firm, British Airways. Conflict is particularly sharp where state enterprises are in direct competition with large private enterprises from other states.

The EU's competition policy has become a powerful force in domestic economic management of its member states. The policy is still being elaborated, but goes further than any other attempt at resolving the subsidy/aid issue between states. Its ability to influence government action and demand repayment of illegal state aids is a marked dilution of state sovereignty. The question arises: why has it been possible to achieve such a result at the European level, when progress has been so difficult at the GATT and in North America? Why have states generally agreed to abide by the decisions of the Commission and the Court?

MORE THAN A MARKET

An EC document boasts that '. . . not only has no other trading partner in the world such an open system of control for dealing with state aids, but also the Community has the strictest control of aids of all major trading blocs' (EC, 1989c: 2). As mentioned above, the control is even stricter than that which exists within the federal states of Canada and the United States! What factors explain this difference?

With regard to other international attempts, the supranational body administering relations between Member States of the EU verges on being a federation, while efforts at the GATT and in the NAFTA are simply agreements between sovereign states. The process of transfering sovereignty has gone further in Europe, allowing for greater forays into issues such as domestic subsidies and state aids. Member States of the EU accept relatively more intrusion into their affairs because there is a commitment to the establishment of a supranational entity. Although progress has been halting at times, with various groups offering opposition, the goal of European integration continues to be political union. This means European state elites are more willing to accept a greater degree of European Union decision making in their domestic economic affairs than other states.

A strong argument can be made that the EU is an example of integrative federalism. Similar to the US or Switzerland, it is a 'constitutional order that strives at unity in diversity among previously independent or confederally related component entities. The goal of establishing an effective central government with direct operation on the people inside its sphere of powers is pursued under respect of the powers of the component entities . . .' (Lenaerts, 1990: 206). Sovereignty is divided, but guaranteed by a common legal order and adjudicated by a supreme court. The Treaty of Rome serves as the EU's constitution. EU law takes precedence over national law, binding Member States (Sipkov, 1988). The European Court arbitrates disputes by delineating the specific, implied, and non-specific powers of the EU with regard to its members.

In the area of state aids, it is crucial that the one state least enthusiastic about supranationality and increased political integration – the UK – is also the one government which stands to gain the most from a strict supranational state aids institution. Having gone through extensive privatization of state companies the UK government has the least to fear and most to gain from a Union policy which increasingly targets the activity of public enterprises. Large UK based corporations such as British Steel and British Airways have been at the forefront of seeking Union action against the practices of other states' public companies. Although they may be frustrated by the pace of change, the Union framework offers them a unique and useful instrument to improve their competitive position against public European rivals.

Conversely, those states with greater direct state intervention correspond with the states that either seek greater integration and supranationality or are most dependent on Union resources. Heavy subsidizers such as Italy, Belgium and Portugal are also countries where the government runs large budget deficits. For example in the 1988–90 period the Italian budget deficit was 11 per cent of GDP and state aid accounted for 28 per cent of that deficit (EC, 1992: 41). Strict Commission policy may have the positive result of forcing the reduction in Italian subsidies that the government itself cannot make. The Italian government cannot reject Commission demands as their membership in the Union is vital for domestic reform. Although the Italians fought hard to preserve their steel industry drastic cuts will be made. The French government has been one of the most enthusiastic advocates of increased integration in the late 1980s and early 1990s. As a large subsidizer it might have an interest in a weak state aid policy, but such a policy would conflict with its goal of increasing supranationality. High and low subsiding governments both have an interest in pushing for a state aid institution that restricts national policy.

Large competitive firms may also benefit from a strict state aid policy. Restricting public enterprises allows private sector competitors such as British Steel to compete against rivals operating under similar commercial restraints. A reduction of specific subsidies allows companies to take investment decisions based upon economic fundamentals rather than being influenced by government incentives. In the short run this might cost manufacturers money in the form of lost government expenditures, but in the longer term should assist in the creation of a more homogeneous and competitive market. State aid policy is part of a larger package of liberalization and competition policy that was instituted primarily at the request of larger European business and retains its support.

A serious potential problem is the strong role played by the European Commission in monitoring and ruling on the potential legitimacy of state aid programmes. The Commission is the most exposed of the Union's institutions to charges of elitism and intrusion into the people's lives. Indeed popular unease or even anger with the Union is usually focused on 'Brussels', which is shorthand for the Commission.[14] As indicated above, the European Commission is a bureaucracy with a difference. Following neofunctionalist strategy the Commission oversteps the (idealized) traditional role of an impartial administrator by becoming a policy initiator. A key group of committed technocrats are tasked with planning (plotting?) methods for expanding Union competence and deepening integration at every turn. At the public level the Commission seems to have its hand in every pot. Rules concerning numerous aspects of daily life from water quality to vegetable size bombard EU citizens.[15] If the Commission was limited to an administrative role it would not arouse so much concern. The initiative power throws it into public scrutiny because it is seen as a cause of so much activity.

The relevance of these problems to state aid policy is that despite public doubts about the Commission's role, it is charged with determining what government spending or aid measures are or are not in the Union's interest. However, unlike domestic legislatures the Commission lacks a democratic base. It is not elected and is subject to loose supervision by the European Parliament. A number of suggestions have been made to shore up its democratic legitimacy including the direct public election of the President of the Commission, increased Parliamentary control of Commissioners or the appointment of Commissioners from the ranks of elected Parliamentarians.[16] All of these steps would serve to increase the democratic nature of the Commission. At the moment it serves as the lightning rod for public discontent which has the potential to undermine its effectiveness in state aid policy should it take on one controversial case too many.

The crisis of the Community in the wake of its difficulty in ratifying the Maastricht Treaty in 1992–3 had little to do with state aid policy. However, the difficult questions posed about accountability, authority, legitimacy, democracy and governance of the new Union will have its effect on the functioning of all of its institutions.[17] The ability of bureaucrats to take vital policy decisions and the inability of people to hold decision makers accountable suggest that public tolerance for expanded activity may be limited. At the very least Union institutions are now more subject to debate and scrutiny.

The unique role of the Union may explain its achievement in subsidy policy in comparison to the GATT and NAFTA, but why is there greater subsidy discipline within the EU than within Canada and the US? EU disciplines were incorporated in the Treaty of Rome at a time when subsidy issues were relatively insignificant compared to the use of tariffs. It is only since the drive to a single market was relaunched in 1985 that the state aids provisions have taken on increased importance and profile. Fortunately for the competition policy Commissioner, the rules were already on the books and it was simply a question of moving vigorously to enlarge their ambit and step up enforcement.

Neither Canada nor the US have similar ready made rules on the statute books that they could use so easily to deal with domestic subsidies. Any attempt to create new rules runs the risk of opening federal–state conflict. Similarly, efforts at stretching present rules concerning federal prerogatives over interstate commerce or acting on behalf of the general good also run the risk of bitter conflict. An additional factor is that the issue of state or provincial subsidy distorting domestic trade does not appear to be viewed as seriously in North America as it has been in Western Europe. However, recent Canadian activity has attempted to take some action in the subsidy field.

In the context of the free trade negotiations with the US the Canadian federal and provincial governments launched an initiative to reduce internal trade barriers between provinces and territories by establishing a Committee of Ministers on Internal Trade in November 1987. Minor agreements were reached in the following years in areas such as the sale of beer and governmental goods procurement, but comprehensive negotiations did begin until March 1993. An Agreement on Internal Trade was signed by First Ministers on 18 July 1994. Its primary purpose was to gradually remove economic barriers to the free movement of people, goods and services across Canada. In addition to eliminating discrimination in a number of areas and promising further liberalization the Agreement provided for a dispute resolution mechanism which would facilitate consultations and conciliation, but would not provide compensation to governments or businesses.

Subsidy concerns are limited to the investment section of the agreement (ITS, 1994: 79–90). Its provisions are rather modest in that its primary achievement is to prohibit subsidies (referred to as incentives in the agreement) being used to lure established industry from one subnational location to another unless it appears that production may move offshore. It also prohibits the use of incentives which discriminate against enterprises that are controlled in other provinces or territories and forbids performance requirements for other Canadian enterprises. In the environmental area Article 610 forbids governments from allowing derogation from environmental measures to encourage enterprises, although some provision is made for firms to comply with government measures. One provision that might influence future behaviour is the establishment of a Working Group on Investment tasked with preparing annual reports on government incentives. This should raise the profile of government activity and may provide fodder for further political activity.

The Agreement acknowledges that incentives are important for economic development, but urges signatories to forgo those which might be excessive or which support economically non-viable production adversely affecting other parties and increasing surplus capacity. Parties are also urged to refrain from bidding wars to attract new investment to their territories. Although a provision is made for consultation, the relatively weak dispute settlement mechanism of the Agreement does not apply to these areas of desired behaviour. In major areas of subsidy activity the Agreement expresses a desire for better behaviour, but avoids legal mechanisms which might enforce or encourage such behaviour. The Canadian efforts at regulating investment incentives demonstrate a new concern about internal subsidies, but highlight its limited possibilities for action in comparison with the EU.

The EU provides an interesting, but most likely unique, example of an institutional structure in which authority to discipline state expenditure is transferred to an international institution. It is unique primarily because the EU is far more than another international institution. Underpinning its operation is a commitment to economic integration and eventual political union. The relatively effective state aid discipline is another step in the neofunctionalist path towards the creation of some form of federal structure. In this case a convergence of interests between supranationalists supporting the transfer of authority to higher levels, and free market intergovernmentalists seeking discipline upon other states' expenditures, permits the operation of a structure which could not be replicated at the GATT or in NAFTA. Because of these unique circumstances it is doubtful that the EU arrangement can serve as an example for other areas of the world.

9 State Transformation and the Global Political Economy

Central to the issue of subsidy disputes discussed in this book is the question 'Who makes the decision about the appropriate realm of government expenditure in advanced industrialized economies?' The traditional notion that national governments make that decision is now only partially correct. In the EU, North America and multilaterally under the GATT and the WTO new structures have been developed to provide stricter disciplines for state spending. Institutions above states are participating in the governing of even the most powerful societies. This final chapter reviews the findings of the present study and attempts to draw out some of their implications. Following an analysis of the relationship between subsidies, liberalization and globalization, attention turns to the transformation of the state and implications for world order.

SUBSIDIES, LIBERALIZATION AND GLOBALIZATION

Subsidy disputes are a product of the drive to liberalization and the process of globalization with which it is bound up. At a systemic level, subsidy disputes highlight both elite and transnational corporate needs for increased liberalization to fuel economic growth and the backlash that such liberalization creates. Subsidies are one area among many where increased liberalization is demanded. It is joined by trade in other fields such as services, investment, government procurement and public utilities. As each of these areas is pried open, there is increasing public pressure to blame others for ensuing economic difficulties.

While subsidy conflict often takes the form of interstate conflict, it also pits broader based social forces against each other. The two primary social forces examined in this study are those that benefit from increased liberalism and those that lose in the liberalizing process. The group that own or work in internationally competitive industries tend to benefit from liberalization, while those in declining industries and the poorer segments of society tend to suffer from liberalization. The less well off may benefit from increased access to some cheaper goods brought about by liberalization, but they also suffer the erosion of social welfare benefits that result from the pressure for increased competitiveness in a time of slow growth.

In the Canadian case, support for the free trade initiative tended to break down along class lines, with the less well off fearing the effects of harmonation with, what this study has labeled, a hyperliberal system. In Canada, those that stood to lose the most from restructuring to a US model offered the greatest resistance, although this was moderated by regional and ethnic divisions influencing Albertans and Quebecois more than fears of harmonization. Except for these two provinces, many people dependent on the social wage sensed the dangers of moving to a hyperliberal system. In the US, industries and workers threatened by foreign competition have sought prosecution of unfair traders as a form of protection. Lacking positive adjustment programs, such as extensive retraining, workers have joined struggling firms to use protectionist laws to reverse competitive disadvantages. Firms that have suffered from numerous economic ills have been able to mobilize the general sentiment for fair trade into assistance for their particular industry. The easiest targets are foreign activities undertaken at variance with US practice.

The Canadian business community (which includes numerous US transnationals) stood firmly behind the move towards liberalization through the FTA *because* of harmonization effects, even when it was clear that their original goal of secure market access would not be reached. The FTA was seen as a means to make Canadian business and society move more quickly in the direction of the US hyperliberal model. It is not clear, however, how far toward the hyperliberal model Canadian neoliberals wanted to move. The Conservative government and business organizations claimed to support 'Canadian' policies of health care and cultural industry protection and ensured that these were not greatly eroded. It is difficult to judge if this was their true position or they simply sensed the political danger in expressing contrary views. The recent rise of the right wing populist Reform Party offers evidence that some in Canada favor a more dramatic move to the hyperliberal model.[1]

US business has been much more differentiated than their northern neighbours. Industries competing against Canadian rivals have used trade laws as protection against too much liberalization and increased competition. Even transnationals in competition with foreign based TNCs have tried to attack rivals. Yet, the upper hand in the US political economy remains with large, liberalizing transnational corporations. The general thrust of US foreign economic policy has been to open markets while conceding specific areas of protection.

In Western Europe the mid-1980s saw a consensus of elite opinion from French Socialists to British Thatcherites that liberalization of the EC through a single market was the key to renewed growth. Pushing forward with liberalization and integration, European government initiatives exceeded the support of many European citizens. In the early 1990s the fragile base of the elite project was revealed as popular opposition to further integration in the form of the Treaty on European Union spread across the Community states. Reeling from a rejection in the Danish referendum and extensive opposition in numerous countries, the Community was forced to confront its democratic deficits and consider subjugating its decision making processes to increased scrutiny.

Social forces benefiting from the move to hyperliberalism and those that suffer from such a trajectory, place competing demands upon the leadership of their states. In the US case this results in demand for protectionist legislation *and* the call for others to liberalize their economies. The public in Canada and the EU press for economic growth *and* shy away from the costs of liberalizing without compensation. Particular areas of activity are valued above the market such as health care and agriculture and popular resistance in these areas can be fierce.

The role of ideology and views of the state are also important in analysing trade negotiations. In Canada, a liberalizing elite entered into the FTA to institutionalize particular economic policies. In numerous cases, trade negotiators from the US and Canada were allied against groups within Canada that favoured a more restricted policy. Transnational alliances were vital to the success of the FTA. Transnational alliances also point to the dual nature of comprehensive trade agreements such as the FTA and NAFTA. Trade deals have both external and internal objectives. The external objective is to increase or secure access to another market. This may be undertaken in an attempt to attract investment or render domestic industry more competitive. The internal objective is to shift the domestic balance of power so that export oriented liberalizing forces have the upper hand. This is accomplished by encasing liberalizing strategies in an international agreement which makes the cost of backsliding exceedingly high.

Perhaps the most interesting aspect of this study is the requirement for the construction of international and/or supranational institutions to govern the increasingly integrated liberal market. Rules need to be created, passions constrained and disputes adjudicated between political entities that remain largely national in character. Acting in response to firms and groups disadvantaged or seeking advantage in the restructuring process that accompanies liberalization, state elites attempt to contain conflicts and satisfy the most powerful domestic constituents. Legalistic and bureaucratic institutions are a useful mechanism for depoliticizing disputes concerning the financial activities of states. However, the creation of such institutions requires a transformation of our understanding and expectation of the state and its role in the global political economy.

TRANSFORMING THE STATE

The state is undergoing change, both by restricting its intervention in the economy to particular forms and by transferring portions of decision-making authority to supranational or international bureaucratic/legal bodies. Study of the subsidy issue reveals that contrary to considerable comment lamenting the increase in protectionism or neomercantilism, state policy in this area is becoming more liberal. The neoclassical liberal desire to see government intervention in the economy subjected to increasing legal constraint is being incrementally realized in subsidy policies. Crucially, this restriction is taking place at an international rather than a national level as envisaged by liberal political theorists. The international agreements form part of a wider 'new constitutionalism' providing for increased restraint upon particular areas of government economic activity (Gill, 1992).

Where can we see evidence of this trend? At the multilateral level, the prohibition of export subsidies on manufactured goods has been a limitation that has existed for some time. The strengthening of the GATT subsidy regime provides increased discipline. Contracting parties will not be able to reject or stall reports as easily as in the past. Subsidy practices are being channeled into broad-based spending programs in areas such as basic research and development, regional development and environmental assistance. By highlighting the concept of specificity in determining the status of a subsidy an effort is being made to shift government expenditure to programs that confer general benefits rather than intervening on behalf of a particular enterprise. The increased powers of the WTO's dispute settlement mechanism will encourage adoption of such policies (Kohona, 1994). In the EU the trend has been towards an increase in horizontal and regional development aid policies and away from sector specific initiatives. These movements should result in a market that is closer to laissez-faire principles and less distorted by government intervention because particular firms or enterprises are not favored over others. NAFTA will have little impact in this area as it concentrates on monitoring domestic legal procedures rather than developing, expanding or enforcing new rules.

Subsidy disputes have confirmed the view of some analysts (Albert, 1992; Thurow, 1992) of an ongoing clash of economic and social development models. The ideal types of hyperliberal and state capitalism have been useful in highlighting areas for comparison. Subsidy disputes tend to pit the US style hyperliberal state model, attempting to return to an idealized notion of laissez-faire capitalism, against a more state capitalist model stressing strategic intervention and activity in the areas of social programs and public ownership. Even countries as similar as Canada and the US, aided by the presence of powerful transnational forces seeking a smooth trading relationship, have been unable to resolve their differences. Public policy in each country is the result of previous domestic political battles and, as such, represents a compromise between contending social forces. Those balances are sensitive matters susceptible to change, but sure to evoke controversy.

A vital aspect of the US federal state is the decentralized nature of the political institutions and importance of trade law in domestic politics. Dissatisfied US interests, whether they be national industries, threatened workers or even transnational companies, use trade law as a tool to attack foreign competition. The US system responds to domestic pressures and concerns as it punctuates the commitment to liberal trade with redress for some of those hurt by such a policy. Politics is at the centre of the trade law system and cannot be avoided. The result in the subsidy field has been that the US political system has highlighted the subsidy 'problem' but also stands in the way of developing institutions that might mitigate conflict. Congressional and industry pressure attacks foreign practices, but blocks both a consideration of domestic subsidy practice and institutional arrangements that might result in a strict limitation of US practice by a higher body.

Space did not permit a detailed examination of contrasting European models of capitalism, but some of the same types of conflict detailed in the Canada–US relationship exist in EU–US relations. The US has advocated a position demanding the removal of subsidy practices that until recently have been quite acceptable in the European context. In the Airbus dispute the conflict has been fought over indirect US subsidies and direct EU subsidies. The examination of internal EU state aids policy in Chapter 8 revealed disagreement between those states with little public enterprise and those states more dependent on public enterprises to fulfill economic or social roles. The struggle within the Union accompanies transatlantic disputes with the US.

Despite the usefulness of the clashing models approach one should not become fixated on this aspect of subsidy disputes for three reasons. The first is that there are some elements of conversion in the system. The rules hammered out at GATT will encourage states to subsidize in the same manner by taking advantage of R&D, regional development and environmental exemptions. Similar to the internal EU experience one could expect national governments to tailor subsidy policies to conform to the new code. In the early 1990s there was a possibility that the US and Western Europe might be moving closer together. The 1992 project firmly moved the European political economy in a more liberal direction. The EU had also accepted increased discipline in the agricultural and aerospace sectors. In the US the Clinton administration took a more explicitly interventionist strategy than its predecessor through a failed attempt to bring in universal health care and a more explicit approach to industrial policy in the R&D field. The November 1994 US election giving the Republican Party a majority in both houses of Congress may reverse the US experiments, but it does seem that the Europeans are moving in a more liberal direction.

A second reason to be cautious of the clash of models approach as a guide lies in the role of economic interests which may not be related to these broader models. The regional disputes across the Canada–US border indicated that it was the presence of the border itself and an environment of intense competition that encouraged firms in one country to target firms in the other. Even if socioeconomic organization had been identical trade disputes would still have occurred as producers sought relief from competition against foreign rivals.[2] In the US–EU relationship, differing models may provide targets for attack, but comparative advantage and levels of competition seem to determine the sectors in which subsidy disputes emerge. The increasing competitiveness and reliance of US agriculture on exports raised concern about European policies. US antagonism to European subsidy practice in the aerospace sector was limited until Airbus emerged as a challenger to Boeing and McDonnell Douglas.

This suggests that the underlying problem may not be with the subsidy policies *per se*, but with the changing fortunes of industries based in the most powerful states. As outlined in Chapter 2, the US trade law system is dynamic and flexible, responding to pressure in one way or another. The tools used may be escape clause actions, antidumping cases or, as documented in this study, countervailing duty investigations. Recent activity has seen Section 301 take on more importance. Competitive foreign interests have little hope of avoiding such action as long as the US system facilitates litigation and economic conditions provide dissatisfied interests.

A third caveat is that each variation of the models is itself under dispute and subject to revision. For example, in Canada some groups may call for scaling back universal health care and more competition, while some US organizations may agitate for universal health care or an industrial policy. Federal systems of government also complicate the notion of a clash between unitary states. Although disagreeing on some issues, federal governments in both Canada and the US tend towards a model encouraging greater liberalization, while subnational levels struggle to influence the market as much as possible. In both countries there is competition between various groups advocating one approach or another. In a similar vein, conclusions about the role of actors also need to be qualified. Corporations seem to strive for a more open economic system, yet they are often the driving force behind protectionism. To be more precise, corporations that are suffering from international competition or sense a commercial advantage from instituting a trade case can drive the process.

The advantage of surveying developments in North America, the European Union and the GATT (now the WTO) is that one can develop a sense of the limits to, and variety of, subsidy solutions and state transformation. The WTO provisions are untested and much will depend upon implementation and application of the law. What appears to have been produced is an increased discipline in the subsidy area, but considerable leeway for continued dispute and confrontation. The WTO arrangements are technically superior and more intrusive than the NAFTA provisions because they apply a new set of common rules rather than monitoring the application of domestic law. Particular areas of spending have been given approval (basic R&D for example), and others discouraged (specific subsidies). The reversal of the unanimity provision in adopting panel reports pushes the system in a more binding and supranational direction. Yet, as with the Tokyo Round provisions, implementation is key. Rumblings from the US Congress indicate that the operation of the system may vary from the original intentions of the drafters. A step has been taken in the direction of building multilateral institutions to adjudicate delicate areas of state expenditure, but it is fragile and may yet be undermined.

In Western Europe, the EU continues to expand its competence despite Maastricht Treaty difficulties. State aids restrictions grow in their intrusiveness, with final decisions in the hands of the Community and the Court. European economic structures are becoming increasingly harmonized and public enterprise cultures undermined. Of the three approaches, the European one is the most elaborate but the least likely to work in other contexts. The distinctive commitment to a community entity involves accepting a greater amount of supranational activity than is presently seen to be possible or even desirable at the multilateral level or in other regions. It would be extremely difficult to separate the state aid provisions from the EU package and apply them to other regions.

In North American arrangements, the state has retained greater decision-making authority, primarily because of the centrality of the US political system. The most the Canadians could achieve was a panel system limited to ensuring existing US law is administered correctly. Even this action has led to disquiet in the US and a Constitutional challenge. The FTA and NAFTA system provides extra protection for the Mexican and Canadian producers entering the US market, but leaves them vulnerable to the protectionist thrust of the laws and potential changes. From the perspective of dealing with subsidy disputes NAFTA ranks behind the EU and GATT systems, but is probably all that could realistically have been achieved. The US reluctance to modify CVD laws is instructive because it applies to trade remedies and other forums.

A similar reluctance also makes multilateral agreements weaker. However, whereas the Canadians had little that would entice the US into limiting its domestic law, the multilateral negotiations offered the prospect of new rules in large markets of potential growth for the US. The EU and US were able to reach agreement on subsidy arrangements because gains in other areas compensated for an imperfect subsidy agreement. The French might have had to compromise on agriculture, but they gained in increased access for their high technology and service sectors. The United States may not have been able to eliminate EU agricultural practices, but they did succeed in moving services on to the agenda and forcing countries such as Japan, Korea and Canada into a tariffication system for domestic agricultural protection

WORLD ORDER

Although subsidy disputes can be both dry and technical, they shed light on a fascinating and crucial struggle. One simultaneously witnesses a drive to liberalize economies and attempts to create institutions and rules to govern the liberal global political economy. Globalization involves the destabilization of societies as economies are exposed to greater and more rapid competition and authority is shifted away from national institutions. The challenge for elites is to create structures for stability while the challenge for citizens is to shape the process in the least harmful direction. An evolving world order of a particular form is under contestation.

National political community maintains its relevance on one level. The restructuring generated by shifts in comparative advantage and capital flows leads to conflict channeled through the political institutions of each territory. This observation was made in Chapter 4 in the context of examining CVD cases and the tendency of US firms to target Canadian crossborder rivals. Even if organizational principles in the two economies are similar there is still an 'us' and a 'them'. Such a proposition opens up a new area of investigation. The clash of models must share its prominence with a series of questions concerning the relationship between freer trade areas and political community. If trade actions are judged to be seriously detrimental to countries entering trade areas, the ultimate solution lies not in tinkering with law (in this case US law), in bilateral subsidy negotiations, or in whole scale harmonization, but in elimination of the state boundary itself. As noted in Chapter 8, Western European states have had a great deal of success dealing with the subsidy issue because of the transfer of sovereignty to a higher level – the European Union. Yet even in this case the process is not complete and institutions are subject to challenge from below.

In contrast to the European model, North American economic integration has been attempted strictly through liberal economic principles. In trying to build free trade areas, the FTA and its successor NAFTA studiously avoided issues outside the concern of liberal economics. There has been no attempt to build a greater political community where issues such as compensation, distribution of costs and wide-ranging legal arbitration can be accommodated. There will be little effort at assisting poorer areas to improve through regional development programs, nor any social charter to set minimum economic rights. It is an attempt to have the integration of markets without addressing important political issues. The failure to address these other issues also limits the ability to create meaningful regulatory bodies. How could either state trust a supranational legal structure to rule on subsidy practices in the face of such different views concerning health care, regional development and cultural industries? Yet, if there is no recourse to a higher body, how can these types of dispute be eliminated?

The disagreements emerging from bilateral subsidy negotiations have their counterpart at the multilateral level. Chapters 6 and 7 demonstrated that GATT subsidy negotiations have been long, difficult and resistant to resolution. The GATT effort to define what is or is not permissible is also fraught with disagreement about the appropriate role of government in the economy. Subsidy practices are embedded in domestic political, social, and economic structures and are not easily changed, despite intense foreign pressure. The ongoing desire to intervene in the agricultural and aerospace fields indicates the difficulties yet to be overcome.

If the Canadian lesson from the FTA experience was that there is an economic cost to maintaining a separate state, the implications for the US in its other foreign relations are much less clear. In Canada, the US faced a relatively weak negotiating adversary: the Canadians simply did not have the clout or will to make the Americans reflect on their domestic subsidy practices. US negotiators and Congressional officials did not pick up on the idea that they also subsidize heavily and that the question of which method is acceptable is one other countries are willing to contest vigorously. The GATT agricultural dispute indicated the potential problems that an overly idealistic US approach can create in demanding that other countries rapidly restructure in accordance with American demands. The potential outcry should other states begin raising objections to US subnational policies under the new GATT agreement may emphasize the inability of US officials to see their own practices as clearly as they see others. By tightening subsidy discipline on the US and its trading partners, the Uruguay Round measures may open new avenues for conflict.

Interestingly, the NAFTA discussion shifted the terms of the institutional debate in North America. In the FTA Canadian opponents of the hyperliberal vision resisted bilateral institution building. In the NAFTA debate similar opposition forces, such as labor and environmentalists, faulted the side accords for lacking institutional muscle while business interests attacked any institution building in this area. It appears that it is the purpose of the institutions governing the increasingly liberalized world economy that is now becoming the subject of debate.

The implications of this trend for international trade negotiations are significant. Negotiations are likely to become more openly political, perhaps reverting to the pre-World War Two standard when issues such as tariff cuts were major lines of division between political forces. The difference today is that liberalization draws resistance from a wide spectrum of groups including the new social movements. With the intensification of liberalization all issues seem to be trade issues. As a result, many more groups are brought into the debate and agreement becomes much more difficult, or if reached, remains open to challenge. From a managerial viewpoint, the liberalization task becomes more complicated as increasingly contradictory demands are placed upon negotiators.

The demands made by environmentalists, organized labor, feminists, nationalists and aboriginal groups will not be easily accommodated by those social forces pressing for further liberalization. Transnational business interests are attempting to build a global political economy that is as liberal as possible in contrast to the demands by the previously mentioned groups. It would not be surprising if the old managerial arguments about governability raised in the national arena are replicated at the regional and multilateral level. Surveying the growing resistance to institutionalized liberalization in the early 1990s, one could imagine a NAFTA, EU or WTO negotiator echoing the views of previous transnational managers that 'in recent years, the operations of the democratic process do indeed appear to have generated a breakdown of traditional means of social control, a delegitimation of political and other forms of authority, and an overload of demands on government, exceeding its capacity to respond' (Crozier, Huntington and Watanuki, 1975, 8).

One is drawn back to the question of sovereignty, understood as the location of final decision making. States are often still viewed as being sovereign in that their citizens continue to hold the state responsible for their security and economic welfare. However, economic integration has increased the influence of global financial and production structures and the domestic policies of other states on the citizens of all countries. To paraphrase Stephen Krasner (1988), there is an intransigent disjuncture between the nature of contemporary sovereignty and the functional requirements of the global economy. It is more accurate to say that globalization creates pressure for sovereignty transfer than to declare that globalization restricts sovereignty. Globalization may make some paths more difficult to pursue, such as Keynesian economic policy or protectionism, but the decision to pursue these policies may still reside with state leaders. In the subsidy field we are witnessing an attempt to dilute national sovereignty by shifting the final decision making authority away from national institutions. It is an attempt to deepen the internationalization of the state to accompany the globalization of production and finance.

Closely linked to the problem of establishing sovereignty over previously separate states is the issue of democratic accountability. Despite the substantial shortcomings of democratic politics in western states, citizens have the ability to exert pressure on their legislatures to change or modify laws. A similar mechanism does not exist at the supranational level. Even in the EU there is concern over the democratic deficit. With a weak European Parliament and relatively strong European Commission, citizens are unable to influence many decisions and rulings that effect their day to day life. Democratic mechanisms are required so that people can give voice to their concerns and steps can be taken to resolve crucial issues through a legitimate process. Blocking or ignoring democratic impulses runs the risk of bottling up frustration, leading to explosive consequences. A transnational order or a 'sovereignty' lacking democratic mechanisms runs the risk of losing its legitimacy in difficult times or requiring its member states to rely on physical coercion rather than persuasion to carry out policies.

This study has described a movement in the subsidy area to the increasing transfer of authority over areas of legitimate state expenditures to levels above the state. Similar activities are taking place and will continue to take place in the realms of labor standards, environmental standards and other aspects of competition policy. The reaction to such activity will force neoliberals to confront a question that they usually wish to avoid – 'Who should rule?' (Pickel, 1989). Perhaps even more difficult is 'How should they rule?' Let us begin with the first question. In the subsidy area, especially in the EU and WTO the trend has been for government leaders, backed by commercial interests, often representing a minority of the population, entering into international agreements to empower bureaucrats and lawyers to take decisions over the appropriateness of government expenditure. Once created, these agreements resemble constitutions in that they embody long term rules about the functioning of the society and the economy. Crucially, these frameworks are created through a process that many would consider unacceptable for constitution making. They are democratic only if one has a very loose notion of the requirements for democracy. One might ask 'Who elected bureaucrat X to determine whether our society can or cannot support agricultural communities in a particular manner?'

The lines of accountability between the citizen, state leadership and international institutions are extended and strained.

If the reply to 'Who should rule?' is a group broader than international bureaucrats and lawyers (albeit with extensive business support) the question becomes 'How should this broader group participate in governing?' To this there is no clear answer, although two methods have been advocated. The first focuses upon democratizing international institutions. In this view democracy cannot function solely on a national basis and must be reconstituted on an international level. David Held (1993: 13–52), an advocate of this position, has labeled it 'Cosmopolitan' and stressed the need to build democratic international institutions. One example would be to modify voting arrangements in the IMF so that decisions are no longer controlled only by the wealthy states (Gester, 1993). The obstacles to such an approach are immense as each institution already supports entrenched interests that are unlikely to acquiesce to such modifications. The resistance of Member States in the EU to increasing the European Parliament's power is an example in the most democratically developed of international institutions.

The other major strain in thinking about bolstering democracy in an increasingly globalized environment is those that identify new social movements as the solution. The social movements referred to in this literature are voluntary, transnational groups trying to influence governing behavior and effect systemic change. The peace and environmental movements are often used as prime examples. They seek to influence both the general public and decision makers on local, national and international levels. They have a global vision, proposing transnational solutions. One of the primary tasks of such movements and the way in which they might contribute to increasing democracy is the creation of a global political community which has a sense of common problems (Brecher, Brown and Culter, 1993; Thiele, 1993).

The merit of this approach is that it proposes the development of a grass roots transnational civil society in response to globalization. Social movements can change behavior, as is demonstrated by the rise of ecological concerns (Bramble and Porter, 1992). They may be successful in lobbying government to change legislation or could lead consumer boycotts of dangerous or unhealthy products. However, the shortcomings of putting too much stress on new social movements should also be clear. Firstly, a lack of concern with political institutions runs the risk of leaving these institutions intact which may frustrate popular measures. Pressure may be brought on politicians, but if they are sufficiently insulated, they may not be influenced. Secondly, this approach may overestimate the ability of people to participate in such organizations. A particular level of income or leisure may be required for effective operation. Those under pressure to make a living wage or simply survive may not be able to participate. The issues championed by such social movements may reflect the desires of relatively privileged groups.

The cosmopolitan and social movement approaches to global democracy are not mutually exclusive if a broad understanding of democracy, as both a procedure and concrete conditions of equality of participation, is adopted. Although Held does not highlight the role of transnational social movements, his earlier theoretical work on national democracy incorporates these organizations (Held, 1987: 289). Their importance seems to be lost as he switches to the global level of analysis. Social movements need not be in opposition to institutional reform, as increasingly democratic and participatory institutions should provide them with increased influence. However, both approaches will have to confront the probability that their initiatives will collide with the major global actors of transnational business. Transnational business already has privileged access to those governments that would be required to agree to international institutional reform. An arrangement that limited their prerogatives would encounter great resistance. While social movements may extol the virtues of global civil society, that space has been and is dominated by the extensive formal and informal contacts of transnational business and their allies.[3]

The questions of who are the rule makers and through what process are rules made are ones of increasing importance to the functioning of international economic institutions. In the subsidy field the most extensive mechanism is found in the EU which embodies a commitment to political integration. Although limited, attempts are being made to increase the institution's accountability. The GATT/WTO arrangements are more modest and more fragile than the EU's. Its lack of legitimacy may well be revealed should sensitive state-level spending in the US be challenged by trading rivals. Critics should be able to mount an effective critique of a remote multilateral institution intervening in domestic affairs. At the North American level little further progress can be expected because of the lack of political community. The gap between the ambitions of international economic managers and national understandings of community and democracy should greatly complicate further institution building in sensitive issue areas such as subsidy regulation.

Some might object at this point that the study has wandered too great a distance from subsidy disputes to a discussion of global democracy. Do international economic agreements and institutions really need to have large democratic elements? Surely the move from discussion of technical matters to value-laden philosophical debates concerning the 'shoulds' of participation not only stretches the notion of interdisciplinarity, but confuses the issue and creates a diversion from the task at hand. Such objections might have carried some weight 20 years ago, but they are of less relevance today. As this study has tried to highlight, subsidy negotiations and their follow-on subjects impinge upon vital political decisions and threaten to modify domestic socioeconomic orders. In treading upon such subjects they have stirred up a hornet's nest of concern and resistance. More and more groups within society are influenced by 'trade' negotiations and, as a result, broader and broader questions will be asked and need to be answered in the future.

Notes

CHAPTER 1 GLOBALIZATION, THE STATE AND SUBSIDIES

1. This is an interpretation that stresses developments in the global political economy. Other work on globalization has stressed the compression of time and space, as well as broader sociological aspects (Shaw, 1994; Robertson, 1992).
2. For an extended consideration of these categories see the work of Robert W. Cox (1987; 1986).
3. James Laxer (1987) uses the terms 'enterprise' and 'enterprise-intervention' to describe similar variations as hyperliberalism and state capitalism.
4. This statement presumes that the interests of domestic societies may not be synonymous with the demands of the international economy as articulated by hegemonic spokespeople.

CHAPTER 2 THE US TRADE LAW SYSTEM

1. This has led one prominent observer (Wolf, 1989: 286) to use 'stupidity' as a possible explanation for trade restrictions!
2. See 'Statement by Forty Economists on American Trade Policy', issued in April 1989 reprinted in *The World Economy* 12 no. 2 (June 1989: 263–4 and Bovard, 1991).
3. Nelson (1989) terms this a shift from distributional to regulatory politics.
4. C. Michael Aho refers to this practice as 'forum shopping'. See 'Comments', (Smith, 1987: 44).
5. Public letter accompanying the release of the 1985 *Trade Barriers Report* (29 October) from United States Trade Representative Clayton Yeutter to Senator Bob Packwood, Chairman of the Senate Committee on Finance.
6. Belgium also brought in a CVD law at this time.
7. Concerns about the protectionist bias in antidumping cases are outlined in Devalut (1990).
8. Having made this point, it is acknowledged that other laws such as the antidumping provision and Section 301 can also be used to change other government activities. Antidumping cases are often aimed at products that are dumped on the world market because of government support such as the European Common Agricultural Policy. Section 301 attacking foreign trade barriers has been used in order to encourage Japan to change its domestic policies in the areas of retail practices and rice policy.
9. VERs are administrated by the exporting country while OMAs are monitored in the importing country.
10. If a country is not a signatory to the GATT code, material injury does not have to be demonstrated. For a clear, detailed discussion about the CVD process see Vakerics, Wilson, and Weigel (1987: 193–270).
11. 'Upstream subsidies' are subsidies given to an input product that is used

in the manufacture of another product, which is then subject to CVDs.

12. 'Certain Softwood Products From Canada', 5 *International Trade Reporter Decisions* (ITRD) (Washington, D.C.: Bureau of National Affairs), 1487.
13. The assumption is that if a subsidy is specifically targeted it will sway a country's comparative advantage in that product, but a generally available subsidy will not have the same effect.
14. Carbon black is used to strengthen natural and synthetic fibres and in the production of some inks. The decision is found in 'Carbon Black from Mexico', 5 *ITRD* 1514–24.
15. For a detailed analysis and severe critique of US practice in this case see Percy and Yoder (1987).

CHAPTER 3 NATIONAL ORIGINS OF CANADA–US SUBSIDY CONFLICTS

1. For a critique of the Hartz–Horowitz debate see Forbes (1987). A brief critique of this cultural/institutional approach is given in Brym and Fox, (1989: 57–66).
2. See Section 36 (2) of *The Constitution Act 1982*, Section 36 (2).
3. Prior to 1984 they were called General Development Agreements (GDA).
4. (Stevenson, 1989: 188). Coincidentally these very Michelin plants became the object of attack via US trade law. The case is examined in Chapter 4.
5. These views are outlined in Report of the Royal Commission on Radio Broadcasting, September 1929. Reprinted in Bird (1988: 41–5).
6. Graham Spry, founder of the Canadian Radio League quoted in Raboy (1990: 40).
7. See the Canadian Associations of Broadcasters attack on the CRTC's Canadian content proposals contained in an editorial in *Broadcaster* magazine in March 1970. Reprinted in Bird (1988: 454–8).

CHAPTER 4 SUBSIDIES AND THE FREE TRADE AGREEMENT

1. Morton (1989: 2) places emphasis on three other factors – Canadian reliance upon exports to the US, perception by both countries that Canada subsidizes to a greater degree, and US reliance on trade remedy laws.
2. As negotiations progressed a second goal of liberalizing the domestic economy gained in importance (Hart, 1989b: 73). This view is also expressed by critics of the trade deal (Warnock, 1988).
3. Another interpretation is that the case was the result of a bidding war between Nova Scotia and Akron, Ohio, with the loser pursuing the CVD process. See Gary Horlick's comments in Smith (1987: 50).
4. The primary decision is 'Oil Country Tubular Goods', 8 *ITRD* 2407–20. Appeals on methodological grounds in 'Ipsco, Inc. v. U.S.', 10 *ITRD* 1267–82, 2379–83.
5. A prominent exception to this thinking has been Gary Horlick, a Washington trade lawyer and Canadian government advisor who has argued that Canada should launch CVD cases against the US to educate Con-

gress about subsidy practices. See his comments in Smith (1987: 50).
6. Some trade analysts have suggested that the fundamental purpose of negotiating trade laws is the establishment of a stable environment for investment decisions. See the comments of Gary Horlick (Smith, 1987: 49). If the dominant value is stability, a managed trade agreement may be able to serve the function as well as a free trade agreement.
7. These figures reflect the number of investigations pending or concluded in each year of the *United States International Trade Commission Annual Report*, 1978–90 Washington: International Trade Commission.
8. The value of exports threatened in the mid-1980s was $7 billion. During this time period Canadian exports to the United States fluctuated in the $100 billion range. (Statistics Canada, 1984–6).
9. The shift towards a free trade strategy and the fit of the business agenda and the Conservative government's policies is explored in McQuaig (1991).
10. The following account of the free trade negotiations is based on Hart (1994); McQuaig (1991), Doern and Tomlin (1991) and interviews.
11. Disputes in areas other than CVD and antidumping go through a process of consultation and arbitration set out in Chapter 18 of the FTA. Diverging views on its utility can be found in Clarkson (1988); Lipsey and York (1988: 93–4); Dearden (1989: 19–30, 31–8).
12. Rodney de C. Grey (1981: 55–67) provides a good discussion of the problems of import diverting versus export enhancing subsidies.
13. 1991 US administration report on the FTA listed some areas of concern, but gave a favorable review to the agreement as a whole (USTR 1991b). For Canada see Doern and Tomlin (1991: 205–42).
14. Interview with USTR official March 1994.

CHAPTER 5 NORTH AMERICAN SUBSIDIES IN THE 1990s

1. In a November 1991 interview an MPEAA official expressed exasperation with 'all this Canadian culture crap' claiming that the dispute is 'basically economic, veiled by culture'.
2. While subsidies in particular sectors may be large Bence argues that overall trade effects are probably minimal as provincial subsidies account for only 0.25 per cent of production sales in 1987–8.
3. See the statement of A. L. Halliday, Chairman, Subsidies and Trade Remedies Working Group, Canadian Department of External Affairs in House of Commons (1989: 7).
4. See the presentation of Gordon Wilson, President, Ontario Federation of Labour (House of Commons, 1987).
5. Morton (1989) proposed dropping the idea of a yellow category. A bilateral commission could be appointed to slot all programs into either the red or green sections, based upon economic analysis. While making reference to the obstacles created by divergent views of government's appropriate role, the author fails to suggest how an *economic* approach will mitigate the dispute.
6. For a sampling of ideas see Horlick and Steger, 1989; Hart, 1989; Hufbauer, 1989.

7. Interviews with Congressional staff members of the House Ways and Means Subcommittee on International Trade, November 1991.
8. Interview with ITC official, March 1994. See Article 1905 of the North American Free Trade Agreement (Supply and Services, 1993).
9. Article 1907: 2 (Supply and Services, 1993).
10. Interview with Mr Miguel Leaman, Minister for Trade Affairs, Mexican Embassy, Washington, March 1994.
11. Interview with USTR Official, March 1994.
12. Interview with Gary Hufbauer, International Institute for Economics, March 1994.
13. An earlier Constitutional challenge to the FTA arrangements had been dismissed in June of 1993 because it had been filed in the district court of the District of Columbia rather than the Court of Appeals of the District of Columbia.

CHAPTER 6 SUBSIDIES AT THE GATT

1. The countries were Australia, Brazil, Canada, China, Cuba, Czechoslovakia, France, India, Netherlands, Luxembourg, New Zealand, South Africa, the Soviet Union, and the United Kingdom,
2. Seven key norms are identified in Finlayson and Zacher (1981). A helpful overview of GATT's difficulties and some possible solutions can be found in Jackson (1990).
3. A useful overview is provided by a former GATT panelist in Pescatore (1993).
4. A clear, concise summary of the GATT experience with the subsidy question can be found in Jackson (1989: 249–73). Dam (1979: 132–47) reviews GATT provisions until the late 1960s.
5. The Michelin Tire Case was examined in Chapter 4.
6. One involved the elimination of the American Selling Price and the other an attempt to reform the antidumping law.
7. Gary Clyde Hufbauer (1983) argues that the 'reef' of subsidies became more visible in the 1970s not simply due to the lowering 'water level' of protection in other areas but because they had actually grown.
8. US House of Representatives, *Background and Status* (Winham, 1986: 119, n.41). Winham's study offers an excellent account of the negotiations. The subsidy issue is treated on pages 116–20, 161–77, 213–23, 359–61.
9. (Rivers and Greenwald, 1979: 145?) Rivers and Greenwald were the American officials at the USTR Office in charge of the subsidy negotiations from 1976 to 1979.
10. The Tokyo Round Subsidies Code and the Illustrative List of Export Subsidies are reprinted in Balassa (1989: 134–62).
11. See Article 9:2a of the subsidies code.
12. (GATT, 1990). For an analysis of the text see Hufbauer (1990).
13. Interview, Department of Commerce officials, November 1991.
14. Canada's subsidy and countervailing measures proposal to the GATT, Section 2(a). The text is reprinted as Annex I in Smith (1990: 171–81).

15. This analysis of the Dunkel Draft's subsidy implications benefited from Hufbauer (1993) and Horlick and Clarke (1993).
16. This qualification led Gary Hufbauer (1993: 16–21) to suggest that another category of 'green/yellow' had been added to the traffic light. Section 8 is usually green, but might slip into the yellow. Similarly, the ability to rebut a charge of serious prejudice may have created a 'red/yellow' category which allows some prohibited practices in exceptional circumstances.
17. Schaefer and Singer (1992) provide a preliminary consideration of the effect of the Dunkel Draft on US states.
18. 2(b)(ii) of Canada's GATT proposals reprinted in Smith (1990: 171–81).
19. A useful summary is in *International Trade Reporter*, 22 December 1993: 2158–9. Greater detail including a profile of institutional arrangements can be found in Behboodi (1994: 133–50).
20. In addition to raising the permitted levels of assistance, the Americans were successful in making a number of other changes which would permit their existing subsidy practices. These included definitional changes, eliminating the need to notify R&D subsidies where it might jeopardize sensitive company technology, and higher subsidy levels for basic, as opposed to applied, research. The last measure was important because it mirrored American practice.
21. For details of the negotiations and background to the dispute see Goodell (1994). The MPEAA bounced back by lobbying the government to keep the EU on its watch list under the Conditions of Special 301 legislation. This would mandate monitoring of further EU activity. The MPEAA appears to have accepted existing EU practice, but is prepared to vigorously contest any new measures. Interview, Director of Federal Affairs, MPEAA, March 1994.
22. 'Senate Finance Committee's Sept. 13 Counteroffer to House Ways and Means Committee's Aug. 22 Offer on Outstanding Differences Over Uruguay Round Legislation', *International Trade Reporter*, 14 September 1994: 1430–2.

CHAPTER 7 AGRICULTURE AND AEROSPACE

1. In 1939 the US instituted import quotas on cotton in response to a bumper domestic harvest and in 1941 granted export subsidies on wheat.
2. Moyer (1993) and Hayes (1993) provide further detail on the Europeans' institutional and policy constraints.
3. Taking a narrow view of agricultural trade as encompassing exports of agricultural raw materials it amounted to just under 3 per cent of non-services trade in value in 1991 (UN 1993)
4. For example, the average and minimum tariff reduction commitments are not contained.
5. Tyson (1992: 204) reports that some US officials believed that Americans should accept the gift of European subsidies while others argued that action against the EC might threaten security interests.

CHAPTER 8 THE UNIQUE EUROPEAN UNION ARRANGEMENT

1. Prior to 1 November 1993 when the Maastricht Treaty came into effect the European Union was known as the European Community. This chapter uses the term European Community when referring to pre-November 1993 events. Other West European efforts to deal with the subsidy issue have taken place in the European Free Trade Association and the European Economic Area. For a comparative analysis see Behboodi, (1994: 56–80).
2. By February 1965 the ECSC had authorized state aid to the coal industry to support social security benefits, partial or total closures and to cover extraordinary expenses during rationalization (Spierenburg and Poidevin, 1994: 604–9).
3. Campbell (1980: 236–48) provides a brief analysis of Articles 92–94.
4. For a description of the state aids review process see Slot (1990).
5. Similar to the situation in Canada, concern has been expressed about the harmonization of technical standards and workplace practices. In many instances, the Community has advanced policy harmonization through the mutual recognition of standards, as opposed to legislating European wide regulations. This has led some to raise the specter of competitive deregulation in the EC (McGee and Weatheril, 1990).
6. UK state aids 1988–90 as reported by the Commission averaged 1.1 per cent of GDP compared to 2.4 per cent in Germany, 2.9 per cent in Italy, and 3.1 per cent in Greece (EC, 1992: 39).
7. (EC 1990d). In May 1993 British Aerospace repaid the British government £57.6 million in returning illegal state aid (*Financial Times*, 27 May 1993).
8. It may have the ability under the Constitution's broad interstate commerce powers. Action would probably have to be motivated by industry complaint – which is unlikely due to the fact that industries are the beneficiaries of bidding wars.
9. The former East German state governments continue to pose a challenge to EU policy. Desperate for employment they are less willing to obey Commission guidelines. In August 1996 the state of Saxony disobeyed Commission policy by offering further grants to Volkswagen, which was threatening to move its investment to Poland or the Czech Republic (*Observer*, 4 August 1996).
10. Definitions of the categories of R&D are provided in Annex I of the Community Framework for State Aids for Research and Development. Interestingly, the Commission indicates in the same annex that it will not challenge the definitions and objectives specified by Member States and will not 'demand or seek strict adherence to predetermined categories or definitions of R&D activities'.
11. Commission Directive of 25 June 1980 on the Transparency of Financial Relations between Member States and Public Enterprises. Reprinted as Annex F in Schina (1987: 202–5).
12. For a review of this policy and a call for its extension until 1996 see 'Request for the Unanimous Assent of the Council under Article 95 of the ECSC Treaty', *Communication from the Commission to the Council* 3 July 1991, SEC(91)1044.

13. Public enterprise activity has also been curbed by another part of the Rome Treaty, Article 90, which stipulates that government companies respect other sections of the Treaty (Bright, 1993).
14. Of those Europeans familiar with the Commission favorable public opinion declined from 54 per cent in 1990 to 39 per cent in 1992 while unfavorable opinion had increased from 18 per cent to 25 per cent. *Eurobarometer* 38 December 1992: 22–5.
15. The EU's constant stream of regulations is easily exploited by the British tabloid press which delights in pointing out seemingly ridiculous rules. For example, the front page of *The Sun* on 21 September 1994 carried a cut-out banana so readers would know the exact size of the latest regulation EC bananas!
16. The problem of the Commission's legitimacy is examined by Featherstone (1994).
17. The shock of near defeat for the Maastricht Treaty sparked a reconsideration of the EU institutions' relationship to the Union's citizens (Duff, 1994; Lodge, 1994; Peterson, 1994; Wallace, 1993; Ross, 1992).

CHAPTER 9 STATE TRANSFORMATION AND THE GLOBAL POLITICAL ECONOMY

1. The Reform Party is examined in three articles in the June 1994 edition of the *Canadian Journal of Political Science* XXVII 2: 213–308.
2. In the United States there may be a floating barrier to imports influenced by general economic trends that resists multi or bilateral legal constraint. Once certain levels of import penetration are crossed or domestic economic activity stagnates, trade law is used to supply relief. Yet, no single factor can be used as a quantitative measure to determine that level. For example, the CVD investigation into Canadian softwood lumber launched after Canada terminated the MOU in the fall of 1991 took place despite the fact that Canadian market share had dropped considerably. In this case US sentiment that Canada was reneging upon an agreement was sufficient to spark trade action.
3. Charles Lindblom's (1977: 170–88) neopluralist work could now be reformulated to stress the privileged position of *trans*national business in domestic political systems.

Bibliography

Aitken, J. (1988) 'Defensive Expansion: The State and Economic Growth in Canada,' in *Approaches to Canadian Economic History*, ed. W. T. Easterbrook and M. H. Watkins, 188–221. Ottawa: Carleton University Press.

Albert, Michel. (1992) *Capitalism vs. Capitalism*. London: Whurr.

Anderson, Perry. (1974) *Lineages of the Absolutist State*. London: NLB.

Andreopulos, Spyros. (1975) *National Health Insurance: Can We Learn from Canada?* New York: John Wiley.

Avery, Donald. (1989) 'Canadian Defence Policy and Economic Relations with the United States, 1939–1988: An Overview,' in *Economic and Strategic Issues in U.S. Foreign Policy*, ed. Carl-Ludwig Holtferich, 121–44. Berlin: Walter de Gruyter.

Bakker, Isabella. (1991) 'Canada's Social Wage in an Open Economy,' in *The New Era of Global Competition*, ed. Daniel Drache and Meric S. Gertler, 270–86. Montreal: McGill-Queen's University Press.

Bakker, Isabella. (1988) 'The Social-Wage and the Canada–U.S. Free Trade Agreement,' in *Trade Offs on Free Trade*, ed. Marc Gold and David Leyton-Brown, 407–14. Toronto: Carswell.

Balassa, Bela, ed. (1985) *Subsidies and Countervailing Measures, Critical Issues for the Uruguay Round*, Washington: World Bank Discussion Papers, 55.

Baldwin, Robert. (1985) *The Political Economy of U.S. Import Policy*, Cambridge, Mass: MIT Press.

Barcelo John J. (1982) 'The Two-Track Subsidies Code – Countervailing Duties and Trade Retaliation,' *Non-Tariff Barriers After the Tokyo Round*, ed. John Quinn and Philip Slayton, 121–52. Montreal Institute for Research on Public Policy.

Beaumier, Guy. (1990) 'Regional Development in Canada,' *Current Issue Review* 88–13E, Ottawa: Library of Parliament.

Behboodi, Rambod. (1994) *Industrial Subsidies and Friction in World Trade*, London: Routledge.

Beigie, Carl. (1970) *The Canada–U.S. Automotive Agreement: An Evaluation*, Montreal: Canadian-American Committee.

Bell, David. (1990) 'Political Culture in Canada,' *Canadian Politics in the 1990s* 3rd edn, ed. Michael S. Whittington and Glen Williams, 137–57, Scarborough: Nelson.

Bello, Judith Hippler and Alfan F. Holmer. (1987) *The Antidumping and Countervailing Duty Laws*, Washington: American Bar Association.

Bence, Jean–François. (1990) 'Analysis of Provincial Transfer Payments to Business in Canada,' *International Economic Issues* April: 25–40.

Bence, Jean-François and Murray G. Smith. (1989) 'Subsidies and the Trade Laws: The Canada–U.S. Dimension', *International Economic Issues* April-May: 1–36.

Bhagwati, Jagdish. (1989) 'United States Trade Policy at the Crossroads,' *The World Economy* 12 4: 439–79.

Bhagwati, Jagdish. (1988) *Protectionism*, Cambridge, Mass.: MIT Press.

Bhagwati, Jagdish and Hugh T. Patrick, eds (1990) *Aggressive Unilateralism: American 301 Trade Policy and the World Trading System*, Ann Arbor: University of Michigan Press.

Binational Secretariat. (1991) United States–Canada Free Trade Agreement, U.S. Section. 'Memorandum Opinion and Order Regarding Binational Panel Remand Decision II.' Extraordinary Challenge Committee. Secretariat File no. EEC-91–1904–01USA, Washington, DC.

Bird, Roger, ed. (1988) *Documents of Canadian Broadcasting*, Ottawa: Carleton University Press.

Black, Edwin R. and Alan C. Cairns. (1966) 'A Different Perspective on Canadian Federalism,' *Canadian Public Administration* 9: 27–44.

Block, Fred. (1977) *The Origins of International Economic Disorder*, Berkeley: University of California Press.

Bovard, James. (1991) *The Fair Trade Fraud*, New York: St. Martin's Press.

Bowles, Samuel. (1982) 'The Post-Keynesian Capital-Labor Stalemate,' *Socialist Review* 12 5: 5–72.

Bramble, Barbara J. and Gareth Porter (1992) 'Non-Governmental Organizations and the Making of US International Environmental Policy,' *The International Politics of the Environment*, eds. Andrew Hurrell and Benedict Kingbury, 313–53, Oxford: Clarendon Press.

Brand, Ronald A. (1993) 'Competing Philosophies of GATT Dispute Resolution in the Oilseeds Case and the Draft Understanding on Dispute Settlement,' *Journal of World Trade* 27, 6 December: 117–44.

Braverman, Harry. (1976) *Labour and Monopoly Capital*, New York: Monthly Review Press.

Brecher, Jeremy, John Brown Childs and Jill Culter eds. (1993) *Global Visions: Beyond the New World Order*, Boston: South End Press.

Bright, Christopher. (1993) 'Article 90, Economic Policy and the Duties of Member States,' *European Competition Law Review* 14, 6 November/December: 263–72.

Brittan, Leon. (1992) *European Competition Policy: Keeping the Playing-Field Level*, Brussels: Brassey's for the Centre for European Policy Studies.

Brown, William Adams Jr. (1950) *The United States and the Restoration of World Trade*, Washington, DC: Brookings Institution.

Brym, Robert J., ed. (1986) *Regionalism in Canada*, Toronto: Irwin.

Brym, Robert J. and Bonnie J. Fox (1989) *From Culture to Power: The Sociology of English Canada*, Toronto: Oxford University Press.

Bulter, Fiona. (1993) 'The EC's Common Agricultural Policy (CAP),' in *The European Community and the Challenge of the Future* 2nd edn, ed. Juliet Lodge, 112–30, London: Pinter.

Buzan, Barry and Gautam Sen (1990) 'The Impact of Military Research and Development Priorities on the Evolution of the Civil Economy in Capitalist States,' *Review of International Studies* 16, 4 October: 321–39.

Cafruny, Alan W. (1989) 'Economic Conflicts and the Transformation of the Atlantic Order: The U.S. Europe and the Liberalization of Agriculture and Services,' in *Atlantic Relations Beyond the Reagan Era* ed. Stephen Gill, 111–37, New York: St. Martin's Press.

Calleo, David. (1982) *The Imperious Economy*, Cambridge, Mass.: Harvard University Press.

Cameron, Duncan, Stephen Clarkson and Mel Watkins. (1988) 'Market Access,' in *The Free Trade Deal*, ed. Duncan Cameron, 46–58, Toronto: James Lorimer.

Campbell, Alan. (1980) *EC Competition Law: A Practitioner's Textbook*, Amsterdam: North-Holland.

Carr, Graham. (1991) 'Trade Liberalization and the Political Economy of Culture: An International Perspective on the FTA,' *Canadian-American Public Policy* 6: 1–54.

Carvounis, Cris C. (1986) *The Foreign Debt/National Development Conflict*, New York: Quorum Books.

Caves, Richard E. (1982) *Multinational Enterprise and Economic Analysis*, New York: Cambridge University Press.

Cecchini, Paolo Cecchini, Michael Catinat and Alexis Jacquemin. (1988) *The European Challenge 1992*, Aldershot: Wildwood Press.

Chen, Jim C. (1992) 'Appointments with Disaster: The Unconstitutionality of Binational Arbitral Review Under the United States–Canada Free Trade Agreement,' *Washington and Lee Law Journal* 49: 1455–99.

Clark, M. G. (1985) 'Nontariff Measures: Perceptions and Reality,' in *Canadian Trade at a Crossroads*, ed. Thomas Courchene, 265–88, Toronto: Ontario Economic Council.

Clarkson, Stephen. (1988) 'The Canada–United States Trade Commission,' in *The Free Trade Deal*, ed. Duncan Cameron, 26–45, Toronto: James Lorimer.

Cohen, Benjamin J. (Spring 1990) 'The Political Economy of International Trade,' *International Organization* 44 2: 261–81.

Comanor, William S. (1990) 'United States Antitrust Policy: Issues and Institutions,' in *Competition Policy in Europe and North America: Economic Issues and Institutions* 34–72, London: Harwood Academic Publishers.

Congress. (1988a) *Approving and Implementing the United States–Canada Free Trade Agreement, Reports and Other Materials*, 100th Cong., 2nd sess., 15 September. Senate, Committee on Finance, United States.

Congress. (1988b) *Hearing on the Constitutionality of Establishing a Binational Panel to Resolve Disputes in Antidumping and Countervailing Duty Cases*, 100th Cong., 2nd sess., 20 May 1988. Senate, Committee on the Judiciary, United States.

Cox, Robert W. (1987) *Production, Power and World Order*, New York: Columbia University Press.

Cox, Robert W. (1986) 'Social Forces, States and World Orders,' in *Neorealism and Its Critics*, ed. Robert Keohane, 204–54, New York: Columbia University Press.

Crichton, Ann and David Hsu. (1990) *Canada's Health Care System* Ottawa: Canadian Hospital Association Press.

Crispo, John, ed. (1988) *Free Trade: The Real Story*, Toronto: Gage.

Crozier, Michael, Samuel P. Huntington and Joji Watanuki. (1975) *The Crisis of Democracy*, New York: New York University Press.

Crump, Jeffrey R. (1989) 'The Spatial Distribution of Military Spending in the United States 1941–1985,' *Growth and Change* 50–62.

Dahl, Robert. (1994) 'A Democratic Dilemma: System Effectiveness and Citizen Participation,' *Political Science Quarterly* 109 2: 23–34.

Dam, Kenneth W. (1970) *The GATT Law and International Economic Organization*, Chicago: University of Chicago Press.
Dearden, Richard G., Michael M. Hart, and Debra P. Steger, eds (1989) *Living With Free Trade*, Ottawa: Institute for Research on Public Policy.
Department of National Defence. (1989) *Challenge and Commitment*, Ottawa, Canada.
Destler, I. M. (1986) *American Trade Politics: System under Stress*, Washington, DC: Institute for International Economics.
Devalut, James. (1990) 'The Administration of US Antidumping Duties: Some Empirical Observations.' *The World Economy* 13 1: 75–88.
Diebold, William Jr. (1959) *The Schuman Plan: A Study in Economic Cooperation 1950–1959*, New York: Council on Foreign Relations.
Difilippo, Anthony. (1990) *From Industry to Arms: The Political Economy of High Technology*, New York: Greenwood Press.
Doern, G. Bruce and Brian Tomlin. (1991) *Faith and Fear: The Free Trade Story*, Toronto: Stoddard.
Doran, Charles. (1990) 'Three U.S. Hypotheses about Culture and Trade in Search of Canadian Validation,' in *Canada–United States Trade Liberalization and Socio-Economic Integration: U.S. Perspectives*, ed. P. P. Proux, 123–37. Halifax, Institute for Research on Public Policy.
Drucker, Peter. (1986) 'The Changed World Economy,' *Foreign Affairs* 64: 768–91.
Duff, Andrew. (1994) 'Building a Parliamentary Europe,' *Government and Opposition* 29 2 Spring: 147–65.
EC. (1993) *XXIInd Report on Competition Policy 1992*, Brussels: Commission of the European Communities.
EC. (1992) *Third Survey on State Aids in the European Community in the Manufacturing and Certain Other Sectors*, Brussels: Commission of the European Communities.
EC. (1991a) 'State Aid Policy: A Key to Greater Cohesion,' *European Commission Press Release* 19 February, IP(91)141.
EC. (1991b) 'The Commission Asks for Repayment of Aid to Toyota,' *European Commission Press Release* 31 July, IP(91)752.
EC. (1991c) 'Approval of Assistance in the New Lander until 1993,' *European Commission Press Release* 26 March, IP(91)270.
EC. (1991d) 'State Aid: Decision on Treuhandanstalt,' *European Commission Press Release* 24 July, IP(91)706.
EC. (1991e) 'New Measures to Increase Transparency for State Aids to Public Companies,' *European Commission Press Release* 24 July, IP(91)707.
EC. (1990a) 'Commission Publishes Second Survey on Aid,' *European Commission Press Release* 31 July, IP(90)664.
EC. (1990b) 'Commission Renews Framework on State Aid to the Motor Vehicle Industry,' *European Commission Press Release* 12 December, IP(90)1006.
EC. (1990c) 'Renault,' *European Commission Press Release* 22 May, IP(90)400.
EC. (1990d) 'Commission Decision on Rover Case,' *European Commission Press Release* 27 June, IP(90)511.
EC. (1990e) 'Commission Approves French Aid Programme For Design of TGV (High-Speed Train) of the Future,' *European Commission Press Release* 25 July 1990, IP(90)637.

EC. (1989a) 'A Bonfire of Subsidies,' *European Commission Press Release* 10 March, IP(89)156.

EC. (1989b) 'Peugeot Repays State Aid Following Negative Commission Decision,' *European Commission Press Release* 14 June, IP(89)452.

EC. (1989c) *First Survey on State Aids in the European Community*, Brussels: European Commission.

EC. (1988) 'Commission Publishes its State Aid Survey,' *European Commission Press Release* 21 December, IP(88)848.

EC. (1985a) *Completing the Internal Market*. Commission. European Communities, Brussels, COM(85) 310 final.

EC. (1985b) 'Community Guidelines on State Aids for Research and Development,' *European Commission Press Release* 19 December, IP(85)594.

EC. (1977) *VIth Report on Competition Policy*, Brussels: Commission of the European Communities.

EC. (1972) *First Report on Competition Policy*, Brussels: European Communities. Commission.

Eisinger, Peter K. (1988) *The Rise of the Entrepreneurial State*, Wisconsin: University of Wisconsin Press.

Evans, Andrew and Stephen Martin. (1991) 'Socially Acceptable Distortion of Competition: Community Policy on State Aid,' *European Law Review* 16 April: 103–4.

Featherstone, Kevin. (1994) 'Jean Monnet and the Democratic Deficit in the European Union,' *Journal of Common Market Studies* 32, 2 June: 149–70.

Feltham, Ivan R., Stuart A. Salen, Robert F. Mathieson, Ronald Wonnacott. (1991) *Competition (Antitrust) and Antidumping Laws in the Context of the Canada–U.S. Free Trade Agreement*, Ottawa: Canadian Chamber of Commerce.

Fennel, Rosemary. (1987) 'Reform of the CAP: Shadow or Substance?' *Journal of Common Market Studies* XXVI 1 September: 61–79.

Finger, Michael. (1990) 'Comments on Negotiating Trade Laws,' in *Canada, the Pacific and Global Trade*, ed. Murray Smith, Halifax: Institute for Research on Public Policy.

Finlayson, Jock and Mark Zacher. (1981) 'The GATT and the Regulation of Trade Barriers: Regime Dynamics and Functions,' *International Organization* 35 4: 273–314.

Forbes, H. D. (1987) 'Hartz-Horowitz at Twenty: Nationalism, Toryism and Socialism in Canada and the United States' *Canadian Journal of Political Science* 20 2: 287–315.

Friedman, Milton. (1962) *Capitalism and Freedom*, Chicago: University of Chicago Press.

Fry, Earl H. (1990) 'The Economic Development Policies of U.S. State and Local Governments: Implications for the Canada–U.S. Free Trade Agreement,' *International Economic Issues* Institute for Research on Public Policy, 41–71.

Fry, Earl H. (1985) 'The Role of State and Provincial Governments in Canada–U.S. Sectoral Integration,' *Canada–United States Law Journal* 10: 169–88.

Gardner, Richard N. (1990) 'The Comeback of Liberal Internationalism,' *Washington Quarterly* 13 3: 23–38.

GATT (1994) *The Results of the Uruguay Round of Multilateral Trade Nego-*

tiations: The Legal Texts, Geneva: General Agreement on Tariffs and Trade.
GATT (1990) 'Agreement (1990) on Interpretation and Application of Articles VI, XVI, and XXIII of the General Agreement on Tariffs and Trade.' MTN.TNC/W/35, Geneva: General Agreement on Tariffs and Trade.
GATT (1953) *International Trade 1952*, Geneva: General Agreement on Tariffs and Trade.
Gavin, Brigid. (1987) 'A "Super Rule" Proposal for Liberalization of Agriculture in GATT – Implications for the EEC,' in *The New GATT Round of Multilateral Trade Negotiations*, ed. Ernst-Ulrich Petersmann and Meinhard Hilf, Boston: Kluwer Law and Taxation Publishers.
Gester, Richard. (1993) 'Proposal for Voting Reform,' *Journal of World Trade* 27, 3 June: 121–36.
Gibbons, Roger. (1982) *Regionalism: Territorial Politics in Canada and the United States*, Toronto, Butterworths.
Gill, Stephen. (1992) 'The Emerging World Order and European Change,' *Socialist Register 1992: New World Order?* eds Ralph Miliband and Leo Panitch, 157–96, London: Merlin.
Gill, Stephen. (1990) *American Hegemony and the Trilateral Commission*, Cambridge: Cambridge University Press.
Gill, Stephen, and David Law. (1988) *The Global Political Economy*, Baltimore: Johns Hopkins Press.
Gill, William J. (1990b) *Trade Wars Against America*, New York: Praeger.
Gilpin, Robert. (1987) *The Political Economy of International Relations*, Princeton: Princeton University Press.
Goldstein, Judith. (1988) 'Ideas, Institutions, and American Trade Policy,' *International Organization* 42 1: 179–217.
Goodell, Jeffrey. (1994) 'Salut, Suckers,' *Premier* April: 131–8.
Goodwin, Cranfurd D. (1988) 'The Heterogeneity of the Economist's Discourse: Philosopher, Priest and Hired Gun,' in *The Consequences of Economic Rhetoric* ed. Arjo Klamer, Donald McCloskey and Robert Solow, Cambridge: Cambridge University Press.
Grant, George. (1986) *Lament for a Nation*, Ottawa: Carleton Library Series.
Gray, John. (1986) *Liberalism*, Minneapolis: University of Minnesota Press.
Grey, Rodney de C. (1982) *United States Trade Policy Legislation A Canadian View*, Montreal: Institute for Research on Public Policy.
Guidi, Robert V., and Michael F. Morrone. (1974) 'The Michelin Decision: A Possible New Direction for U.S. Countervailing Duty Law,' *Law and Policy in International Business* 6: 236–66.
Haas, Ernst B. (1958) *The Uniting of Europe: Political, Social and Economic Forces, 1950–1957*, Stanford: Stanford University Press.
Haglund, David G., ed. (1989) *The Defence Industrial Base and the West*, London: Routledge.
Hancher, Leigh. (1994) 'State Aids and Judicial Control in the European Community,' *European Competition Law Review* 15, 3 May/June: 134–50.
Hardin, Herschel. (1974) *A Nation Unaware: The Canadian Economic Culture*, North Vancouver: J. J. Douglas.
Harris, Richard. (1989) 'Market Access in International Trade,' in *Trade and Investment Relations Among the United States, Canada and Japan*, ed. Robert M. Stern, 263–92, Chicago: University of Chicago Press.

Hart, Michael. (1994) *Decision at Midnight: Inside the Canada–U.S. Free-Trade Negotiations*, Vancouver: UBC Press.
Hart, Michael. (1989a) *The Canada-United States Working Group on Subsidies: Problem, Opportunity or Solution?* Carleton University: Centre for Trade Policy and Law.
Hart, Michael. (1989b) 'The Future on the Table: The Continuing Negotiating Agenda under the Canada–United States Free Trade Agreement,' *Living With Free Trade*, ed. Richard G. Dearden, Michael M. Hart, and Debra P. Steger, 67–131, Ottawa: Institute for Research on Public Policy.
Hartz, Louis. (1964) *The Founding of New Societies*, New York: Harcourt, Brace and World.
Hartz, Louis. (1955) *The Liberal Tradition in America*, New York: Harcourt, Brace.
Hawes, Michael K. (1986–7) 'The Steel Industry: Change and Challenge,' *International Journal* XLII: 25–58.
Hawley, Jim. (1987) 'The Internationalization of Capital: Banks, Eurocurrency and the Instability of the World Monetary System,' in *International Political Economy* ed. Jeffry A. Frieden and David A. Lake, 269–84, New York: St. Martins Press.
Hayek, Frederick A. (1960) *The Constitution of Liberty*, Chicago: University of Chicago Press.
Hayes, J. P. (1993) *Making Trade Policy in the European Community*, New York: St. Martin's Press.
Hayward, Keith. (1986) *International Collaboration in Civil Aerospace*, London: Frances Pinter.
Held, David. (1993) 'Democracy: From City-States to A Cosmopolitan Order?' in *Prospects for Democracy* ed. David Held, 13–52, Cambridge: Polity Press.
Held, David. (1991) 'Democracy, the Nation-State and the Global System,' in *Political Theory Today* ed. David Held, 197–235, Stanford: Stanford University Press.
Held, David. (1989) *Political Theory and the Modern State*, Cambridge: Polity Press.
Held, David. (1987) *Models of Democracy*, Cambridge: Polity Press.
Hendriks, Gisela. (1988–9) 'Germany and the CAP: National Interests and the European Community,' *International Affairs* 65 1 Winter: 75–87.
Hinsley, F. H. (1986) *Sovereignty*, Cambridge: Cambridge University Press.
Hoekman, Bernard M. (1989) 'Agriculture and the Uruguay Round.' *Journal of World Trade* 23 1 February: 83–96.
Hollander, Samuel. (1979) *The Economics of David Ricardo*, Toronto: University of Toronto Press.
Horlick, Gary N. and Peggy A. Clarke. (1993) 'The Dunkel Text Subsidies Code,' unpublished paper.
Horlick, Gary N., and Debra P. Steger. (1989) 'Subsidies and Countervailing Duties,' in *Making Free Trade Work*. ed. Peter Morici. 84–101. New York: Council on Foreign Relations Press.
Horlick, Gary N. and Geoffrey D. Oliver. (1989) 'Antidumping and Countervailing Duty Law Provisions of the Omnibus Trade and Competitiveness Act of 1988,' *Journal of World Trade Law* 23 3: 5–49.
Horowitz, Gad. (1978) 'Notes on Conservatism, Liberalism and Socialism in

Canada,' *Canadian Journal of Political Science* 11 2: 383–9.

Horowitz, Gad. (1966) 'Conservatism, Liberalism, and Socialism in Canada: An Interpretation,' *Canadian Journal of Economics and Political Science* 22 2: 143–71.

House of Commons. (1989) *Minutes of Proceedings and Evidence of the Standing Committee on External Affairs and International Trade* Issue No. 23: 72, 7 November, Canada.

House of Commons. (1987) *Minutes of Proceedings and Evidence of the Standing Committee on External Affairs and International Trade*, Issue No. 63:12, 7 December, Canada.

House of Commons. (1986) *Minutes of Proceedings and Evidence of the Standing Committee on External Affairs and International Trade* (Ottawa: House of Commons), Issue No. 38: 17 November, Canada.

Hudec, Robert E. (1990) 'Enforcement Powers: U.S. Dairy Quotas,' in *The GATT Legal System and World Trade Diplomacy* 2nd edn, 181–206. Salem: Butterworth Legal Publishers.

Hudec, Robert E. (1988) 'Legal Issues in US–EC Trade Policy: GATT Legislation 1960–1985,' in *Issues in US–EC Trade Relations*, Robert E. Baldwin, Carl B. Hamilton and Andre Sapir eds, 15–59. Chicago: University of Chicago Press.

Hufbauer, Gary Clyde. (1993) 'GATT Discipline on Domestic Subsidies and Implications for State and Provincial Governments,' unpublished paper.

Hufbauer Clyde. (1990) 'Subsidies,' in *Completing the Uruguay Round* ed. Jeffrey Schott, 93–107, Washington, DC: International Institute for Economics.

Hufbauer, Gary Clyde. (1989) 'A View of the Forest, Subsidies and Countervailing Measures,' *World Bank Discussion Papers* No. 55 ed. Bela Balassa, 11–25. Washington, DC, World Bank, 1989.

Hufbauer, Gary Clyde. (1983) 'Subsidy Issues After the Tokyo Round,' *Trade Policy in the 1980s* ed. William R. Cline, 327–60, Washington, DC: Institute for International Economics.

Hufbauer, Gary Clyde, Diane T. Berliner, and Kimberly Ann Elliott. (1986) *Trade Protection in the United States: 31 Case Studies*, Washington, DC: Institute for International Economics.

Ingersent, K. A., A. J. Rayner and R. C. Hine. (1993) 'Agriculture in the Uruguay Round: From the Dunkel Draft and Blair House Agreement to the Final Act,' University of Nottingham: Centre for Research in Economic Development and International Trade.

Innis, H. A. (1956) *The Fur Trade In Canada*, Toronto: University of Toronto Press.

ITRD (1988) 'New Steel Rails from Canada,' *International Trade Reporter Decisions* 12 Washington, DC: Bureau of National Affairs, 1412–29.

ITRD (1988) 'In Re New Steel Rail from Canada,' *International Trade Reporter Decisions* 12, Washington, DC: Bureau of National Affairs, 1753–64.

ITRD (1984) 'Certain Fresh Atlantic Groundfish from Canada,' *International Trade Reporter Decisions* 8 Washington, DC: Bureau of National Affairs, 1853–97.

ITS (1994) *Internal Trade Agreement*, Ottawa: Internal Trade Secretariat.

Jackson, John H. (1990) *Restructuring the GATT System*, New York: Council of Foreign Relations.

Jackson, John H. (1989) *The World Trading System*, Cambridge, Mass.: MIT Press.

Jackson, John H., Jean-Victor Louis, and Mitsuo Matsushita. (1984) *Implementing the Tokyo Round National Constitutions and International Economic Rules*, Ann Arbor: University of Michigan Press.

Johnston, Catherine. (1988): 'What's at Stake in the Multilateral Trade Negotiations?' *Global Business Issues* 1, 1 December: 1–4.

Karger, Howard J. and David Stoesz. (1990) *American Social Welfare Policy*, New York: Longman, 1990.

Kelly, William B. (1963) *Studies in United States Commercial Policy*, Chapel Hill: University of North Carolina Press.

Keohane, Robert O. (1984) *After Hegemony*, Princeton: Princeton University Press.

Keohane, Robert O. and Joseph S. Nye. (1977) *Power and Interdependence*, Boston: Little, Brown.

Kock, Karin. (1969) *International Trade Policy and the GATT 1947–1967*, Stockholm: Almqvist & Wiksell.

Kohona, Palitha T. B. 'Dispute Resolution under the World Trade Organization,' *Journal of World Trade* 28, 2 April: 23–47.

Krasner, Stephen. (1988) 'Sovereignty: An Institutional Perspective,' *Comparative Political Studies* 21, 1 April: 66–94.

Krasner, Stephen. (1976) 'State Power and the Structure of International Trade,' *World Politics* 28 23: 317–48.

Krugman, Paul R. ed. (1986) *Strategic Trade Policy and the New International Economics* Cambridge, Mass.; MIT Press.

Lake, David. (1988) *Power, Protection, and Free Trade: International Sources of U.S. Commercial Policy, 1887–1939*, Ithaca: Cornell University Press.

Langille, David. (1987) 'The Business Council on National Issues and the Canadian State,' *Studies in Political Economy* 24: 41–85.

Langille, Howard Peter. (1990) *Changing the Guard*, Toronto: University of Toronto Press.

Lasok, Paul. (1986) 'State Aids and Remedies under the EEC Treaty', *European Competition Law Review* 7 1: 53–82.

Laux, Jeanne Kirk, and Maureen Appel Molot. (1988) *State Capitalism: Public Enterprise in Canada*, Ithaca: Cornell University Press.

Laxer, James. (1987) *Decline of the Superpowers*, Toronto: James Lorimer.

Lenaerts, Koen. (1990) 'Constitutionalism and the Many Faces of Federalism,' *American Journal of Comparative Law* 38: 205–63.

Leslie, Peter. (1987) *Federal State, National Economy*, Toronto: University of Toronto Press.

Lindberg, Leon N. (1963) *The Political Dynamics of European Economic Integration*, Stanford: Stanford University Press.

Lindblom, Charles. (1977) *Politics and Markets*, New York: Basic Books.

Lipietz, Alain. (1987) *Mirages and Miracles: The Crisis of Global Fordism*, London: Verso.

Lipset, Seymour Martin. (1990) *Continental Divide: The Values and Institutions of the United States and Canada*, New York: Routledge.

Lipset, Seymour Martin. (1970) *Revolution and Counterrevolution*, New York: Anchor Books.

Lipsey, Richard G. (1988) 'The Free Trade Agreement in Context,' *Trade Offs on Free Trade*, ed. Marc Gold and Leyton-Brown, 67–78. Toronto: Carswell.

Lipsey, Richard G., and Robert C. York. (1988) *Evaluating the Free Trade Deal*, Toronto: CD Howe Institute.

Lithwick, N. Harvey. (1986) 'Federal Government Regional Economic Development Policies: An Evaluative Survey,' in *Disparities and Interregional Adjustment*, ed. Kenneth Norrie, 109–57, Toronto: University of Toronto Press.

Lodge, Juliet. (1994) 'The European Parliament and the Authority-Democracy Crises,' *Annals of the American Academy of Political and Social Science* 53, 1 January: 69–83.

Mackintosh, W. A. (1988) 'Economic Factors in Canadian History,' in *Approaches to Canadian Economic History*, ed. W. T. Easterbrook and M. H. Watkins, 1–15, Ottawa: Carleton University.

Magder, Ted. (1989) 'Taking Culture Seriously: A Political Economy of Culture,' *New Canadian Political Economy*, ed. Wallace Clement and Glen Williams, 278–96, Montreal and Kingston: McGill-Queen's University Press.

Maier, Charles. (1994) 'Democracy and Its Discontents,' *Foreign Affairs* July/August: 48–64.

Markusen, Ann. (1990) 'American Military Spending: Impacts on Industrial Structure, Regional Development and Trade with Canada,' in *Canada–United States Trade Liberalization and Socio-Economic Integration: U.S. Perspectives*, ed. P. P. Proux, Halifax, Nova Scotia: Institute for Research on Public Policy.

Markusen, Ann, Peter Hall and Amy Glasmeier. (1986) *High Tech America*, Boston: Allen & Unwin.

Marshall, Patrick. (1989) 'Unfinished Business: The Problem of Subsidies,' *Editorial Research Reports* 18 December: 684–92.

Mathijsen, P. (1975) 'Competition Laws which Apply to Member States,' in *Competition Policy in the UK and EEC*, ed. Kenneth D. George and Caroline Joll, Cambridge: Cambridge University Press.

McDonald, Bradley J. (1990) 'Agricultural Negotiations in the Uruguay Round,' *World Economy* 13, 3 September: 299–327.

McGee, Andrew and Stephen Weatheril. (1990) 'The Evolution of the Single Market – Harmonization or Liberalisation,' *Modern Law Review* 53 September: 578–603.

McGilly, Frank. (1990) *An Introduction to Canada's Public Social Services*, Toronto: McClelland & Stewart.

McLachlan, D. L. and D. Swann. (1967) *Competition Policy in the European Community*, London: Oxford University Press.

McQuaig, Linda. (1991) *The Quick and the Dead*, Toronto: Viking.

Milner, Helen V. (1988) *Resisting Protections: Global Industries and the Politics of International Trade*, Princeton: Princeton University Press.

Monnet, Jean. (1978) *Memoirs*, trans. Richard Mayne, New York: Doubleday.

Moran, Theodore H. and David C. Mowery. (1991) 'Aerospace,' *Daedalus* 120 4: 135–54.

Morgenthau, Hans J. (1973) *Politics Among Nations* 5th edn, New York: Alfred A. Knopf.

Morris, Robert. (1985) *Social Policy of the American Welfare State*, New York: Longman.

Morse, Edward L. (1976) *Modernization and the Transformation of International Relations*, New York: Free Press.

Morton, Colleen S. (1989) 'Subsidies Negotiations and the Politics of Trade,' *Canada–U.S. Outlook* 1 1: 1–43.

Moyer, Wayne H. (1993) 'The European Community and the GATT Uruguay Round: Preserving the Common Agricultural Policy at All Costs,' in *World Agriculture and the GATT*, ed. William P. Avery, 95–118, Boulder: Lynne Rienner.

MPEAA. (1990) 'Comments of The Motion Picture Export Association of America on The North American Free Trade Agreement.' Washington, DC: Motion Picture Export Association of America.

Muth, Robert. (1988) Brief submitted to the House Ways and Means Subcommittee on Trade *United States–Canada Free Trade Agreement Hearings* February 9, 26, 29, March 1, 11, 25, 1988, 285.

Nagle, J. C. (1976) *Agricultural Trade Policies*, Lexington: Saxon House.

National Planning Association. (1991) 'National Health Care: Is it the Answer?' *Canada–U.S. Outlook*. 2 4. Washington, DC.

Naylor, David C. (1986) *Private Practice, Public Payment Canadian Medicine and the Politics of Health Insurance 1911–1966*, Montreal and Kingston: McGill-Queen's University Press.

Nelles, H. V. (1974) *The Politics of Development: Forests, Mines, and Hydro-Electric Power in Ontario, 1894–1941*, Toronto: Macmillan.

Nelson, Douglas. (1989) 'Domestic Political Preconditions of US Trade Policy: Liberal Structure and Protectionist Dynamics.' *Journal of Public Policy* 9: 83–108.

Niskanen, William. (1990) 'Forward,' in *Arms, Politics and the Economy*, ed. Robert Higgs, New York: Holmes & Meier.

Nozette, Stewart and Robert Lawrence Kuhn, ed. (1987) *Commercializing SDI Technologies*, New York: Praeger.

Ohana, Gilad Y. (1989) 'The Constitutionality of Chapter Nineteen of the United States–Canada Free-Trade Agreement: Article III and the Minimum Scope of Judicial Review,' *Columbia Law Review* 89 4: 897–919.

Ontario. (1988) *The Question of Secure U.S. Market Access in the Canada–U.S. Free Trade Agreement*, Toronto: Ministry of Trade and Technology.

Pallberg, Robert L. (1993) 'Why Agriculture Blocked the Uruguay Round,' in *World Agriculture and the GATT*, ed. William P. Avery, 39–54, Boulder: Lynne Rienner.

Pauly, Louis W. (1994) 'Promoting a Global Economy: The Normative Role of the International Monetary Fund,' *Political Economy and the Changing Global Order*, eds Geoffrey Underhill and Richard Stubbs, 204–15, London: Macmillan.

Pearson, Charles S. (1989) *Free Trade, Fair Trade?* Washington, DC: Johns Hopkins Foreign Policy Institute.

Pendakur, Manjunath. (1990) *Canadian Dreams and American Control*, Detroit: Wayne State University Press.

Percy, Michael B., and Christian Yoder. (1987) *The Softwood Lumber Dispute and Canada–U.S. Trade in Natural Resources* Halifax: Institute for Research on Public Policy.

Perez, Carlota. (1985). 'Long Waves and World Structural Change: New Perspectives for Developing Countries,' *World Development* 13 1: 441–63.
Pescatore, Pierre. (1993) 'The GATT Dispute Settlement Mechanism,' *Journal of World Trade* 27, 1 February: 5–20.
Petersmann, Ernst-Ulrich and Meinhard Hilf. eds (1987) *The New GATT Round of Multilateral Trade Negotiations*, Boston: Kluwer Law and Taxation Publishers.
Peterson, J. 'Subsidiarity: (1994) A Definition to Suit Any Vision?' *Parliamentary Affairs* 47, 1 January: 116–32.
Phillips, Peter W. B. (1990) *Wheat, Europe and the GATT*, New York: St. Martin's Press.
Pickel, Andreas. (1989) 'Never Ask Who Should Rule: Karl Popper and Political Theory,' *Canadian Journal of Political Science* XXII 1 March: 83–105.
Polanyi, Karl. (1957) *The Great Transformation*, Boston: Beacon Hill.
Quinn, John J. (1988) 'A Critical Perspective on Dispute Settlement,' in *Trade Offs on Free Trade*, ed. Marc Gold and David Leyton-Brown, 407–14, Toronto: Carswell.
Raboy, Marc. (1990) *Missed Opportunities*, Montreal and Kingston: McGill-Queen's University Press.
Rapkin, David P. and Aurelia George (1993) 'Rice Liberalization and Japan's Role in the Uruguay Round: A Two-Level Game Approach,' in *World Agriculture and the GATT*, ed. William P. Avery, Boulder: Lynne Rienner.
Reich, Robert. (1983) 'Beyond Free Trade,' *Foreign Affairs* Spring: 773–805.
Ricardo, David. (1992) *The Principles of Political Economy and Taxation*, London: Everyman's Library.
Richards, John, and Larry Pratt. (1981) *Prairie Capitalism* Toronto: McLelland & Stewart.
Richardson, David J. (1990) 'The Political Economy of Strategic Trade Policy,' *International Organization* 44 1 Winter: 107–33.
Rivers, Richard R., and John D. Greenwald. (1979) 'The Negotiation of a Code on Subsidies and Countervailing Measures: Bridging Fundamental Policy Differences,' *Law and Policy in International Business* 11: 1447–95.
Robertson, Ronald. (1992) *Globalization, Social Theory and Global Culture*, London: Sage.
Rosecrance, Richard. (1986) *The Rise of the Trading State*, New York: Basic Books.
Ross, George. (1992) 'After Maastricht: Hard Choices for Europe,' *World Policy Journal* IX 3: 487–513.
Ross, Malcolm. (1989) 'A Review of Developments in State Aids 1987–88,' *Common Market Law Review* 26: 167–92.
Royal Commission. (1964) *Royal Commission On Health Services* Vol. 1, Ottawa: Queen's Printer.
Rubin, Alissa J. (1994) 'Overhaul Issue Unlikely to Rest in Peace,' *Congressional Quarterly Weekly Report* 52 38 October: 2797–801.
Ruggie, John Gerard. (1982) 'International Regimes, Transactions, and Change: Embedded Liberalism in the Postwar Economic Order.' *International Organization* 36 2: 195–231.
Rugman, Alan M. (1986) 'U.S. Protectionism and Canadian Trade Policy,' *Journal of World Trade* 20 4: 363–80.

Rugman, Allan M. and Andrew Anderson. (1989) 'Subsidies in the U.S. Steel Industry: A New Conceptual Framework and Literature Review,' *Research Programme Working Paper*, Toronto: Ontario Centre for International Business.

Rugman, Alan M. and Andrew Anderson. (1987) *Administered Protection in America*, London: Croom Helm.

Savoie, Donald J. (1986) *Regional Economic Development: Canada's Search for Solutions*, Toronto: University of Toronto Press.

Schaefer, Matt and Thomas Singer. (1992) 'Multilateral Trade Arangements and U.S. States,' *Journal of World Trade* 26 6: 31–59.

Schina, Despina. (1987) *State Aids under the EEC Treaty Articles 92 to 94* European Competition Law Monographs, Oxford: ESC Publishing.

Schmitt, Hans A. (1962) *The Path to European Union: From the Marshall Plan to the Common Market*, Baton Rouge: Louisiana State University Press.

Schott, Jeffrey J. ed. (1990) *Completing the Uruguay Round: A Results Oriented Approach to the GATT Trade Negotiations*, Washington, DC: Institute for International Economics.

Schott, Jeffrey and Murray Smith. (1988) *The Canada–United States Free Trade Agreement: The Global Impact*, Washington, DC: Institute for International Economics.

Shaw, Martin. (1994) *Global Society and International Relations*, Cambridge: Polity Press.

Shipman, William D, ed. (1986) *Trade and Investment Across the North East Boundary*, Montreal: Institute for Research on Public Policy.

Sinclair, Timothy J. (1994) 'Passing Judgement: Credit Rating Processes as Regulatory Mechanisms of Governance in the Emerging World Order,' *Review of International Political Economy* 1 1: 133–51.

Sipkov, Ivan. (1988) 'The European Economic Community: A Sovereign Entity Under Its Own Legal Order,' *International Journal of Legal Information* 16 3 Winter: 177–89.

Skilton, T. E. (1993) 'GATT and the Environment in Conflict – the Tuna–Dolphin Dispute and the Quest for an International Conservation Strategy,' *Cornell International Law Journal* 26 2: 455–94.

Skogstad, Grace. (1992) 'The State, Organized Interests and Canadian Agricultural Trade Policy: The Impact of Institutions,' *Canadian Journal of Political Science* XXV 2 June: 319–47.

Slot, Piet Jan. (1990) 'Procedural Aspects of State Aids: The Guardian of Competition Versus the Subsidy Villains?' *Common Market Law Review* 27: 741–60.

Smiley, Donald V. (1987) *The Federal Condition in Canada*, Toronto: McGraw-Hill.

Smiley, Donald V. (1980) *Canada in Question: Federalism in the Eighties* 3rd edn, Toronto, McGraw-Hill Ryerson.

Smith, Margaret. (1989) 'Subsidies and United States Trade Law: The Application to Canada,' *Backgrounder* BP-215E, Ottawa: Library of Parliament.

Smith, Murray, ed. (1990) *Canada, The Pacific and Global Trade*, Halifax, Institute for Research on Public Policy.

Smith, Murray G., ed. (1987) *Bridging the Gap: Trade Laws in the Canadian–U.S. Negotiations*, Washington, DC: Canadian-American Committee.
Smith, R. P. (1988) 'The Significance of Defence Expenditure in US and UK National Economies,' *Defence Expenditure and Regional Development* ed. Michael J. Breheny, London: Mansell.
Spero, Joan Edelman. (1988–9) 'Guiding Global Finance,' *Foreign Policy* 73: 114–34.
Spero, Joan Edelman. (1985) *The Politics of International Economic Relations*, New York: St. Martin's Press.
Spierenburg, Dirk and Raymond Poidevin. (1994) *The History of the High Authority of the European Coal and Steel Community*, London: Weidenfeld & Nicolson.
Statistics Canada (1984–6) *National Trade Estimates*, Ottawa.
Steger, Debra P. (1988) 'Dispute Settlement,' in *Trade Offs on Free Trade*, ed. Marc Gold and David Leyton-Brown, 182–7, Toronto: Carswell.
Stern, Paula and Paul A. London. (1990) 'Deficits in Trade and Leadership,' *Washington Quarterly* 13 4: 105–17.
Stevenson, Garth. (1989) *Unfulfilled Union*, Toronto: Gage Educational Publishing.
Stokes, Bruce. (1991) 'Tinseltown Trade War,' *National Journal* 23 February: 431–8.
Stone, Charles F. Stone. (1988) 'International Trade,' in *Challenge to Leadership*, ed. Isabel V. Sawhill, Washington, DC: Urban Institute Press.
Stone, Frank. (1984) *Canada, GATT And the International Trade System*, Montreal: Institute for Research on Public Policy.
Stopford, John and Susan Strange. (1991) *Rival States, Rival Firms*, Cambridge: Cambridge University Press.
Strange, Susan. (1988a) 'The Future of the American Empire.' *Journal of International Affairs* 42 1: 1–17.
Strange, Susan. (1988b) *States and Markets*, London: Pinter.
Strange, Susan. (1985). 'Protectionism and World Politics.' *International Organization* 39 2: 233–59.
Supply and Services Ministry. (1993) *North American Free Trade Agreement*, Ottawa.
Supply and Services Ministry (1988) *Free Trade Agreement*, Ottawa.
Swann, Denis (1992) *The Economics of the Common Market* 7th edn, London: Penguin.
Swinbank, Alan. (1993) 'CAP Reform, 1992,' *Journal of Common Market Studies* 31, 3 September: 359–72.
Tangermann, Stefan. (1987) 'Proposals for a "Rule-Oriented" Liberalization of International Agricultural Trade,' in *The New GATT Round of Multilateral Trade Negotiations* ed. Ernst-Ulrich Petersmann and Meinhard Hilf, 243–64, Boston: Kluwer Law and Taxation Publishers.
Thurow, Lester. (1992) *Head to Head*, New York: William Morrow, 1992.
Thiele, Leslie Paul. (1993) 'Making Democracy Safe for the World: Social Movements and Global Politics,' *Alternatives*, 18 3 summer: 273–305.
Tilly, Charles, ed. (1975) *The Formation of National States in Western Europe*, Princeton: Princeton University Press.
Treddenick, John. (1989) 'The Economic Significance of the Canadian Defence

Industrial Base,' in *Canada's Defence Industrial Base*, ed. David Haglund, London: Routledge.

Tuohy, Carolyn J. (1988) 'Medicine and the State in Canada: The Extra-Billing Issue in Perspective,' *Canadian Journal of Political Science* XXI, 2 June: 267–96.

Twiggs, Joan E. (1987) *The Tokyo Round of Multilateral Trade Negotiations*, New York: University Press of America.

Tyson, Laura D'Andrea. (1992) *Who's Bashing Whom? Trade Conflict in High Technology Industries,* Washington, DC: Institute for International Economics.

Urban Institute. (1986) *Directory of Incentives for Business Investment and Development in the United States in the United States, A State by State Guide*, Washington, DC.

UN. (1993) *Handbook of International Trade and Development Statistics*, New York: United Nations.

USTR (1991a) 'United States Announces Action on Canadian Lumber Imports,' *Press Release* 4 October. Office of the United States Trade Representative: Washington, DC.

USTR (1991b) 'The United States–Canada Free Trade Agreement Biennial Report,' United States Trade Representative: Washington, DC.

Vakerics, Thomas V., David I. Wilson and Kenneth G. Weigel. (1987) *Antidumping, Countervailing Duty and Other Trade Actions*, New York: Practicing Law Institute.

Vallenti, Jack. (1990) 'How a GATT can Kill You.' Remarks at the Los Angeles World Affairs Council, 7 November.

Vernon, Raymond. (1966) 'International Investment and International Trade in the Product Cycle,' *Quarterly Journal of Economics* 80: 190–207.

Viatte, Gerard and Frederic Langer. (1990) 'Agricultural Reform: A Hesitant Start,' *OECD Observer* 165 August/September: 4–8.

Viner, Jacob. (1923/1986) *Dumping: A Problem in International Trade*, New York: Kelly.

Walker, RBJ. (1993) *Inside/Outside: International Relations as Political Theory* Cambridge: Cambridge University Press.

Wallace, Helen. (1993) 'European Governance in Turbulent Times', *Journal of Common Market Studies* 31, 3 September: 293–304.

Warnock, John W. (1988) *Free Trade and the New Right Agenda*, Vancouver: New Star Books.

Weber, Max. (1958) *From Max Weber: Essays in Sociology,* eds H. H. Gerth and C. Wright Mills, New York: Oxford University Press.

Webster, Judith, ed. (1977) *Voices of Canada*, Burlington: Association for Canadian Studies in the United States.

Whitaker, Reg. (1977) 'Images of the Canadian State,' in *The Canadian State*, ed. Leo Panitch, 28–68, Toronto: University of Toronto Press.

Wilcox, Clair. (1949) *A Charter for World Trade*, New York: Macmillan.

Wilson, Dorothy. (1987) 'The Welfare State in America,' in *Welfare Abroad: An Introduction to Welfare Provision in Seven Countries* ed. Roslyn Ford and Mono Chakrabarti, 29–65, Glasgow: Scottish Academic Press.

Winham, Gilbert R. (1990) 'GATT and the International Trade Regime,' *International Journal* XLV: 796–822.

Winham, Gilbert R. (1988) 'Dispute Settlement and the Question of Subsidies,' in *Trade-Offs on Free Trade* ed. Marc Gold and David Leyton-Brown, 205–11, Toronto: Carswell.

Winham, Gilbert R. (1986) *International Trade and the Tokyo Round Negotiation*, Princeton: Princeton University Press.

Wishlade, Fiona G. (1993) 'Competition Policy, Cohesion and the Co-ordination of Regional Aids in the European Community,' *European Competition Law Review* 14, 4 July/August: 143–50.

Wolf, Martin. (1990) 'What We Need From the Uruguay Round,' *World Today* 45.

Wolf, Martin. (1989) 'Why Voluntary Export Restraints? An Historical Analysis,' *World Economy* 12 3: 273–91.

Wrobel, Marion. (1990) 'Canada–U.S. Steel Trade,' *Current Issue Review* 88–2E Ottawa: Library of Parliament.

Young, R. A., Philippe Faucher and Andre Blais. (1984) 'The Concept of Province-Building: A Critique,' *Canadian Journal of Political Science* XVII 4: 783–818.

Zacher, Mark W. (1992) 'The Decaying Pillars of the Westphalian Temple,' in *Governance Without Government: Order and Change in World Politics* eds James N. Rosenau and Ernst-Otto Czempiel, 58–101, Cambridge: Cambridge University Press.

Index